Back Roads Home

The true story of a family: lost and found

Wrapped around this vivid biography of an unknown but fascinating cowboy is an intimate portrait of one family's struggle with adversity. Karen Moderow's fast-paced, fiction-like narrative moves seamlessly from history to inspiration. This family and their special story of personal growth will be long remembered.

> Woodrow W. Leake, Ph.D., CAE
> *President & Chief Executive Officer*
> **Brain Injury Association of Georgia**

Back Roads Home is a tender story of lessons learned about love, integrity, and faith. It is a good read for those of us who deal with pain in our families and need to discover new depths of grace.

> Dr. Jimmy R. Allen, *author*
> *Burden Of A Secret*
> *Former President,*
> **Southern Baptist Convention**

Karen Moderow and her family show that with God's help, every generation can be the great one.

> Loren Cunningham
> *Founder,* Youth With A Mission

Back Roads Home.

The true story of a family lost and found

KAREN MODEROW

Kelly —

To someone who has
walked in our shoes.
May this book remind you
of the special gift of family you
experience in your own life.

Karen Moderow
7/24/03

PRESS

ACW Press
Phoenix, Arizona 85013

Grateful acknowledgment is made to the following for permission to reprint previously published material:

"Eagle's Wings" by Reuben Morgan/*Hillsong Publishing* (adm in the US and Canada by Integrity's Hosanna! Music)/ASCAP. Used by permission.

Excerpt from "What A Day That Will Be" by Jim Hill © copyright 1955, Ben Speer Music/SESAC (adm by ICG). All rights reserved. Used by permission.

Some names have been changed to protect the privacy of certain individuals.

Cover design: northcutt & associates
Interior design: Pine Hill Graphics
Author photographer: Deborah Whitlaw
Map design: Allan Dutch

Packaged by ACW Press
5501 N. 7th Ave., #502
Phoenix, Arizona 85013
www.acwpress.com
The views expressed or implied in this work do not necessarily reflect those of ACW Press. Ultimate design, content, and editorial accuracy of this work is the responsibility of the author(s).

Library of Congress Cataloging-in-Publication Data
(*Provided by Quality Books, Inc.*)

Moderow, Karen.
    Back roads home : the true story of a family lost and
found / Karen Moderow. -- 1st ed.
    p. cm.
    ISBN 1-892525-93-3

    1. Moderow, Karen. 2. Moderow, Karen--Family.
3. Choate, Alva Houston. 4. Spiritual biography.
5. Desire for God. 6. Self-realization. 7. Grandparents--
Death--Psychological aspects. 8. Bereavement--Religious
aspects. I. Title.

BL73M634A3 2003   248.8'66'092
                        QBI33-767

Printed in the United States of America.

To Joseph

My heartfelt thanks...

To Andy Scheer who mentored me as a writer...

To Mary Beth Bishop, Gaydell Collier, and Ann Starr who encouraged me...

To Elaine Wright Colvin whose passion for this book spurred me into action...

To Elizabeth DeBeasi for the gifts of friendship and excellence she brings to my life...

To Sharon Brookshire, my sister and most trustworthy critic, for challenging me...

To my family for loving me.

Table of Contents

Time Line — Alva Houston Choate

1903
Alva Houston Choate is born in Indian Territory before statehood in what would become Davis, Oklahoma.

1923
Alva returns home to the farm after chasing the rodeo and working in the oil fields.
Alva courts Cora White.
Cotton crop fails and the Choates lose their farm.

1927
The Choate and White families buy a sawmill together.
Alva and Cora marry on March 4, 1927.
Six months later, both families lose everything.
Alva and Cora go to Hobart, Oklahoma, to pick cotton.
Alva is hired by Lee Brazil to handle outlaw mules.

1928
They move to a big, rent free house, but are soon robbed.
With Cora pregnant, they move to Maud, Oklahoma, to be near her mother.
First child, Marie, is born November 18, 1928.

1929
Alva works near Seminole in the oil fields.
In December, Alva and Cora find God in the Valentine Revival in Hobart, Oklahoma.

1930
Second child, Atha, is born in Maud on September 28, 1930.
The family moves to Byers, Texas, to be near Alva's brother, Pernie.
Alva works three years for John Adair on the farm.

1932
The third child, Kern, is born.

1933
Alva moves the family to Oklahoma to start a turkey ranch. It fails.
They return to Seminole where Alva works the oil fields in Oklahoma City.

1935
Alva and Cora work with Sister Hartwell in Byer's revival meetings.

They pick cotton in the fall to support themselves.
In August, Alva becomes foreman of the Blackwell Ranch in Wichita Falls, Texas.

1939
Old man Blackwell dies.
Alva continues working farm for one of Blackwell's sons for another year and then is fired.

1940
Family moves to Arizona in January looking for work.
In June, with Cora in poor health, they return to Wichita Falls.
Alva works for Ben Blackwell, the other son.

1942
Family moves to Byers at the end of the year to help Sister Hartwell start a church.
Alva works in a filling station for a year, then gets on with the county doing roadwork.

1949
Unable to keep pace with the hard physical labor, Alva returns to Wichita Falls to work for his cousin, Watts, in his jeep dealership. He stays there ten years as parts manager.

1959
Watts sells the dealership. Alva drives a cattle truck intermittently for the next two years.

1961
Alva becomes a maintenance man at Faith Apartments and begins building up a freelance carpentry business.

1963
Alva is hired to manage Circle R Stables—what would later be known only as "the barn."
He and Cora move onto the property.

1965
Alva leases the barn himself and begins serious horse-trading.

1980
June 20—Cora dies.

1982
Alva moves to Midtown Manor.

1998
Alva leaves Midtown Manor for nursing home.

Map

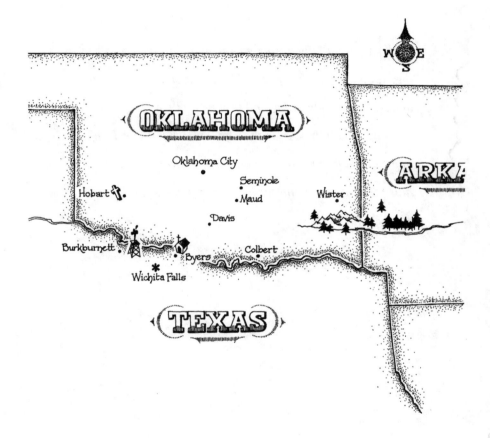

Daily our grandfathers are moving out of our lives… When they're gone…the eloquent and haunting stories of suffering and sharing and building and healing and planting and harvesting—all these go with them, and what a loss. If this information is to be saved at all, for whatever reason, it must be saved now; and the logical researchers are the grandchildren.

Eliot Wiggington

Alva Houston Choate, 1983

Spring
1985

Midtown Cowboy

My plane, a tiny prop with a screaming engine, bucked wildly as it descended into the north Texas city of Wichita Falls. *Rough ride,* I thought, but I welcomed it because it meant I was almost home. I scanned the open, flat land below me and wondered about my connection to this place. I was only two when my family left Texas for California, yet this was where I returned when life pressed in on me.

I could hardly wait to see my grandfather again. At eighty-two he was still the epitome of the Texas cowboy. I pictured him in western Levis, wearing a leather belt with a wide, ornate buckle. I had often watched him walk from the trailer to the barn, tilting his Diamond Horseshoe hat downward to shield his eyes from the Texas sun. Though his legs were bowed from years of riding, he walked briskly, his finely stitched boots grinding the baked clots of dirt beneath him.

Papa's boots and hats were always the highest quality. Some might think that extravagant, but for a real cowboy, they were tools of the trade. Only the best would stand up to the abuse meted out by the fierce rain and dust storms he confronted in the course of his work. He was wiry and stood only 5'6", but as he often said, "I never saw a man who could out-work me."

I knew the image playing in mind differed greatly from reality. Papa no longer worked cattle on a ranch. The barn was no longer his. The years had long ago removed him from the life he loved. Only the boots, the hat, and the memories remained to reflect the cowboy life he once cherished; yet he was still a cowboy. I thought he always would be.

After Mama, my grandmother, died in 1980, Papa stayed on at the barn for two more years. Mama would have been proud of him—we didn't think he'd last two months without her. But the work kept him going. Regardless of his grief, there were horses to feed, groom, and train, and he rose to the occasion.

Papa had hoped to run the barn with the help of Margie, a young woman he and Mama had loved through tough times as a teenager. A loser husband had recently left her with two boys to raise alone, and for her, to work the barn with Papa was a dream come true. She was as passionate about horses as Papa was. But it wasn't to be. A hernia operation followed by the discovery of thyroid cancer ended the most rewarding season of Papa's life. Though the operation to remove the cancer was successful, his recovery was tedious and complicated.

Papa's greatest fear was that he would be a burden to his children, so once he realized he could no longer handle the stable, he wasted no time in looking for a new home. He applied to live at Midtown Manor, a senior citizens' apartment building, even before it opened. When the time came for him to move, my aunt imagined herself literally pulling Papa from the barn with his spurs dragging the ground. But he surprised her by accepting the change from barn living to high-rise residency with regal dignity.

When I was younger, my grandfather and I were not close. My mother, Papa's middle child, died when I was nineteen. It was then I began my regular treks back to Texas—desperate for any connection to my mother. I needed to be where I could hear the stories she heard as a child. To be held by arms that had held and loved her. Just being with my grandparents, spending my days as she must have spent hers, gave me comfort. But when my grandmother also died, I felt adrift once again and stopped coming.

I had never related to my grandfather except through my grandmother. In my family, like most, the women kept the relational home-fires burning. But my grandfather was the one who was left and I was hoping we could find common ground. I was a little nervous about how things would go since we seemed an unlikely match for friendship. I was thirty-five; he was eighty-two. We had seldom even shared a personal conversation. I really didn't know much about him. I had heard he'd been no saint in younger years. That, of course, intrigued me. The only thing I knew about him first-hand was that he had a great sense of humor.

One of my earliest memories of Papa was his telling how he accidentally butchered a woman's favorite flower.

This lady had flowers all over everywhere and I was putting up some valley tin on her roof. You know how valley tin goes along the roof valleys for water to run down? Well, at the end I had to cut it kind of three-cornered. What made it so funny was that old widow woman—and I knew her real well—she was one of these outspoken women, always everything had to be so and so.

I started to put that valley tin in and she said, "Now I don't care what you do to the rest of these flowers around here but you be sure you don't do anything to this one." I looked down and below, way off to side of me, was the biggest flower I ever seen. I don't know what kind of flower it was but it had a blossom on it as big as a man's face. So I said, "Okay," and I'm thinkin', What's she worryin' 'bout? We're nowheres near that flower. So while she was a'standin' right there, I cut that tin and threw the scrap off the roof. Well, that piece o' tin turned 'round two or three times, floated out to the side and just decapitated that flower. That ol' woman seen what it done, but she looked up at me and never said a word. Took her about five minutes to get to where she could talk again. Any other time she'd a bawled me out, but that got her so. I didn't throw that tin towards the flower, the wind just caught it and carried it off over there. But I just about fell off the house, laughin'.

Papa got in trouble many times over not being able to resist a hearty laugh. But, more than it hurt him, it got him through many tough situations. As for me, I needed a little laughter in my life, and I knew that had a lot to do with why I had come. I knew bits and pieces of Papa's life. He'd been through hard times, and though he was struggling with the loss of my grandmother, I'd heard he was coping well. I wondered how he kept any joy in his life when his heart was breaking.

So here I was. I had been married for fifteen years and was floundering. My boys, ages eight and six, were becoming more assertive every day. I took their quest for independence as a personal assault. I felt alone, abandoned, and uncertain about my identity, my marriage, and my ability to parent. I needed a place where I could get my bearings. I wasn't quite sure how spending a week in a senior citizen's apartment building with an eighty-something cowboy was going to provide that, but I sensed I was right where I needed to be.

Midtown Manor

Aunt Marie met me at the Wichita Falls Municipal Airport. Papa still had his white '77 Chevy, but he only drove where he was familiar. The airport, though just ten minutes from Midtown Manor, wasn't on his route. I didn't know my mother's older sister well. In fact, we had probably only met two or three times in our lives. Frankly, I was surprised that she would take off work to come pick me up. I lived in Stamford, Connecticut, just outside New York City—where if you needed a ride somewhere, you hailed a taxi. You certainly didn't bother someone you hadn't seen in years, even if she was your aunt. She greeted me warmly though, as if being family was enough in itself to merit special treatment.

Though she towered over my five-foot frame, anyone could see we were related. Her small face, hazel eyes, even her smile looked very familiar. The lines around her eyes and mouth were deeper than mine but gave me the eerie sensation of looking at myself twenty years from now. Like me, she wore her reddish hair short. Hair like ours didn't have the good sense to curl but waved unevenly at the mercy of several cowlicks around the hairline. Fortunately, the natural look that was now in style worked in our favor, and neither my aunt nor I made any attempt to protect our hairdos as we battled the wind on the way to the car.

Instead, we fell into lively conversation searching for any treasure of family information the other might hold. But our exploration ended abruptly as Aunt Marie pulled into a sweeping drive in front of a tall, glass front building. *This can't be where Papa lives,* I thought. Texas is known for its low-lying brick structures that, for the most part, hold their own in the destructive tornadoes that frequent the area. This was not the one-story cottage I had expected.

Midtown Manor stood as the only high-rise in what used to be the old downtown area of Wichita Falls. Thanks to the construction of Sike's Mall, Main Street was a ghost town now. To the east, there were a couple of large manufacturing buildings and two or three mainline churches where the majority of the community attended years ago—before fundamental and charismatic forces swept across the city. A few government buildings, and Wichita General—where I was born—rounded out the old downtown. But to the west, immediately surrounding Midtown Manor itself, were blocks and blocks of tenement housing. The senior citizens' apartment building was to be the corner piece for revitalizing the downtown area, but not much had happened in the past three years.

It was not safe. Crime was a problem and the vulnerable citizens of Midtown Manor were easy targets for predators. Still, the few small business—especially the restaurants that struggled to hang in there—gave just enough stability to the place to give everyone hope.

There was Luby's just off Ninth Street. And Pat's, a hamburger joint Papa loved. A block or two down the street from Midtown Manor, Pat's was the hangout for men like Papa who were mobile enough to get there. "Best hamburger in town" was the official critique given by Wichita Falls' citizens.

At this point though, I'd never heard of Pat's. I was busy just trying to absorb the fact that my grandfather was living in a high-rise. I pulled my bags from the trunk of my aunt's car and followed her toward the main entrance of the building. In spite of my initial misgivings, I had to admit the building looked sturdy and it positively gleamed. The heavy glass doors opened and Papa came toward us.

His cowboy hat kept pace with his jaunty walk—a distinctive swagger. He had the same wry smile and mischievous look in his eye that I remembered.

"Hello, hon," he said softly. Then held me as though I were so precious I could break. I was surprised by his tenderness and by the tears that sprang to my eyes. Papa had never been much of a touchy-feely guy. Kind, yes. Thoughtful, yes. But he kept his emotions tight. His vulnerability took my breath away.

My aunt went on her way while Papa picked up my heavy bag and escorted me through the entrance. Residents were sitting in neat rows on the sofas and chairs lining the walls of the lobby. We were greeted with a chorus of "oohs" and "aahs."

"That's her," somebody whispered. "That's his granddaughter come from back East."

"Well, Cowboy, did she finally git here?" asked one of the men.

"This here's Deets," Papa said to me.

Deets, a big guy with sandy hair and faded freckles, stood up to shake my hand. He wore a short-sleeved shirt that revealed thick and burly arms. "Nice to meet ya."

"Your granddaddy shore has been lookin' forward to your coming," said a woman who was later introduced to me as Ida.

She was as thin as a beanpole and propped on top of her head was a wig of such poor quality it seemed made of brown cotton candy. But she—like the other four or five whom I later learned spent hours in the lobby to see what they could see—seemed happy for Papa's good fortune. It was clear that to have a visitor, someone who actually stayed in the apartment with you, was a high honor.

Papa walked slowly and regally through the lobby, nodding graciously to those who addressed us, but saying little. He put his free hand under my elbow, directing me gently but firmly toward the elevator with the same authority he'd often used to guide an uncertain colt to the barn.

At the sixth floor, we were greeted by a deep humming sound I couldn't identify.

"That's Betty," Papa said. "She keeps things clean around here."

Stepping out of the elevator, I saw a woman who looked to be in her early sixties. She had unnaturally black hair teased into a beehive and wore a T-shirt with jeans as tight as I had ever seen. She was attached to a giant buffing machine with which she was polishing an already shining floor to a higher gloss.

Papa introduced us briefly, then nudged me onward. "They're pretty careful around here now," he said. "A few months ago we had a couple of con artists get in here saying they were selling one thing and another. Quite a few folks wrote checks but it was just a rip-off."

As Betty eyed me from down the hall I realized Papa had been letting her know I was "legit."

I noticed the doors of the apartments we passed were alternately painted bright green, yellow, or peach. Papa stopped at apartment 610, a green door. His name was engraved neatly on a brass plate—Alva H. Choate. Opening a leather key chain, he selected a key and inserted it deftly into the lock until the deadbolt turned. The oversized door opened into a generous hallway that held the aroma of breakfast sausage even though it was late afternoon.

I walked past the kitchen on the left and into the living room just beyond it. Two large windows straight ahead were covered by heavy, short cream drapes but offered the potential for light and expansiveness. And the apartment, painted a pale green to coordinate with the door, was clean and neat as a pin. *Not bad*, I thought. Papa had found a nice little place for himself.

Nestling In

Papa invited me to make myself at home—a task easier said than done. There wasn't much space to put things so they'd be accessible but not in the way.

"Hon, I just hate that you're gonna have to sleep on that old couch," Papa said as he half pointed to a large floral sofa with the back of his hand. "It's all I got."

I remembered that sofa well. Even though they bought it used, my grandmother had been proud of it. It was yellow and green, made of a terry cloth fabric that at the time seemed luxurious to her. Its matching chair sat about two feet in front of the window but the drapes were pulled tightly "so that the sun don't get to it," Papa said.

Papa was paranoid about sun fade. He was convinced that the main reason he always got the highest marks possible on his monthly inspections was because everything in his apartment looked as good as the day he moved in. "A lot of people here have had their walls painted two or three times, but they've never had to do a thing to mine," he would brag. The comment was always followed by his explanation of how the sun would ruin everything in the room if you let it. It took me a while to realize it was his way of telling me not to open the drapes. He was addressing the situation before it came up. It was a lecture I needed because the first thing I would have done was thrown them open.

I thought it ironic that a man who had spent so many years out in the sun would be so intent on keeping it out, but I think it was Mama's influence asserting itself from the grave. My grandmother had to be the cleanest person on God's earth. She wasn't a fussy housekeeper, but she was diligent. No matter how poor or shabby their conditions, Mama kept a clean house, and she trained Papa for domestication with the same fervor with which Papa trained horses.

My grandmother fully appreciated that Papa's love in life was working with livestock, but she didn't like being around animals herself. She hated the smell of "that ol' barn." She was willing to move anywhere, to live under any conditions necessary for Papa to practice his trade, but she was determined to keep the smell of the barn out of her house.

The result was that Papa must've pulled his boots on and off more than any person in the history of mankind. There was perpetually a sheet of newspaper near the front door for Papa to set his boots on before entering the house. I never heard him question the inconvenience. It was a house rule and he accepted it. Whether it was a point of contention early on in their marriage, I don't know. By the time I was old enough to notice, it was obvious Papa took pride in having a home that reflected the grace of the woman he loved.

Though my grandmother kept an immaculate house, I don't remember her slaving away night and day in endless rounds of dusting and vacuuming. She was busy but without the frazzle that characterized my days. There always seemed to be plenty of time for talking, shopping, or just sitting out on the porch with a glass of iced tea in the late afternoons.

I remember coming to see Mama and Papa once when I was in my early twenties. It was harvest time. Mama and Papa always had a big garden and there were a few weeks in the fall that were "make or break" time. What wasn't saved in those precious days soon became garbage. We'd been working hard every day canning and freezing. After a few days, I was exhausted. I was also worried about my grandmother who had a heart condition. I could tell she was weak.

Between the garden and the company, we hadn't had a moment to stop. For an out-of-the-way place, they certainly had a lot of people coming and going. Four or five visitors had already been by that day and it wasn't yet 3:00 in the afternoon.

"I think I'm going to lie down a minute," Mama said when things finally quieted down.

"Sounds good to me," I said. "Maybe I'll do the same." I went to my room but no sooner did my head hit the pillow than I heard a knock at the front door. I hurried out and met a young woman in her late twenties. Dark hair. Cowboy boots. Smelling of the outdoors. "Yes?" I asked quietly, hoping not to disturb Mama.

"Is Miz Choate in?" she asked.

"Yes, but she's resting right now. Can I help you?"

"My name is Alice. My husband and I used to have a horse here at the barn, and I just wondered if I could see her for a minute?"

I was annoyed. Was there no peace? But just as I was about to ask if she could come back later, I heard Mama say, "Alice! Good to see you. Come on in." Before I knew it, Alice was sitting on Mama's floral sofa drinking a Dr. Pepper, boots and all.

I realized then that though Mama loved her house, people came first. In that regard, I was nothing like her. I was seldom available for anyone, even my husband or children. It was always, "Not now. Just a minute. Let me take care of this first…" Whenever it was inconvenient, I was quick to dismiss them just as I wanted to dismiss Alice.

Over the years I often saw Mama and Papa change their plans to accommodate someone in need, or simply a neighbor who wanted to visit. Their welcome always gave a moment of dignity to whoever crossed their path. I saw that "giving" people find a way to give whatever is needed at the moment, and my grandparents were giving people. I, in a painful moment of recognition, realized that I was not. I preferred to be selfish. I would take the nap to an unexpected visitor any day.

Now, as I pulled my suitcase behind the large floral chair in Papa's living room, I knew much had not changed. I had come to see my grandfather because I needed something from him. Instinctively, I felt he could give me that place of belonging I desperately desired. I wanted a home, but I wasn't interested in giving one to anyone else at the moment.

I continued making my nest—rearranging cleaning supplies in Papa's huge bathroom closet to make room for my toiletries—while Papa sat in his worn recliner waiting patiently.

I'm a nest builder by instinct. Even when I go to a hotel the first thing I do is unpack. And the next thing on my agenda is to eat. So, of course, no sooner had I found a home for my things than hunger began to gnaw at my stomach.

"Have you eaten yet?" Papa asked, as though reading my mind.

"No," I replied. "I thought I'd wait and see if you were up to going out."

His eyes sparkled as he got out of his chair and reached for his hat. "Then let's go. I haven't had a bite since breakfast."

I couldn't believe he'd waited all day to eat, but that was to become his usual routine when he was expecting me. It motivated me to schedule my arrival earlier rather than later in the day, something I doubt he intended but pleased him nonetheless.

"So where do you want to eat?" I asked.

"How 'bout Piccadilly? They've got just about the best food there is."

My heart sank. I was tired of traveling and Piccadilly was a good thirty minutes on the other side of town, but I hesitated. Papa was sensitive. Years earlier when my older boy, Michael, was a baby, I had complained about not having a high chair for him. Twenty minutes later, Papa arrived with one in his pickup. "He's always quick about anything like that," said my grandmother, "so I have to be careful what I say."

I, in contrast, was quick to want my way. But wanting to make a good impression, I decided not to push it this time. Instead I said, "Sure, what else have we got to do?"

So we got in the truck and headed down Kemp Street toward Sike's Mall. I've always loved cafeterias anyway; it's the good memories of family gatherings there, I guess. In Texas, they do cafeterias right, and the food at Piccadilly was excellent, especially their yeast rolls.

We returned before sunset, full of chicken fried steak and peach cobbler, ready to nestle in for the night. Even with the drapes drawn, the sun still gave enough light to illumine the pictures on his walls: a sketch of a cowboy on a bucking bronco; a large photograph of the American Quarter Horse displayed prominently over the sofa; and a colored print of the Last Supper. That picture looked out of place in Papa's bachelor quarters, but it hung above the tiny two-seat kitchen table in the living room, in deference to my grandmother. It was the only picture she ever owned. Next to his recliner was a photo calendar. It starred Papa himself riding Paige, Margie's horse, on his eighty-second birthday.

Papa sat down, reached for the silver bootjack under his recliner then began to take off his boots. "They didn't much think I could still mount a horse," he commented when he saw me looking at the calendar, "but I didn't have no trouble at all."

I noticed he looked more at ease on the horse than he did sitting in his chair. Out of respect for the moment, neither of us said anything. It was his last ride and we both knew it.

Then, signaling the beginning of a nightly ritual, Papa reached for the large black Bible he kept on the telephone table beside his chair. I sat on the sofa, my feet tucked under me and listened to Papa's gravelly voice as he read aloud from Psalm 57.

"My heart is fixed, O God, my heart is fixed: I will sing and give praise," he began. But Papa never could just read. After a few verses he'd stop and comment on their meaning, or tell a story about how a particular passage touched his life. That night he began to tell me how the Lord "fixed" his heart. Fixed it because it had been broken and ugly before God saved him. Fixed it by making him steadfast, giving him a purpose, so that he was able to serve God faithfully for so many years.

I just listened, enjoying the sound of his voice and the security of being enveloped by his faith—a faith I longed for but did not fully own.

Pool Sharks

The next morning, I woke up about 8:00 A.M., vaguely aware of someone's presence. I opened one eye and saw Papa sitting in his recliner watching me. He had been careful not to wake me, but he was clearly ready to start the day. We agreed to share kitchen chores. He would cook; I would clean.

The national clamor over eggs and heart disease came too late to benefit Papa, who began every day of his adult life with a breakfast of sausage, biscuits, eggs, and oats.

"I don't eat the way I used to," he said to me as he carried two heavily laden plates to the table. "When I was workin' on the range, I'd eat four eggs every morning. Now I only have two." He seemed to think that was concession enough.

For me, it was the beginning of an unwanted ritual attached to each visit—a weight gain of five pounds a week. But I never could settle for a bowl of cold cereal with a big farm breakfast staring me in the face.

Now a farm breakfast is not to be confused with a Texas breakfast. A Texas breakfast includes crispy fried potatoes and gravy along with eggs, sausage, and biscuits. This calorie-laden feast was a family tradition. The farm breakfast, a shortened version of our beloved Texas breakfast, was temptation enough. So I ate and gained and considered it as much a part of the cost of the journey as the airfare. Fly now, pay later. Some things are worth the experience and a farm breakfast was one of them.

As I dawdled over my second cup of coffee, I got the distinct feeling Papa had some agenda in mind. Finally, he came out with it.

"The boys play pool every morning 'bout ten, if you're interested," he said. "Sounds good," I said looking at my watch. I thought we had plenty of time to shower and dress. But Papa, who couldn't stand to be late for any-thing, spurred me into action. By 9:45 we were headed for the rec room. As we exited the elevator, we met the same group who'd greeted us the day before, plus a few newcomers.

"Howdy, Cowboy! You always did have a way of gettin' the pretty girls," said one stooped, white-haired man. "Looks like you've done gone and done it again."

"Can't keep 'em away when you're as good lookin' as I am," Papa coun-tered, tilting his hat slightly to the side.

I later learned you could tell a lot about a cowboy from the way he wears his hat. "If a cowboy wears his hat over his eyes," Papa said, "it means he's mad or out of humor. If it's sitting back on his head, he's feeling happy-go-lucky. A little sideways means he's cocky. And if it's all crushed in, watch out—he's either drunk or looking for a fight." This morning, it seemed Papa was feeling pretty jaunty.

No explanation of who I was was needed. That information had been delivered from door to door with an efficiency UPS would envy. So, Papa basked in the warmth of their greetings, allowing me to get a better feel for the place that was now his home.

The lobby was filled with an assortment of artificial plants and trees, something I hadn't noticed yesterday. Still, as intended, the greenery sug-gested life and care. A large glass case full of handmade crafts and quilts told me this was an active place. The crocheted blankets and intricate quilts could have fetched a good price in the northeast, had they not contained some of the most awful color combinations I had ever seen. Lime green and yellow with accents of baby blue and pink was one that was repeated often. I wondered if age had dimmed the maker's ability to differentiate colors or if someone simply enjoyed being lavishly unconventional.

The quilts conveyed a cheerful sense of time warp and screamed "old fashioned." Because the quilts lacked the sophistication of timeless classics, they would never be treasured outside these walls. But they were not made with an eye toward profit or use, but for the simple joy of creating. It was a luxury I hoped was appreciated.

Though I loved creative ventures, I found little time to nurture that part of myself. I wanted to write but, except for a few poems, some halting attempts at journaling, and occasional PR work for local charities, I did little. Between my family responsibilities and the mundane, every nook and cranny of my life was filled.

"We have a quilting group that meets three times a week," volunteered a small woman sitting in a wheelchair beside the case. But her eyes twinkled as she held out her hand to me. "I'm Patsy. We turn out a lot of these," she said nodding toward the case.

"I guess so," I said, imagining a storeroom full of unused quilts representing years of work. As much as I valued the creative process, I could never see myself investing the time and effort into a project that had no future.

"We'd better git going," Papa said, eyeing a big clock on the wall.

"Cowboy, you playin' pool with the boys this morning?" Patsy asked.

"Yep," Papa said, taking my elbow and turning me toward the hall. "They're probably waiting for us by now."

And they were. The boys, as they were known at Midtown Manor, consisted of four men who gathered at 10:00 A.M. and 4:00 P.M. every day to play pool. They were the elite of the building. Healthy, witty, aloof, these men literally lived for the four hours a day they shared in each others' company. They weren't particularly good friends. In fact, Virgil, noted for his bad disposition and big appetite, was downright hard to get along with, according to Papa. But the boys' camaraderie eased any pettiness like oil in a machine.

As we entered the room, a short, bald man wearing brown polyester pants walked briskly in front of us. Leading with his stomach, he walked in prissy little steps to a large closet beside the kitchen. It had to be Virgil. He pulled down a heavy box of balls from the shelf and again passed us, his crepe-soled shoes squishing softly. "'Bout time you got here," he mumbled to Papa.

Six or seven women and one man sat around a long folding table in the middle of the room, smoking cigarettes and drinking coffee. In the center sat a large platter of glazed donuts, covered by a deep plastic lid. The cracks in the glazing told me the donuts were a day old—at least—but the residents seemed to be enjoying them.

Papa spoke to each person before directing me toward some comfortable chairs at the far end of the room. "Have a seat there hon," he instructed me. "I have to get my stick." He went to the closet, pulled out his own cue stick from the corner, then joined me.

The other two men were already there, watching Virgil. One of them winked at me but said nothing. The other man introduced himself as Walter. His eyes smiled behind wire-framed glasses, and I liked him immediately.

Virgil began to rack the balls in quick, efficient movements, almost like he was showing off. With each motion, the buttons on his small-checked, long-sleeved shirt strained to cover their territory.

"You can play for me," Papa said, handing me his stick.

"No," I protested. "I'm here to watch y'all play. Go ahead." I could almost hear them sigh with relief. So, I settled in to watch the game, wondering where that little "y'all" had come from.

"Boone, you break," Papa said. I gathered Boone was the man I had not yet met, and it looked like he and Papa were partners. The balls scattered cleanly.

"We got the little ones," Boone said as one solid ball dropped into the pocket. He then pocketed two more. The next one he missed.

Walter giggled, took his own shot and missed. That sobered him up immediately. "Shoulda went," Walter said shaking his head.

Papa walked around the table to line up his shot. "Yep, but it didn't go," he said. Papa sunk another solid ball then proceeded to run the table. I was stunned. Papa had always had great coordination, but I never thought about it translating into his being an excellent pool player.

I knew for a fact he had not played the game while my grandmother was alive; she would have disapproved with a capital D. For the most part, pool was played in dingy beer halls, and the mere hint of that association would have sealed its fate as an X-rated activity in her book. Though Mama was a very quiet and nonjudgmental woman, she held a high standard for herself and family. She was adamant about refraining from even the appearance of evil. Apparently, Papa's views were a little more flexible.

This time Boone racked and Virgil broke, hitting the balls so hard they practically flew off the table. Virgil made four or five of the most incredible shots I had ever seen: going around and over balls; banking impossible combinations; drilling one ball after another into the pocket. He seemed unstoppable. Then he missed a shot and his winning streak was over as quick as it started.

"It ain't right. It ain't right," he complained as he watched his beautiful game go down the drain. The banter and the play continued with Papa and Boone easily winning the next three games. Then Virgil, who was by now very ticked off, suddenly remembered he had something important to do.

"Probably goin' down to the food bank to get some of that moldy cheese," Boone said dryly as he racked up the balls again. "You play for him," he nodded at me. "Me and Alva will split up."

I had no idea at the time, but with his invitation, the key to Midtown Manor had been given to me. Boone was the unofficial king of the Manor, I would learn. The residents respected and fawned over Papa, but they feared Boone.

"Boone's one of the few people in here I'd care for being friends with," Papa told me afterwards, "but he's always got some woman in his place. He's pretty fond of the bottle, too, and I'm not interested in either one."

Yet something about Boone appealed to Papa. Though Papa never dabbled in the seamier side of life after he became a Christian, I had a feeling Boone's rough lifestyle may have reminded him of his friends from cowboy days. I could understand why he might long for them.

Boone was a man of few words, but if he didn't like you, your stock in the hierarchy of Midtown Manor plummeted like a stone. A sarcastic comment under his breath, a long stare, and you were history.

To be accepted by Boone was the ultimate compliment, and, though I didn't fully appreciate the honor he'd given me by asking me to play, it paid immediate benefits. I was "in." I was now an unofficial member of the boys' club.

Boone had welcomed me solely out of respect for my grandfather, with no concern about my level of play. But after watching the amazing display from the four of them, I was suddenly very nervous. Still, not being one to sit on the sidelines, I stood up to join them. Mustering all the confidence I could, I resolved to make my grandfather proud of me.

Rough Start

"Let's see if we can't go the rest of the week without fixing supper at home," Papa said to me one morning. "Sounds great to me," I laughed. I realized I had laughed more in the past four days than the last four years. It felt great. Freeing. *And what is it you want to be free of?* The question came unbidden. My gut twisted because the answer was unacceptable: I felt trapped. Why, I wasn't sure. I loved my family but was consumed by a loneliness so profound it was all I could do to function. Because of it, my kids were getting the short shrift.

A flash of anger rose up in my throat. They needed more. Deserved more. But I couldn't help it. What I gave wasn't enough. Nothing was ever enough and now I had no more to give.

I once saw a book titled *I'm Dancing As Fast As I Can.* I thought, *Perfect description of me,* only I felt I was about to take a giant tumble on the dance floor. Every choice for my family seemed to come out of my hide. I stayed home with my kids because I had wanted to, but something was missing. I didn't know what it was, but the lack of it was killing me.

At least I was finding some respite being with my grandfather. I couldn't remember the last time someone cared about what I thought. Or enjoyed the pleasure of my company just for my own sake. Not as a wife or a mother. Just as a person. Unique and interesting in my own right.

It made me angry to think how much of me had been stripped away. I loved to laugh, but my kids sure didn't know that. I just couldn't get the sadness out of my heart even around them. I often wondered if God saw how I felt. *Do you care about what's happened to me?* I wanted to scream. Lately these angry prayers seem to well up from some dark place inside myself. But, as I cleaned Papa's kitchen, I deliberately brushed these thoughts away, along with the crumbs on the countertops. I didn't even want to think about all that now.

Papa came into the room, smelling fresh and manly. His white starched shirt with long points on the collar had three pearl buttons on the cuffs and one button on each western-style pocket. He looked great. Crisply ironed dark gray slacks. A dress leather belt with a large silver buckle. And, of course, black cowboy boots.

I had forgotten that Papa never went into town without dressing up. He wore work clothes to work and dress clothes for anything else. Fortunately, I had packed a couple of skirts along with my usual sporty attire and seeing Papa was dressed to the nines, I opted for one.

As we headed out for the cafeteria, Papa said, "I always did like to see a lady in a pretty dress."

My face warmed at his words. Back East, a man would get his face slapped for such a comment, but I was sick of political correctness. He intended it as a compliment and I accepted it as such.

We got into Papa's old Ford, which practically drove itself to Piccadilly. Sike's Mall was always busy but we were lucky to find a parking place near the cafeteria entrance. I didn't bother trying other locations. Papa liked to park in one particular area; if there wasn't a place, we would just drive around till one opened up. Ordinarily, this little quirk would have driven me crazy, but, surprisingly, I didn't mind. It was nice to gear down a bit.

My stomach was growling in anticipation of food, but I knew parking was just the first obstacle to eating. We could hardly make it through the mall's main entrance for all the people who knew Papa.

"Hey, Cowboy, how's it going?" was the usual greeting followed by witty comments or good-natured teasing. The men would tell me stories about Papa and pass along any new tidbit of news to him. Family business, horse business, and church business were the topics of interest.

A tall thin man with a huge Adam's apple met us and shook Papa's hand and mine enthusiastically. "Mister Choate, did you hear ol' Barnes is sellin' his place? He's moving to Fort Worth to be near his kids." The man was chawing on a toothpick so I knew he'd already enjoyed his lunch.

I was wishing we could get on with our own meal, but Papa was in no hurry. Yes, he'd heard. There weren't many things Papa hadn't heard already but that was because he was a diligent networker. He liked being "in the know."

A bowlegged cowboy with a paunch stopped us next. "Cowboy," he said after the usual preliminaries, "my daughter's lookin' for a gentle mare, if you come across one."

"How old is she?" Papa asked.

"'Bout ten."

"She ridden much?"

"Naw, just a few months."

Papa nodded slowly. "Then you don't want something with a lot of spirit in her. Call Jake Ward. He's got an old sorrel that's pretty good turned. Small. He might be ready to let go of her."

Grateful, the man went on his way and at last we were free to make our way to the line.

Breathing deeply to take in the aroma of fresh bread, I worked my way slowly down the line of sumptuous food. Something wonderful comes over me when I enter the threshhold of a good cafeteria. Maybe it's all the choices. Or the clientele—mostly down-to-earth folks I feel comfortable around. It might be just the anticipation of favorite foods. For whatever reason, I love it.

Most Sundays that I could remember, Mama and Papa ate at the cafeteria. It's a memory that entices me yet. Maybe if they'd belonged to the country club I'd have had an affinity for that way of life, but I didn't. Too bad. It might have helped.

Instead, thanks to my husband's successful corporate career, the country club arena is exactly where we found ourselves. We moved easily there but were marginal members. Though we enjoyed the lifestyle, that environment tended to mirror many of the social and political dynamics of the workplace that we found unappealing. Social standing wasn't an issue at Piccadilly.

"Thank you, Mr. Choate," said the smiling clerk at the end of the cafeteria line as she handed him our bill. Papa took it quickly. He'd let me know from day one there would be no sharing of expenses. He was the gentleman; he would pay. I waited for him to tuck the ticket into his shirt pocket, then together we picked up our trays, steaming with southern fare flanked by tall glasses of iced tea. Walking gingerly, we scanned the room for a booth, which, like the parking place, we were also willing to wait for, if necessary. We snagged one just as its previous occupants were leaving.

A small dark woman appeared to wipe off our table. She looked like she might be part Hispanic as well as American Indian. That was something I loved about Texas—the mixture of those two races.

Both Papa and Mama were Indian, and, though you could never tell from my coloring, my mother had been very dark skinned. Her hair was raven black. Coarse. Her facial features very Indian. From her I had inherited thick hair, high cheekbones and a petite frame. And that was about it. But I am drawn to people with brown skin—a partiality I would attribute to my mother.

This woman looked to be about the age my mother would have been had she lived. I greeted her warmly and she responded with a shy hello but kept busy at her work. She moved quickly to another table leaving Papa and me to our meal.

"Papa, don't you think that woman looks like my mother?" I asked.

"Maria? Can't say I ever thought about it. Known her for years. But now that you mention it, yeah, she does favor Atha a bit."

There was a sharp pinch in my stomach at the sound of my mother's name. It had been years since I had heard it spoken. I felt a pang of loneliness for her I had not felt in some time. Time had done its work to heal the pain, but forgetting had brought a pain of its own. I wanted to remember my mother. To sense her influence in my choices. To treasure her quiet spirit, shy smile, and laughing eyes. I never wanted to forget her. Yet I had forgotten her. Day by day. Year after lonely year. I no longer gave the loneliness her name and it occurred to me that perhaps I should. Though common sense told me what I felt could never be filled by one person.

She died at thirty-nine.

Would I feel I had done my share of living had I only five years left? I wondered. That was a sobering thought I wasn't ready to answer just yet, so I returned to the present. I wanted to hear about Papa's life. I had missed the chance to know my mother's. I was nineteen when she died, old enough to have asked and understood. But even though I knew she was dying, at the time it never occurred to me that knowing would matter.

"Papa," I asked, "what was your life like when you were a teenager?"

But as I asked the question, my own memories returned. Caring for my mother. Loving her. Waiting for her to die. I snapped at my brother, my sister. Closed off from the world. I turned down the parties at school—partly because I didn't want to long for what I couldn't have and partly because I recognized my time for giving to her was quickly passing. I wanted to give, but to her only. Everything else I resented. Outside I looked like a saint. Inside, my heart locked down, frozen in fear. I couldn't imagine what normal teen years would be like.

"When I was a teenager," Papa's gruff voice interrupted my thoughts, "I was workin' for my daddy. He was one of the most successful farmers in the county."

"Really?" This was news to me. For most of their lives, my grandparents had just enough to get by. Even then, they wouldn't have made it except for the credit extended to them by local stores. It never occurred to me there could have been a time when they lived differently.

Yeah. My daddy, Thomas Choate, was what they called a scientific farmer. At one time he farmed cotton and corn on seven hundred acres of rich river bottomland, in the heart of what is now Texoma Lake. Every one of Poppa's six boys had the finest horse and saddle that money could buy. But none of us got much schoolin'.

If I coulda got some education things might not have been so rough. But Poppa had a stroke when I was in fifth grade, and I had to quit school to work in the fields. I was sixteen before I had the chance to go back.

When Poppa got better he said, "Alva, I'll pay for any kind of learnin' you want. I can afford to do it now." So I went back but not for long. I was so far behind I had to study with the little bitty kids, and I couldn't stand the humiliation. I got most my learnin' on the job. But I got to where I could figure the lumber for a house as good as any college guy.

Soon after his daddy was able to work again, Papa went out on his own. He took a job in the oil fields and, as far as I can gather, sowed some wild oats, though he kept the specifics to himself. "I don't want nothin' in my life to be a stumblin' block to any of the grandkids," he explained. As it turned out, they didn't need a stumbling block; they made the same blunders without any help whatsoever.

Papa's freedom allowed him to follow the rodeo to his heart's content. "There weren't no money in it in those days," he said. "We just rode for the love of it." Yet after he became a Christian, he wouldn't even go to the rodeo. "I know what goes on there," he would say, shaking his head.

After a couple years of the wild life with no let up in sight, Poppa started getting worried. One day he rode out to where his son was working. "Alva, if you'll come home and work the farm with me, I'll buy one of those new tractors from McCormick Deering," he said. "I've already talked to them and they'll let me pay it out by the month." In today's terms, the bribe was the equivalent of a little red sportscar. And it worked. My grandfather returned to the farm.

Yellow Rose of Texas

After Papa moved back to the farm to help his daddy, it became obvious there was something more than a new tractor in which he was interested. A family named White had rented a few acres from Thomas and helped him pick cotton during the harvest season. The Whites also had a beautiful daughter. "They lived within hollerin' distance from us," Papa said.

We both had big families. A lot of the kids was about the same age, and when I came home to visit one weekend my daddy wanted me to meet them. So they come over. That's the first time I saw Cora. She was real quiet. Kind of bashful. But when I saw her, I thought she was the prettiest girl I'd ever seen. Yeah, Cora was real pretty. Course I never thought about marryin' her or nothin' like that then 'cause she was only fifteen and I was twenty or twenty-one.

We had one of those gramophones that sat in one of those great big ol' cabinets. And we had waltz records, two-step records, and rag records 'cause we all loved to dance.

There was always a dance in town on the weekends, and me and Earl used to go every Friday night. We'd work the fields all day, come home, clean up, and get back on our horse without even eating supper. All the guys would pay the fiddler a dollar each—a day's wages—and we'd dance till two or three o'clock in the morning.

I stopped goin' after me and Cora got together. She was so shy she wouldn't dance in a public place. She was a great little dancer though. Real light on her feet. That's the first thing I noticed about her.

Well, when her and her family come over that time, we put on them records and I danced with Cora the whole time. I stayed home about a week or so and they came over every night. I went back to work then, and it was a year later before I come back. Then it was to stay. The first thing I made a point to find out was if the neighbors had moved. They hadn't. Cora was sixteen by then, but still too young for me so I tried to forget her. For several months I just run here and yonder, dating one girl then another, but it didn't help.

Cora had a girlfriend named Peyton Morrison who was older. I knew Cora's parents wouldn't let me go with Cora 'cause she was so young, so I just started going around with Peyton and Cora to church or back or somethin' like that. Well, all the folks thought I was talkin' to Peyton but I didn't care nothin' for her. It was Cora I was interested in. Finally we got up the nerve to let people know we was sort of courtin'. Her mother didn't say nothin' about it so I started goin' with her steady.

I was crazy about her and I guess she was crazy 'bout me too 'cause we never had one bit of trouble. We planned to marry after the next harvest, but then things started going against us.

My daddy farmed all that good land there and was doin' real good for a long time, but we hit two years where the boll weevils ate the cotton up. Poppa had tractor rigs, seven teams, and hired hands, and for two years he paid out and didn't get nothin' back. He had to mortgage everything he owned just to get seed for the third year's crop. That year, the cotton came in big—purdiest crop I ever seen. The field looked just like a snow bank, far as the eye could see.

Well, we had a bunch of hands pickin' cotton and when the first wagon was loaded with bales, Poppa drove off to the gin. Before long, he's back, all red and angry. He says, "Alva, call the pickers in and let them weigh up. Then open the gates and let the cows out in the pasture." I thought he was crazy 'cause them cows would trample the crop. Then he told me what had happened.

The price of cotton dropped overnight, and for us, the bottom fell out of everything. Poppa said, "The last two bales we took in lacked

two dollars payin' for the pickin' and the ginnin'." There was no point
in just watchin' it ruin in the field, so we let the cows in.

It was 1924 when the cotton market failed—and with it went Papa's
hopes for marrying Cora White. "I love you," he told her, "but I got no way
to support a family."

I thought it ironic that it never occurred to Joe or me, both college students, to view lack of income as a reason for postponing marriage.

When Joe asked for my hand in marriage, my father asked him, "Do
you think you can provide for my daughter?" I still can't help laughing
when I think about my cautious, pessimistic, soon-to-be-husband, owning
nothing in this world but a 1967 VW bug, looking my father straight in the
eyes and somberly assuring him, "Yes, I do."

At twenty-one and nineteen, we thought if all else failed, we could both
work at McDonald's and make enough to get by. So we married. Joe had a
semester left at California State University at Fullerton then four years of
law school. I was a sophomore at the local junior college. With part time
jobs, we not only had to pay our living expenses, but all of our own college
tuition. The amazing thing is that somehow we did it.

Joe made another commitment to my father that night. One I didn't
learn about until twenty years into our marriage. "If anything happens to
Karen. If she becomes sick or disabled, I'll never leave her," he said. "I will
love her and take care of her the rest of her life."

That blew me away. It's one thing to marry someone assuming you're
going to have a great life together—being an optimist, that was my perspective. It's another thing to marry expecting the worst—being a pessimist, that was Joe's.

On the day we declared our vows, I had committed to stay by Joe "in
sickness and in health," but I hadn't really thought it through. My vow
came from my head. His was from the heart. Had we known the degree to
which these commitments would be tested, I doubt either of us would've
had the courage to proceed. But on a rainy, Saturday night in January 1970,
we were just two kids who thought we could handle anything together.

Though we had absolutely no vision for the future, we sensed in each
other an unusual amount of perseverance and determination. Not for one
moment did I question whether either of us would quit school if things got
hard. Neither did Joe. And we didn't.

Unlike Mama and Papa's courtship, ours was anything but love at first
sight. Joe and I dated briefly in high school when his family began attending

my father's church. In fact, I was the first girl to ride in his little blue VW beetle. Joe picked up his new car that afternoon then swung by to pick me up for a beach party. When we left the Huntington Beach pier late that night, I hopped into the front seat with my dirty feet, sprinkling sand all over his new cocoa mats. Though he didn't let on at the time, he wasn't pleased.

I've often reminded him that after that night he shouldn't have been surprised that I was forever bringing something unsettling into his life. I think he married me because deep down he wanted someone who could have fun without worrying about getting sand on the cocoa mats. Someone who would nudge him to enjoy life without sweating the details. I married him because he *did* sweat the details and that allowed me to be more free. Anyway that little scenario pretty well depicted what would become the dynamic of our marriage.

All the potential problems were evident from the very beginning. Of course, we didn't recognize them as such, and I didn't think much about it when we first dated because it didn't look like our relationship was going anywhere. Joe had a great sense of humor, but I lost interest when we weren't successful in getting past that superficial level. Interpreting it as not "clicking," I moved on. I doubt we would have ever gotten together had I not left the country.

The summer after I graduated from high school, I went on a three-month missions trip to Nicaragua. As a friend, Joe wrote to me faithfully and, for the first time, gave me glimpse of the person he really was. I could tell he worked hard. Took college seriously. Was driven to succeed. And had picked up on the fact that the way to my heart was through my family.

Joe took my brother to the beach every day. He teased my little sister. And brought my mother pies, courtesy of a girl he was dating who worked at Marie Callender's pie shop. For my family, notorious sweet lovers, that was definitely a good move.

Meanwhile, Joe's hilarious descriptions of family events helped assuage my homesickness and provided much needed relief from the physical hardships I was experiencing in Central America. My girlfriends, wanting to know what was so funny, conned me into reading the humorous parts to them. Soon, I wasn't the only one looking forward to Joe's letters. By summer's end, he'd gained quite a fan club, me among them.

I returned home in September to find that a steady diet of tortillas and peanut butter had plumped me up two dress sizes. Not having looked in a mirror for three months and wearing nothing but mumu-style cotton dresses in the jungle, I'd had no clue. Being young, it didn't take me long to lose the weight, though I never again regained that little girl, string bean shape I'd had before.

Joe, in contrast, had gotten leaner. At 6'4", he couldn't have weighed more than 160 pounds. He was deeply tanned with short hair, bleached white by the California sun. But it was his intelligence—burning behind cool aquamarine eyes—that captivated me. I've always thought Joe was the smartest man I've ever met. I loved the way he could spar with me about everything from the classics to current events. He was well read, a brilliant debater (almost a necessity in my vocal, aggressive family) and a creative thinker.

But I saw something else in his eyes that both concerned and drew me: a deep sadness I couldn't reach. He'd been deeply wounded, but I was convinced that in time he would let me in so I could, of course, make it all better. I was wrong about that, but it would take me years to accept defeat.

I wasn't wrong about everything though. I sensed something special in Joe. He lacked confidence in himself, but I had enough for the two of us. Even though he had no financial resources—not even a college degree yet—I knew he was destined for success in a big way. I didn't know if it would mean financial gain or not, but for me, that was beside the point. It was the adventure that intrigued me. Joe was going somewhere and I wanted to go with him. I felt we'd be good partners in business as well as life.

On the night he proposed to me, Joe took me to the church in which I had grown up. After slipping a small diamond ring of white gold on my finger, he read to me from 1 Samuel 7:12.

"Then Samuel took a stone and set it up between Mizpah and Shen, and called its name Ebenezer, saying, 'Thus far the Lord has helped us.'"

This act—choosing a scriptural principle to guide our life together—touched me deeply. I tended to observe life in the realm of symbols and ideals, something I was pleased Joe understood. But more important, the acknowledgment of our dependency upon God to help us, whatever our future might hold, was like laying a massive cornerstone for the foundation of our home.

We knelt at the altar, the darkness of the sanctuary broken only by the shimmer of gold emanating from a large cross and the candlesticks on the communion table. We didn't know it at the time, but that table held all the lessons we were destined to learn in the years ahead. I knew the litany by heart: "…this is my body which is broken for you…" The lessons would come harder. Sacrifice. Commitment. Love. The life, the body, and blood of one for another. It was an exchange I embraced then without understanding.

Fall
1987

Roots

As I sat in Papa's living room, listening to the account of my grand-parent's early years of marriage, my first impression was that their beginning was very unlike Joe's and mine. But on second thought I changed my mind. The pressures were different; theirs was a scramble for physical survival, mine was for emotional balance—but it was a fight for survival nonetheless.

By 1930, Papa's family wasn't the only one in trouble. The bottom would fall out for the whole nation. I couldn't relate to what it must have been like to wake up one day and have no job, no food, and no hope of get-ting either. But I did know what it was like to have the bottom fall out and feel like there was no future.

My mother died six months after Joe and I married, and with her went a big chunk of the foundation of my life. My father, consumed by his own grief was not able to fill the gap. Frantically, I looked to Joe for the security I'd lost, only to find he was as overwhelmed as I was.

I muddled through several years as Joe finished law school and began a corporate career. We moved a couple of times. Had our two boys. And around every corner I expected to find that elusive "something" that would fix whatever was wrong inside of me. I liked moving (one time we moved three times in two years) because it helped take my mind off the alarm screaming in my gut that something wasn't right.

It was when we stopped moving that it all came crashing down. Emptiness. Fatigue. Headaches. Tears. I couldn't get past them. I kept what sanity I had by escaping whenever I could. So when my aunt called to tell me there was going to be a first ever Choate family reunion, I jumped at the chance to go.

I brought David, my younger son, with me. Since he was only eight— young enough to miss a little school—it seemed a good opportunity for him to meet the family. The travel was rough: seventeen hours going, twelve hours returning.

We left in the midst of an ice storm in New York only to be greeted by high winds in Texas. The little plane from Dallas to Wichita Falls tossed us up, down, and sideways with drops twice that of a roller coaster. I was scared to death. David was mostly worried about throwing up. "Mom, it's up to here," he said, pointing to higher and higher places on his throat. I gave him a barf bag and hoped for the best. Thankfully, he made it and so did the plane.

In spite of my good intentions to see Papa on a regular basis, it had been two years since my last visit. I'd been busy trying to pull myself out of depression. I'd tried working part-time selling real estate but the kids' chronic allergies and ear infections kept me home half the time. Instead of being a release, juggling home responsibilities with work demands was making me even more frazzled. I talked to everybody who would listen, but no one seemed to understand.

"You've got to take time for yourself," they said. And my question was, "And just who is supposed to take care of the kids while I take time for myself?"

There didn't seem to be such a thing as a reliable babysitter. Several months after the fact, Michael told me that the husband of our sitter had drawn a handgun and threatened to shoot their thirteen-year-old son in front of them. I called the sitter and cancelled our arrangement, but I trembled for days thinking of the danger my kids had been in. So, what were my options? My closest family was three thousand miles away and co-oping wasn't worth the pain of having twice as many kids in my house the next day.

"I feel like a time bomb ready to go off," I told Joe, often in quick, staccato words. Each morning I would wake up and swear I would be different. I prayed God would help me cope. I would not complain to Joe. I would be kind to the kids. I would…I would…I would…But I couldn't. And I was still shaking from an episode a few days earlier.

My kids were up early as usual, but instead of cleaning their rooms and getting dressed as they were supposed to do, they came downstairs to play. They were happy, full of energy, and playing sweetly together. We had breakfast and I sent them to get dressed. But when I went to their room a half hour later, both were still in their pajamas and the room was a mess. I lost it. I started in on them, following them around as they tried to keep up with my orders. I yelled. They moved slowly. So slowly I wanted to scream and I did. I kept going after them. Not hitting, but wanting to. Crying, until I got them as upset as I was, which was what I wanted, I guess. The moment I let them go, they ran out the front door, full of their anger as well as mine.

I felt terrible about it. Even if the outburst was about teaching them to be responsible (which I knew it wasn't), why did I have to do it that way? A mother should be the one person a child could count on to be encouraging. To be kind. But I was not kind to my children. That day, I was mean. A tyrant. I apologized to them but was sick wondering if the memory of an out-of-control mom could ever be erased. And it seemed to be happening more and more.

I was tired of trying to make Joe understand that some darkness burned inside me—smoldering like live coals, consuming everything about me that was light and good. It took all I had just to get up in the mornings, let alone plan something for myself like a trip to Texas. Had it not been for the extra motivation of a family reunion, I doubt I would have made it.

But now that we were here, I was glad. Papa's warmth embraced us the moment we saw him. He showed off David to the waiting gallery in the lobby of Midtown Manor then ushered us up to his apartment.

"David, you look pretty sharp in those cowboy boots," Papa said taking in my son's western attire. "But where's your hat?"

"Don't have one," David said, rocking back and forth on his boot heels.

Papa bent down so they were eye level. "What was that?" he asked.

"I said I don't have one."

Papa shook his head. "Well then, we're going to have to do something about that." He stood up, walked to the hall closet, and slid a beautiful felt cowboy hat off the shelf. "Why don't you try this one on? There's a mirror in there," he said, pointing toward the bedroom.

David ran to the mirror and put on the hat. "This is great!" he said, checking his profile on first one side then the other.

Papa chuckled, fiddled with the brim, then settled the hat slightly to one side. "It's a little big, but it'll do."

The hat became David's constant companion as we went about our daily routine—farm breakfast, pool, and Piccadilly. The three of us played a good bit of pool by ourselves, and, of course, we watched Papa pace the boys. We didn't have quite as many trips to Piccadilly as usual, though, because we were flooded with lunch and dinner invitations. For some reason, Papa didn't seem as enthusiastic about them this time, but he went along with it knowing all the relatives wanted to see David.

As the day of the reunion approached, I was primed for a meaningful connection with those who shared my heritage. For several weeks I had been immersed in family history, taking hours of notes and recording Papa's recollection of various family members and events.

I was born in 1903 in Davis, Oklahoma, just out from Sulfur. It was Indian Territory then, before statehood. We was part Indian. Cherokee. We coulda gotten our rights if it hadn't been that the papers for our tribe was transferred for some reason from Muskogee to Gainesville and the courthouse burned down, along with all our records. We have traced them to Muskogee. They have them at Muskogee showing up to Earl, me, and Pernie on the records. All our names was on the record. My daddy had his record, but it was Mama Brasher's family records that got burned up. Mama Brasher, my mother's mother, was a full-blooded Indian.

All the tribes had different strips. The Cherokee Strip, the Chickasha Strip. It was our strip, the Cherokee Strip, that was missing. They had the proof that we had the Indian rights but we couldn't get it.

Now Lester Watts, his mother was a Brasher—Emmy Brasher— and when he married, his wife went to Muskogee. She went as far as she could go with it. She had proof we were on the records but couldn't get the papers to get the rights.

I don't know why they transferred the papers out of the territory. Really nobody knows. It may have been some dirty work that was done way back. Anyway, they claimed that that was where the papers was destroyed years ago and all the proof was burned up. We tried several times but we never could get the papers.

Both Mama and I was Cherokee. That's where our family gets that dark complexion. Edwin. Teresa's boy. In all the family there's at least one that shows up. Pernie. Now Pernie really showed up. Johnny Choate. And Atha. Yeah, Atha was real dark complected.

I was intrigued by my Indian heritage and proud of it, but it was a heritage of another kind that took me by surprise when the day of the reunion finally rolled around. We gathered at what was generously termed the picnic area of Lake Arrowhead Park. In truth, it was a covered 30' x 70' rectangle of concrete set in the middle of nowhere. A dirt buffer of ten or fifteen feet surrounded the perimeter, keeping the underbrush at bay. The site was quite a distance from the park entrance, and the lake was nowhere in sight. Somebody said it was "just down a ways" from our campground, but only a fool would walk through the surrounding briar scrub, even with boots, to find it. It looked like snake heaven to me.

A few vehicles were already there—mostly trucks. A few big American cars. And people began to fill the patio, toting an assortment of lawn chairs, coolers, and barbecues. As people arrived, my aunt introduced them to David and me. Some I knew. Papa's two sisters, Winnie and Lois. Lois, the youngest of Papa's eight siblings, was now in her late seventies. I warmed to her immediately because she reminded me so much of Papa. Tiny, dark haired, spry, with a gleam of mischief in her eye. All of Aunt Marie's family were there. My cousins. Most looked like clean-living people, but there was also a group of strangers who, as Papa would say, "looked like they'd been rode hard and left out to dry."

These people had lived. You could tell from the hardness in their eyes as they smoked one cigarette after another and from the gaudy tattoos sported by men and women alike. Their language. The attitudes. I'd been around rough people before so they didn't offend me. If anything, I was drawn to people whose lives had been more exciting than my own. Maybe this explained why. If I could have seen into the future of my family, I would have had to acknowledge it was more of an affinity than an attraction of opposites.

What caught me off guard was the fact that these people were family. I couldn't believe that within one generation there could be such a divergence of culture. From various conversations the facts emerged. There was a lot of interest in someone who was in the state penitentiary.

"Papa, what was he in for?" I asked.

"What?" Papa asked, leaning toward me.

I repeated the question and he stiffened in his chair.

"Counterfeiting," he admitted, drawing his mouth into a tight line, and would say nothing more.

As people gathered into familiar groups, chatting about past love affairs, jail terms, and rehab facilities, I could only hope the Texas tendency for exaggeration had kicked in big time. It felt like there were more crooks, alcoholics, drug addicts, and moral reprobates on that one cement pad than one would find in any one place in the country—except maybe a jail yard.

In Texas, others put a lot of stock in your "people." When a young woman started dating, one of the first questions her family was likely to ask was, "Who are his people?" One of the highest compliments a person could receive was for someone to say, "She comes from good people." It was a reference not just to physical or financial status, but to the character and reputation of the family in the community.

That these were "my people" gave me pause for concern. It's not that I thought Papa, my aunt, my mother, or their families were any better than my other relatives, but it was clear that somewhere along the line Papa had taken his family in a different direction. Somehow he managed to live his life unmarked by crime and addiction. They did not. What made the difference?

When I asked Papa about it later he answered without a moment's hesitation. "The Lord," he said simply. "It was the Lord."

Every night me and Cora would read the Bible together. Never failed. Cora studied in the morning while I was working. Then when I'd come home at noon, she would have dinner ready. We would kneel at the table and pray. Then I'd sit down and eat while she read out of the Bible. And we'd shout and cry and in between I'd eat till I had to get up and go to work. After I left, then Cora would eat, and that was how we lived the most of our life.

We lived together fifty-two years. Over fifty years of those we was Christians and I don't know of a time that we ever went to bed without me and her prayin'. We never went to the table without offering thanks. Sometimes we'd start giving thanks for the food and just keep prayin'. The Lord was so real to us that it woulda been for anyone to backslide in the Christian environment we had in our home.

This was the heritage I had always taken for granted. Ever since I could remember, I knew God existed and that I wanted to know Him. It wasn't until I was an adult that I realized not everyone felt that way. A man once told me, "You don't know how lucky you are. I want so much to believe in God and I can't. I never have." He wondered if that "knowing" was a gift, and I've come to believe that it is. I see it now as a kind of grace, though I have no clue as to why I was given it. I did nothing to deserve it. But I wonder if the spiritual foundation laid by my grandparents and parents made it possible.

I was a preacher's daughter so I knew the Bible backward and forward. What I didn't know was how the truth of the Bible made any real difference in someone's life. Somehow Papa claimed that truth had led him and Mama to make choices that resulted in a better way of life for them and for their children.

Still, it was sobering to own the other influences on our family—the vices and weaknesses tightly woven into our heritage. I must have had a shocked look on my face because, as I sat in a flimsy patio chair contemplating all this, my aunt came and sat beside me. She took a bite of mustard greens then picked at her baked beans. "Well," she said with a smile playing at her lips, "what do you think of your roots?"

Cowboy

Papa's cowboy life lent a legendary quality to the less colorful side of our family tree. And his passion for horses set him apart from his contemporaries. Most people fled the ranch or the farm at the first opportunity, but not Papa.

We once asked him, "If you could live at any time in history, when would it be?" He said, "I guess it would be in the days of the pioneers going out West in covered wagons. The horse and buggy days—before the invention of the automobile." To which my grandmother replied, "Well, you didn't miss it by much."

True. Papa was born at the end of that era, but he would have been perfectly content had it continued to the end of his days. From an early age, Papa realized he had a gift with horses.

"All the guys would run off to play ball of some kind and they'd ask me to come along, but I'd always rather monkey around with some horse. I used to train 'em to do all kinds of things. Had this one horse I trained to not walk over a rope."

"Now why would you do that?" I asked.

"No reason except to prove I could do it," he said.

Soon Papa realized if he could train a horse to not step over a rope, he could teach him to do something a little more practical. One of his favorites was training a horse to follow him like a dog would his master.

I was in town one day with my horse. I started walkin' around takin' care of my business and wherever I'd go, that horse would go. I never had to tie him up or anything. Some of the men standing around said, "Look at that horse. He's followin' that guy." I told them I'd trained him that way, but one of them said, "He's not followin' you, he's followin' them mules."

Well, a fella was leading a pack of mules goin' the same direction we was. But I was with a friend who had a one-horse wagon, so I got in his wagon with him and told him, "Now just drive off," and he did. He drove through the alley, then down the main street, and went on down to his house—and that horse was right behind me. He weren't followin' no mules. He was followin' me.

I would train a horse just like you would a kid. I'd talk to him. Let him know what I wanted. I'd call him to me. Maybe he'd take a step or two and I'd praise him. Pretty soon I stopped trainin' horses to do tricks, though, and trained them to work with cattle.

I'd teach a horse to cut a cow out from the herd by working with the horse alone first. While I was riding him, I'd shut him down right quick and make him turn back till I got him where I wanted to be. Then we'd do it with a cow. Got so he'd know when I wanted to cut a cow out from the herd and every time that cow would take a step in the wrong direction, my horse would step in front of him and cut him off here, cut him off there. He'd just stand in front of the cow till we let him turn back. That's how I trained "cuttin' horses." With a good horse, the two of us could go out and bring a cow in from the pasture by ourselves.

Papa would've been happy to work with livestock the rest of his life, but, as often happens, what he needed to do conflicted with what he loved to do. He built roads, worked in the oil fields, picked cotton, sold trucks, drove trucks, worked construction, did maintenance work, and anything else he could do to make enough to feed his family.

That wasn't unusual for his generation, but what impressed me about my grandfather was how he managed to keep such a strong sense of himself in the midst of it. No matter what he did to earn a living, Papa was a cowboy. According to his family, he didn't fret about future goals, his potential, or personal fulfillment. He just worked hard, prayed, and kept a sharp eye out for the opportunity to do what he loved.

Amazingly, he was often able to make a living working with livestock when no one else could. There is a proverb that says, "A man's gifts make room for him." That axiom proved true for Papa. Opportunities seem to just fall into his lap, and when they came, he took them—but never held them tightly.

Papa was always a risk taker. Perhaps because he started out a farmer and believed "farmin' is the biggest gamble a man can make," he grew up accepting calamity and change as a part of life. Papa would walk away from anything if staying meant compromise. He was convinced that if one thing didn't work out, another would.

Like everybody else, Papa floated from job to job during the Depression, moving between Texas and Oklahoma following rumors of work. By now he had three kids and did whatever was necessary to keep body and soul together. But being an entrepreneur at heart, Papa could never resist the temptation to make a go of things on his own.

The truth is, he failed at everything he tried that didn't involve horses or livestock. In 1933 he moved the family to Oklahoma to start a turkey ranch but it never got off the ground. Instead, he did some itinerate preaching and ended up in Seminole working in the oil fields of Oklahoma City.

Two years later, the woman preacher who had led Mama and Papa to God wrote and asked them to come to Byers. She was trying to get a church started and needed help. Mama and Papa, both fervent Christians by then, jumped at the opportunity. Papa's brother, Pernie, lived in Byers. He and his wife, Evie had also become Christians and were enthusiastic about working together with Alva, Cora, and Sister Hartwell.

Papa knew Byers would need pickers for their cotton crop that fall, and he figured they could make enough to get by. By all outward standards, it was a foolish move—giving up a steady job in the oil fields for low-paying, backbreaking work. But once my grandparents became convinced God was leading them in a particular direction, there was no stopping them. As it happened, it was while in Byers that Papa landed one of the best jobs of his life: foreman of the Blackwell ranch.

Foreman

Old man Blackwell—that would be Brice Blackwell I—was president of the Wichita National Bank and part owner of the All American Oil Refinery. I heard he finally sold the refinery for five million dollars, but he made most his money in cattle. He had one of the largest ranches around those parts—before it got taken over by the bank, oh, musta been around 1980. His kids run it into the ground with their drinkin' and carryin' on. But in 1935, the Blackwell Ranch was one of the most prosperous ranches in these parts.

Old man Blackwell raised the cattle, and Brice II, the boy, was in charge of the farming. The ranch had ten big farms of about four thousand acres, and each farm had at least one hired man and a family or two. All together there was twenty families on the ranch. Blackwell was lookin' for a manager to run the ranch. I heard 'bout it—it was August—and I went to his office in Wichita Falls to hit him up for the job.

I applied but didn't hear nothin'. There was ten or twelve men who was tryin' to get that foreman job. But there was this rancher in Byers that knew me. He knew I could handle stock, and Blackwell knew him, too. One day Blackwell was out that way and dropped by to see him.

It was just the Lord that he talked to that rancher 'cause there wasn't many people in Byers that knew me then. Anyway, that rancher told him, "My head man has just passed away, and I'm gettin' ready to go hire Choate myself."

Well, Blackwell got in his car and came to my house just as hard as he could tear. We lived in a little ol' house where we'd been pickin' cotton. He drove his big yellow Cadillac nearly up to the front porch and said, "I've decided to hire you, so just go on down and move onto the ranch."

That was music to my ears. There was a bunch of Hardings that owned a lot of land down there, and one of their boys was tryin' to get that foreman job. I just knew somebody like that was gonna get it. I could hardly believe it.

So, we moved down there with all we had, and we got a pretty fair housekeeping outfit. A couch, a chair. A new oil range. We bought that from the mercantile in Byers. Then we went to Wichita and bought a bill of groceries—'bout a week's supply. The job paid thirty dollars a month, and they fed our chickens, our hogs, our milk cows and things like that. They had the finest land you ever saw, so we had big gardens. We didn't have to buy much. There was no electric bill 'cause we didn't have electricity—we used kerosene lamps. We had a wood stove and cut our own wood. And I wasn't there too long when I got raised to forty-five dollars a month. I was making eight-five dollars a month when I left there. Then most people all over the country was working for a dollar or a dollar-fifty a day. I'd have fifty hands working on the ranch and they'd get a dollar a day.

Papa had that job for five years, working cattle for the old man and the farm for Brice II. When the old man died, Papa continued in the same job for about a year until Brice II fired him for refusing to work on Sundays. The firing was a blow to him. But by now I recognized one constant thread running through Papa's life: a commitment to God, his family, and his passion—horses. All his choices were made in light of those priorities, in that order, regardless of the cost.

I had some trouble with that priority system; I just couldn't see how it played out. If God and family—the first two priorities—were all consuming, how did one ever get around to number three? I hadn't even had time to discover my passion, let alone pursue it. There was so little of me left, but that "little" was fighting for all it was worth to be seen and heard.

Yet I couldn't deny that it worked for Papa. By putting God first, he was a better provider, and more fully the man God created him to be. I started thinking about what it would mean for me to abandon myself to God that way. To stop trying to carve out my own place in the world. To give myself first to the task of loving God (whatever that meant) and trust that in discovering God I would discover myself.

I envied Papa's self-assurance. Unlike me, he never seemed to struggle with who he was. He was a cowboy. He knew it and so did everyone else. But who was I?

I couldn't help wondering how Joe and the boys perceived me. Did they see me as neurotic? Miserable? Depressed? It saddened me to admit that while these descriptions would be accurate, not one would give a single clue about who I really was.

As for how to change that, I had no idea. Intuitively, I knew God had to be part of the equation. He made me. He, more than anyone, knew what made me tick. But my struggle didn't center on whether or not God created me. My question was, *Does He care about me?*

It had been a long time since I'd felt cared for. Looking back on it, I realized that even as a child I'd often been depressed. Though my family loved me, in my mind, it was for what I did, not for myself. They saw me as the serious, brooding one. Though true, it was an assignation I resented. I knew there was more to me, but moodiness was the face I showed to the world. Since the real me had never seen the light of day, I had nothing else to offer.

I handled my anger about my place in the family by making myself useful; I couldn't imagine anyone wanting to be around me for any other reason. Later, my mother's illness and death gave me the perfect excuse to drown myself in "doing," and I did that admirably.

After Joe and I married, I thought, *At last, someone who will love me for myself.* But I had married a man who had a hole inside him very much like mine, and he was busy filling it in the way he thought best: work and more work.

Though I continued to pressure Joe for nurturing and acceptance, my needs always seemed to end up on the back burner. "After I finish school," he promised. Later it was, "As soon as I get established in my job, then there will be time for us."

Somehow, in spite of the depression, I remained optimistic. I hung in there believing that somewhere along the line, my day would come. I cried, begged, and threatened, but nothing changed. And seven years passed.

I remember clearly the day I began to lose hope.

I was in my obstetrician's office in Greenwich, Connecticut, enduring what I hoped would be the last prenatal exam before the birth of my son, Michael. The doctor removed the rubber gloves from his hands and dropped them in the plastic-lined container behind him. He turned slowly to face me.

"I'm sorry, dear," he said, crossing his arms and stooping slightly to look into my eyes. "There's been no change. The baby just isn't ready yet, and even though I think there's a 90 percent chance you will have a Cesarean section, I don't want to jump the gun."

Dr. Wyatt was a kind man in his early sixties. He wore his white hair in a crew cut, like a Marine Corps sergeant—a look that belied his gentleness. He knew my situation and understood the implications of his words: *I could be having my first child alone.*

Dr. Wyatt took my hand then patted it. I tried to control my emotions, but, disarmed by his genuine concern, tears spilled down my cheeks and dropped in big heavy splotches on my shirt.

We'd just moved to Connecticut two months earlier. It had been a difficult move. Though it was a promotion for Joe, the high cost of living placed us under great financial strain. We had no friends yet, I missed our families, and no respite from my loneliness was in sight.

I knew Joe would not be around for day-to-day involvement in the baby's life. He'd been assigned a long-term case in Canada that would begin the following week, and he would commute home on the weekends. The bottom line was, there was a good chance he wouldn't be there for the baby's birth.

The sky was dark as I drove home. A violent summer storm had come through earlier, leaving muddy streams that dirtied the streets. I pulled into our narrow driveway trying to ignore the grating sound of wet gravel grinding beneath my tires. Then I saw the rain had flooded our drive and front yard. There was no way to the house except through the water.

Opening the car door, I stomped defiantly into the giant puddle directly under me and slammed the door behind me. Dirty water flowed over my shoes, drenching my socks and the hem of my cheap maternity pants, but I trudged on through to the next puddle. And the next. By the time I reached the house, I felt like everything lovely in my life had leached into the soggy mess.

I'd been right after all. No one cared. What should have been one of life's most joyful times was turning into a nightmare. There were no friends to celebrate with. No excited grandparents or aunts and uncles to share the waiting. No supporters to encourage me in my new role as a mother. I felt those losses deeply. But to be alone at the birth of our baby—that, I didn't think I could bear.

I was enraged at God and my husband. "Is this how You take care of me?" I screamed when I got in the house. There was no reply. I cried until the tears turned to steel and the anger gave me the strength to accept what had been reality for me over and over in my life: There was no one I could count on but myself.

Unknown to me, Joe had determined that nothing would keep him away from being with me when the baby was born. Scrambling at work, he'd made arrangements to fly home the moment I went into labor. But he told me none of this. He withheld his heart and thoughts from me in case something happened and he couldn't get back.

Joe's greatest fear was that he would disappoint me. He didn't realize I could have handled the unexpected; it was thinking that he didn't care enough to give the baby and me priority that destroyed me. But he lived out that terrible time in his own fear, and I lived it out in mine.

As it turned out, I did have a Cesarean and Joe was there. But the terror of that experience stayed with me. And with it a growing bitterness against Joe.

I found motherhood overwhelming. I'd had a long labor before the Cesarean and was weak. When all my help flew home after three weeks, I panicked at the realization that I would be alone with a newborn twenty-four hours a day. But I had no choice. Without support or family, once again, it was up to me. So I bucked up and did what I had to do.

I probably would have gone on like that forever—unhappy but managing—except that I simply wore out. Joe drew from me. The kids drew from me. Finally, I had nothing left to give. I knew God was supposed to be able to fill the hole inside me, but, the truth was, I didn't trust Him any more than I trusted Joe.

And now I was tired. Tired of being used. Tired of not measuring up. Tired of trying. There wasn't enough of me as it was, and giving my life to God felt like signing up for one more set of expectations.

Even though I believed God was "present" in some theological sense of the word, that was no longer enough. I refused to be comforted. What was the point if in the end you were still alone?

My fear was that to God, I was little more than a pawn in His kingdom. Another expendable worker. What I wanted to know was, *What would happen if I gave God my heart? What would He do with it? Leave it exposed and vulnerable to the forces of life? Use it to accomplish His ends with no concern about how they impacted me? Or would He hold my heart in His hand and protect it with all the power of heaven?* I decided unless the latter was true, I wasn't interested.

Good Eatin'

It was Papa who fed my spirit during this time, and I hungrily took all he had to offer. It didn't surprise me that our favorite place of connecting was the dinner table. Humor, memories, thoughts, information, and feelings flowed easily there. Our words ladled from one heart to another like Mama's delicate white gravy on mashed potatoes. Smooth. Warm. Soothing. So unlike the thick paste globbed over heavy biscuits by restaurants advertising "southern cooking" that it seemed sacrilegious to call it by the same name.

Being with Papa, it was obvious where my love for good food came from. Food has always been a big deal in my family. We love eating out. My boys do, too, so at least one family passion has been transferred to the next generation.

As a child, I knew our family was in deep financial trouble when there was no money to eat a modest meal out once a week. We had all the saving tips down—always share and, of course, no drinks, appetizers, or desserts. Our meal may have been meager, but we enjoyed it.

We loved home cooking, too. My mother was a wonderful cook, and because of the delightful times spent in the kitchen together, laughter and a comforting sense of well-being will forever mingle with the aroma of food for me.

Those in the diet industry scream that such connections are precisely why America struggles with obesity, but I disagree. From birth, eating provides a pleasant bonding experience between mother and child. Our food sources broaden with age, but I think that innate association—between the food, the one who provides it, and those who partake—still exists.

In fact, I've wondered if obsessive eating isn't the result of the opposite. Food ingested without love. Without community. Without the nurturing of the soul along with the body. I do know that as a family—parents, children, aunts, uncles, and grandparents included—our best times have been those spent around the dinner table. We love to eat, and I make no apology for it.

I've noticed that people, like animals, tend not to eat when they're nervous. Most of us need a certain comfort level before we can relax and enjoy a meal. So, I consider it a privilege when others share my table or ask me to share theirs. But that was something I learned.

Both my grandmother and my mother, masters of hospitality, were quick to invite others into our circle. As a kid, I resented it. But now, seeing how Papa's eyes brightened at the thought of a meal with a companion, I began to understand why they couldn't turn anyone away. And I understood why, for Papa, the hardest thing about living alone was eating alone.

Not that he did anything to help himself. Though he was lonely, he was very picky about his eating partners. He wouldn't consider eating with someone he didn't like. In fact, he wouldn't even eat with someone he felt neutral about. If you weren't on his A-1 list of companions, he'd starve before there would be any breaking of the bread. Papa went along with Mama's hospitality so long as she did the cooking. But he wasn't interested in straying too far from the barn even then.

One thing he hated was church potlucks. "You wouldn't believe what people bring to those things," he complained. "Used to be the women folk would bring the best they had. They woulda been ashamed to bring some casserole made out of soup, or a cardboard carton full of store-bought chicken like they do now. I'd have to make sure I got in line first because after the first bunch or so got through all of mother's food would be gone. You could just look at her food and know it was good."

For Mama, cooking was an expression of caring. One day while I was visiting, a woman from the church called to say a distant relative of a nominal church member had died. "Do you think you could fix a meal for the family tonight?" she asked. As always, Mama said yes. In two hours' time, we had loaded into Papa's pickup truck a basket of fried chicken, dishes of mashed potatoes, green beans, corn, a batch of cornbread, and a large banana pudding. Papa then drove the precious cargo to the home of the bereaved family as if it were a Brink's car filled with gold.

I said, "Mama, I can't believe you would go to this much trouble for someone you hardly even know."

"It says in Ecclesiastes 'Whatever your hand finds to do, do it with all your might,'" she reminded me. "I think that means if you're going to do something, you ought to do it right."

I've often regretted the awareness that came with that experience. It cured me of the temptation to bring anything store-bought to anyone else's home and has caused me great inconvenience more than once.

Still, I began to appreciate how a meal can communicate almost any attribute one desires. Lovingly prepared and freely offered, it can communicate compassion and acceptance. But it can also convey negative emotions. In the book *Like Water for Chocolate*, people experience whatever emotion the cook feels as she prepares the meal. An entire wedding party becomes ill when served a wedding cake laced with the sorrow and bitterness of a sister's broken heart.

This allegory reminded me that all home cooking isn't necessarily good. Such was the case in my husband's family. His father, an angry man who often took out his anger on Joe, once bragged that he took care of his son no matter how much he disliked him.

"I fix that boy two eggs every morning and never say a word to him," he said. It was not, however, a meal that went down easily. As a young man, my husband developed severe gastrointestinal problems—including colitis—that almost took his life. Was there a connection? We couldn't help but wonder.

Papa would never eat a meal under those circumstances. He hated to eat alone, but unless eating involved going someplace where there was quality food, respect, and camaraderie, eat alone he would.

Though he was begged and cajoled, he refused to attend any of Midtown Manor's frequent suppers and potlucks. About once a quarter, Boone would organize the men to fix a big breakfast. Papa would go to that, but as for the rest of it, you couldn't pay him to attend.

As we waited for the elevator one afternoon, I read a notice announcing a chicken-fried steak dinner with all the fixings. "Papa, wouldn't you like to go to this?" I asked. He took one look at the flyer and tersely said, "No!" Neither of us said anything till we got to his room.

"I'll tell you why I don't go to those things," he said in a lets-get-this-straight-once-and-for-all voice. "To begin with, half of these ol' ladies can't see, so there's no tellin' what they put in them pots. And not all of them keep their apartments as clean as I do. I know that for a fact, 'cause the manager says so. Then you see 'em waddlin' down the hall with these big ol' dishes. Stuff sloppin' out one side and then the other." He shook his head. "Nothin' about that appeals to me."

I couldn't blame him. Put that way, it didn't appeal much to me either.

"And I see what they take home, too," he continued. "Some of these folks is willing to eat anything so long as it's free. Once a week we get big boxes of food from the trading commodities. Oh, there's lettuce and tomatoes. Sometimes fruit. Eggs. Big slabs of cheese. They don't bring it over here 'less it pretty nigh gone, but when it comes, you can't hardly get in the rec room for all the people. Beats all I seen—all of 'em fightin' over that rotten food. I'm not interested in eatin' with anybody who wants to eat rotten food," he declared.

Though Papa was by his own admission "more particular than most," there were two places that met his criteria—Piccadilly and Pat's. He and Mama ate at the cafeteria often during their years at the barn. Now that he lived on the other side of town, Luby's was much closer, but it was worth it to him to drive to where he was known.

He'd never been to Pat's until he moved to Midtown Manor, but it quickly became his home away from home. We finally made it there one afternoon, and I saw why Papa liked the place. It was as clean as a whistle and they treated him like a king.

There were several free tables on the left side as we entered, but Papa hesitated to take one. There was a quick flurry of activity on the right, though, and a customer was soon on his way. We were ushered to this table, and I later learned that someone had been sitting at Papa's usual spot.

"Hey, Mr. Choate, how ya doin' today?" asked a pretty young woman at the counter.

"That's Christie, Pat's daughter," he said as we were seated. Pat was in the back cooking. Cooking his order, it turned out.

They were enacting a ritual carefully observed on both sides. As soon as they saw Papa walk in the door, they started preparing his order. Small hamburger—no onions—on a soft bun, warmed, not toasted. Half order of French fries, not too done. And a medium Dr. Pepper.

"Just order a half order of fries," he whispered to me across the table. "They just about give me a full order anyway."

"Sorry you had to wait, Mr. Choate," Christie said as she rolled back the used pages of her order pad. "You're a little late today, so we didn't think you were coming." After a little small talk that concluded with a hearty endorsement for Pat's milk shakes, I placed my order. One chocolate milk shake with a small cheeseburger, and half order of fries. Grilled onions on the burger.

"Papa, that was great," I said afterwards pushing back from the table.

"I didn't know you liked hamburgers or I'd a brought you here sooner," he said. "I thought maybe you was accustomed to meat and vegetables every night."

I said I wasn't and didn't elaborate. It seemed like the more tense things got at home, the less I wanted to eat there. But here, I was ravenous.

Concern that I get my vegetables wasn't the only reason Papa hesitated to take me to Pat's. It was the area. Papa warned me not to go after dark. "It's not safe," he said.

It sent chills up my spine to think he usually walked to Pat's. I wasn't sure we were safe in broad daylight, but, whether we were or not, I agreed with him that the food was worth the risk.

Something I was beginning to realize about Papa was that risk had always been a part of his life he enjoyed. As I recalled his "farmin' is the biggest gamble there is" statement, it occurred to me that the "gamble" part was what he liked. Maybe that's what made him such a remarkable Christian. I was drawn to Christianity out of a need for security. For my grandfather, it was the adventure. He didn't get all upset about his life being turned topsy-turvy when he and Mama "got the call" to go to Byers. He relished it.I was the opposite. True, I was sick at heart about my life, but I was but too afraid to change anything. *Did I really think some act of God could turn things around? Maybe. But was that what I really wanted?*

I pondered the tension between security and adventure—another paradox for which Christianity was famous. Most change involved pain, something I didn't want to sign up for without a guarantee that, in the end, it would be worth it. *How could I embrace the adventure unless I were confident that everything would work out okay in the end?*

I couldn't, I concluded. Not unless God could be counted on to keep me safe in the midst of the turmoil—as well as work out what otherwise seemed impossible. So, it was back to the old trust issue.

I knew of one concrete example where God had come through. The way Papa became foreman of the Blackwell Ranch was not chance. It was a miracle—one family's equivalent of Moses parting the Red Sea. Yet, for me, spectacular acts of grace and goodness were totally out of the realm of my awareness.

I remember once sitting with my grandmother as she told me about a Scripture the Holy Spirit had highlighted in her reading that morning. I was curious. Though I'd dutifully read the Bible through the years, it seemed dry. The words never "spoke" to me as she claimed. They certainly never made my eyes shine with excitement as hers did at that moment.

When I asked her about it, she said, "When you tell God that you accept the sacrifice of Jesus for your sin, and give over your life and everything to Him, then God's Spirit comes and lives inside you. If you pay attention, He'll tell you everything you need to know. When you read the Bible, certain parts will stand out—like someone underlined it with a pen—and you'll know it's God's word for you."

It seemed pretty simplistic to me. "I've been a Christian for a long time, so why haven't I experienced it?" I asked.

"You have to listen and then act on what you believe God has said. If you ignore His Spirit, He'll stop talking to you. But the more you obey, the more He'll speak to you."

How could I tell her I'd been trying to obey my whole life and all it had gotten me was more emptiness? Why was it different for her? It's not that things were easy for her and Papa. In fact, I knew that, at that moment, they were in financial trouble. Mama was sick a lot, and they had no insurance. I'd heard her and Papa praying about it early that morning.

"Look," she said, turning to Psalm 78, "this is what I've been reading. God has brought His people through the desert. They've not been without food, water, or clothing for even a day but the Scripture says, 'Yes, they spoke against God: They said, "Can God prepare a table in the wilderness?"'"

My grandmother took the question of the Israelites as a challenge. "Karen, God *can* prepare a table in the wilderness," she assured me with conviction. I never learned how their financial situation was resolved. What stayed with me was this: from the moment she felt God had spoken to her, Mama considered the matter as good as settled. She stopped worrying. The subject of finances didn't come up again, and she and Papa walked around as though someone had dropped a $100,000 check off for them that afternoon.

Over the years, that little phrase—"Can God furnish a table in the wilderness?"—echoed through my mind many times. But now, knowing what I did about Mama and Papa's lives, I realized their ability to trust God in hard times wasn't based on sentiment or tradition. They had experienced the desperateness of poverty, fear, and need many times. And they had found God faithful.

The doubter in me said, *If God had given my husband a great job in the middle of the Great Depression, maybe I'd believe in miracles, too.* Wanting to believe, I searched for a modern-day challenge and found it closer than I expected. It was my relationship with my husband. Our marriage, like my personal pilgrimage, was a desert journey that I traveled with weariness and a growing sense of hopelessness. Can God furnish a table in the wilderness? *We'll see*, I thought.

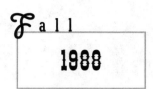

Fall
1988

Bridges

I had both boys in tow the next time I came to Wichita Falls. "I can't believe this is an airport," Michael said. "It's so small." But it didn't take them long to appreciate the convenience. To pick up our rental car, all we did was walk out the front door. It was to the right. Unlocked.

"This is great!" David said. Fresh from New York's La Guardia airport, this place seemed as foreign to them as Africa.

They were oblivious to the flat land we drove through with its layers of brown and scrub. All they wanted was to see Papa. Their excitement pleased me. Though they barely knew him, they loved him already.

They were displaying something I've often observed in children: a kind of blind, fervent love of family—both known and unknown. It seems instinctive. Like a genetically based emotional connection that lasts until a real relationship can be established. Maybe it's given to ensure that children will have some means of survival within the family even if parents should die. That was how it worked for me. It bridged the gap of years and time when I sought out my grandparents after my mother's death.

For that reason, I've always felt an obligation to guard the innocence of those relationships. My boys would chatter for weeks in anticipation of a vacation spent with aunts, uncles, and cousins they saw but once or twice a year. It was a love beyond what could be explained by the amount of time spent together. That kind of love was a gift I'd purposefully nurtured between my children and their great grandfather, and as they ran to embrace Papa, I knew it was theirs.

Yet I knew the fantasy of a cowboy grandfather could only go so far. I wanted them to *know* the man they loved on untried faith. I wanted them to experience the color and rhythm of Papa's speech as he spun the stories of his past and their heritage. To feel his hand on their heads in blessing. To see their smiles reflected in his laughing eyes. To receive affirmation through the power of Papa's words and the simple presence of his life.

For this, I journeyed home once again. And for another reason as well. I'd made some changes in my life about which I was excited, and it made me long to see Papa. For one, I'd decided to give God an honest chance. My search for Him would no longer be from a skeptic's heart. I would come to Him asking for understanding, not demanding that He prove Himself to me.

It seemed strange to talk about finding God when a part of me had known Him forever. But my religious life had been a string of clichés interspersed with flashes of true faith. I'd had moments of powerful connection with God: after my mother died and when David, born with hylan membrane disease, lay in intensive care for almost a week.

During such crises, my faith took on substance. I'd even had one year of spiritual awakening where God seemed close and real. Also, gathering with believers for Sunday morning worship was profoundly moving for me. Without that, I doubt my shell of a faith would've lasted as long as it had. But for some time now, there had been a wilderness so vast that I questioned whether I'd really known anything of God at all.

Even my decision to trust God now was not born so much of faith, but frustration. The incongruity between what I'd experienced of God and what His Word said was available to me was no longer acceptable. How could God be "my rock, my fortress," yet not seem sufficient when it was time to get up in the morning and face the day?

And how did I justify the breakdown in relationship with those closest to me—Joe and the boys? Our home was a sad, barren place. Joe and I seldom fought. Distance and sarcasm were just as effective. And though I cried for my boys, they were tears of anguish, not love.

For years, my love for Michael and David lay buried inside some deep, unreachable cavern. Still, every day I tried to show the love I didn't feel, and I prayed they wouldn't realize that I planned trips to the park so I could mentally fly away while they played—that "sweethearts" and "honeys" spoken too brightly masked the truth that I wanted to be anywhere but there.

Every day their little faces looked up to mine for any crumb. Michael, quiet, with his wide, all-seeing blue eyes. David, with small green eyes almost always closed with laughter. It broke my heart just to see them.

The first step I took in my spiritual journey was to get help for my depression. I felt I needed the perspective of an insightful professional to challenge both my view of myself and my view of God. Something was wrong. I didn't know what. But I knew what I wanted.

I wanted what my grandfather had. A simple faith that would stand no matter what. Something I could measure everything else against. My attitude. My choices. My theology. Jesus' words from Matthew 22:37-38 kept coming back to me, "You shall love the LORD your God with all your heart, with all your soul, and with all your mind. This is the first and great commandment."

I knew I didn't love God that way, but I wanted to. It occurred to me that the love I had for God was not unlike what my boys now felt for my grandfather. It was good as far as it went, but it was based mostly on an inherited emotional tie. It wasn't meant to last a lifetime. Its purpose was to keep me where I belonged until my own relationship with God took root.

I'd staked my life on godly principles many times. Tithing. Trusting Him for financial matters. Even claiming the promise of His help at the beginning of my life with Joe. I offered what I had to God—obedience and good deeds—until I just ran out of steam. I knew He wanted all of me, but I felt there was no "me" to give.

This was the issue I was attempting to address. I was going in a lot of different directions to see what "took"—counseling, a Bible study, even a writer's conference to explore the possibility of writing professionally.

I was on a journey to find God and myself. If what my grandmother said was true, then God's Spirit—the Holy Spirit—would teach me everything I needed to know. He could put the pieces together and help me discard things that weren't true or helpful.

I didn't tell Papa any of this outright. He would've listened, but talking about self-esteem and identity issues with Papa would've been like speaking to him in Latin. It wasn't important that he understand the steps I'd taken. I knew what they were. Baby steps. Scary, but exhilarating enough to loosen the chains of depression just a bit.

This was the first time I would come to see Papa when I wasn't completely overwhelmed. And I had a purpose. By bringing my children, I hoped they'd see the difference between someone religious and someone who truly loved God. I knew instinctively they weren't one and the same.

Deuteronomy 6:7 implies that life's spiritual lessons are best learned in the course of ordinary living. "You shall teach them diligently to your children," wrote Moses the prophet, "and shall talk of them when you sit in your house, when you walk by the way, when you lie down, and when you rise up."

These lessons weren't something that could be explained as much as lived. But maybe the veracity of my grandfather's faith would influence my children—just as spices rubbed into a wooden bowl subtly flavor whatever it contains. Perhaps he could give them what I could not.

That's why it seemed important for my boys to see Papa on his own turf. The stories of how he and my grandmother trusted God and were not disappointed seemed so much more real when I saw where they had lived and worked and struggled to raise a family. It made me want to believe. I hoped the firmness of the cracked, rutted soil and the vastness of the land would come to symbolize for the boys—as they had for me—all I hoped for: a foundation sure enough to build a home on.

The Barn

The first place the boys wanted to see was the barn. That rustic, sturdy structure was an anomaly. It was a slice of life as it used to be, preserved in the epicenter of Wichita Falls' most modern structures. Its official name was the Circle R Stable, but we never called it anything other than "the barn." It was there that Mama and Papa spent their happiest years. And it was there, while snapping beans and baking cobblers with my grandmother, that the seeds of my faith were watered and nourished.

Papa said that in 1963 a doctor and an insurance man had taken a lease on the stable. "They had fifteen to twenty horses of their own there and they were taking in renters."

One of them had one boy and the other had three, so they figured they could do it themselves. But they found out pretty quick that workin' a barn involves a lot of hard labor. So they was huntin' somebody to run it for them.

Somehow or another, they got in touch with a friend of mine, Kern Pieratt, and they tried to hire him. That's how desperate they was. Kern said, "No, I don't know nothin' about horses, but I've got a friend that knows more about them than anyone I know." And he told them about me.

When I went out there to look things over, I liked what I saw right away. The barn needed a lot of work but it was large and sound, and there was a small tack room off it. The only problem was that they wanted me to live at the stables in an ol' bunkhouse near the front of the property.

Now, Cora and I had lived in some sorry places over the years, but the bunkhouse wasn't much more than a shed. It had a shower and a kitchen of sorts, but it was run down pretty bad. So, I went to the doctor and said, "What would you think about us settin' up a trailer there in front of the bunkhouse?"

He thought a minute then said, "I guess as long as you're willin' to go to the expense and trouble it's okay with me." So, Mama and I found us a used, single-wide mobile home, and we gave ten thousand dollars for it. Of course, it was clean and in good shape. I sunk some cement pads in real deep to set it on, and within the week we was livin' on the property.

I guess we musta put that trailer in a good location 'cause all the bad weather just seemed to go right around us. When that tornado came through here in 1979, Sike's Mall across the road was almost leveled. Forty-nine people was killed and hundreds of folks lost their homes, including Marie. It liked to tore up the whole town, but it skipped right over us. Every year we'd see storms blowin' by and wreckin' everything in sight, but we never got hit bad. Things went just about as good as you coulda asked for all the time we lived there.

At first, I had nothing to do with the business end of things. I was just a hired hand. But after a couple years, the doctor and the insurance man got tired of playing cowboy and told me they weren't going to renew their lease.

Well, that was what I'd been hoping for.

The next day I went to see the owner and said, "You know, I'd be interested in leasing the barn myself." 'Course I was praying he didn't already have other plans. He shrugged his shoulders and said, "It's all the same to me. I just don't want to worry with it." We settled on the terms and before I knew it I was walkin' out the door with a lease and a smile.

I paid the owner a set amount every month. After that, it was up to me to run things however I thought they oughta be run. I paid for feed

*and all the expenses for maintenance and what-not, but whatever
was left over was mine to keep. I'd heard different ones had leased out
the barn over the years and none of them had run a profit. But I was
pretty sure I could make a go of it.*

Papa said one of the best things he did was to make the barn a "girls
only" stable. "I learned pretty quick that when you get the girls and guys
together you spend all your time trying to break up the monkey business,"
he explained. And once parents realized there was a safe place for their
daughters to ride, they beat the doors down to board their horses there. In
no time most the stalls were filled. Papa taught riding and roping, and
finally, he was able to do what he loved best—trade horses.

The barn was located on a dirt lane called Lake Park Drive, off the
frontage road of Southwest Parkway. It was just a cut in the pasture that
even the U.S. Mail had trouble finding. Mama and Papa's closest neighbor
was the state mental hospital whose escapees provided them with
numerous adventures both scary and funny. And Holliday Creek, one of
the best fishing spots in the county, was on their land.

A friend of Papa's who loved to fish, set out lines and kept them sup-
plied with as much fish as they wanted. Once when I was visiting, he
brought a sixteen-pound catfish and gave us an excuse for a party. We rus-
tled up as many family members as we could find and fried catfish all
evening. When it was all said and done, twelve of us somehow gathered
around Mama's table and enjoyed a meal as fine as offered by any gourmet
restaurant.

But the most anticipated event at the barn was the annual trail ride. I
missed out on that experience—something I regret to this day. Papa and
the girls would leave at sunrise and return to the barn at dark, filthy and
starving. Waiting for them would be a feast of my grandmother's fried
chicken, and for dessert, cherry cream pie. Her pies seemed to spark as
much excitement as the trail ride itself. Whenever I met someone who had
been out at the barn during Papa's tenure, the subject always got around to
Mama's cherry cream pies. They were that good.

Papa did his best to see that each of his grandkids had good memories
of the barn. It was never too much work to saddle up a horse for one of us
to ride, even though he knew we were poor investments as future cowboys.
We lacked either the opportunity or the interest. But he told me I was a naturally good rider and praised me so much that I considered myself a fair
horsewoman.

Brown Jug was probably the best cow horse Papa ever had, and, as long as Papa owned him, he was mine to ride. It wasn't until years later that Papa admitted he gave me Brown Jug because the horse was smart enough to compensate for my lack of experience. So much for my competence.

When we rode, we'd take the culvert under the highway and cross to the acres of open land on the other side. We kept hearing someone was going to build on the property, and one day, in spite of our displeasure, the rumor became fact.

The last time we rode there, Joe, my brother Edwin, and I, along with Jerry (a family friend), wove our horses in and out of the sprawling foundation of what would become Sike's Mall. It was an interesting day. Jerry was almost a beau of mine long ago. He loved to sing and was doing his best to find tunes we could sing in three-part harmony. The reason it was three-part and not four was that Joe is a monotone.

Joe wasn't thrilled about how things were going. Not only did he feel excluded—and mortified that the rest of us actually seemed to enjoy singing to the top of our lungs in the middle of a construction site—he was worried sick about his horse.

"Papa, I think I'm too big for this horse," Joe had said as he sat uneasily on a huge, docile white horse named Rex.

"Naw, that horse is used to carrying big ol' ladies heavier than you," Papa assured him. "He's just spoiled." As my grandfather eyed Joe and Rex meandering out the gate, Rex did seem totally overwhelmed by his burden. He shifted his haunches dramatically from one side to the other as if changing gears.

"Rex!" Papa yelled, "Cut that out!" Rex stopped and looked back toward Papa as if to say, "Do I have to?" With a resigned sigh, he resumed walking with a gait as straight as Brown Jug's. Still, Joe was convinced he was making his poor horse miserable. Rex, sensing a sensitive soul, made the most of it, and started in on his old routine just as soon as Papa was out of sight. We all began to wonder if the horse was truly on his last legs.

Finally, Joe said, "I can't take this any more." We didn't know if he meant the singing or the horse, but, in any event, he decided to head back home. What happened next would surprise no one who is familiar with horses, but as city slickers, we were caught unaware.

The moment Joe turned Rex toward the barn, the horse that could barely put one foot in front of the other suddenly flew as though he had wings. With Joe looking like a flopping Raggedy Andy doll astride a white beast, the two thundered out of sight. It ended with us roaring in laughter and Joe vowing never to ride again.

The next time we came to Texas, the mall was too far along to accommodate the likes of us, and after riding free, trotting around the arena didn't appeal much. So, we didn't ride. Then Papa left the barn, and we hadn't been back since. But now that the boys were with me, I was hoping we could ride there one more time. At nine and eleven, Michael and David were the perfect ages for this experience.

Fortunately, Margie, Papa's "cowgirl" daughter still boarded a horse there. So, the next day Papa and I, along with two very excited boys, met her at the barn. The boys, in jeans and boots bought for the occasion, took turns riding Paige, a beautiful, well-trained quarter horse.

Papa showed them how to sit tall in the saddle. How to hold the reins loosely, but in front so you could tighten them at a moment's notice. How to shift your weight a little to one side or the other to let the horse know what direction you wanted her to go. In between rides the boys sat on the corral fence, their legs hooked behind the rails like they belonged. They listened and laughed with us as Papa and I retold our favorite barn stories.

Papa, who'd been looking frail when we arrived, seemed to gather energy just being there. Margie came over to give him a hug before we left.

"Mr. Choate, any chance you'd have time to come with me to look at a saddle? I think I found a good one but I'd like you see it before I buy it."

A few days earlier, she'd asked Papa to go check out a horse with her, and he felt bad that he couldn't. "It was a couple hours away," he explained, "and it hurts my neck bein' in a car that long." But the saddle trip was doable and he was delighted. So was Margie. Everybody in town knew that whoever walked into a business establishment with Alva Choate was likely walk out with a good deal.

I was glad he agreed to go. He needed a boost to his confidence. The past year had been difficult for Papa. Though he had recovered physically from thyroid surgery, he seemed shaken.

One night he told me, "When I left the barn and moved into Midtown Manor, I had ten thousand dollars in the bank—more money than I'd ever had in my life. I felt like a rich man. I thought I'd be able to take care of myself without being a burden to any of the children." His eyes filled with tears. "But it's all gone. Between the hospitals and the medicines, it's all gone. That's why I sold my truck. Sold it for $2,100 and told Marie to take me down to the funeral home. I bought a policy with it so when I die, the kids don't have to pay for nothin'."

He cleared his throat. Talking was difficult and the slightest irritation sent him into a coughing spell, but he continued. "Now I don't know if I'm gonna be able to stay here. If I don't get my strength up, I can't. I always said

I didn't want to go to a nursing home, but I'd rather do that than go live with one of the kids."

I relayed this conversation to Joe when we spoke on the phone later. "Papa's trying so hard," I said, "but I don't think he's going to be able to live independently much longer."

"He can't get around?"

"No, it's not that. He's just weak. He doesn't have the strength to fix a meal. Or by the time he does, he's too tired to eat it."

"What a terrible place for him to be in." I heard compassion in Joe's voice. Suffering himself from increasing episodes of colitis, he understood that kind of deep exhaustion. But his next words caught me off guard. "Do you think he would come live with us?" he asked.

For a moment I couldn't answer. "You would do that?"

"Of course," he said, "he's your grandfather."

After hanging up, I thought about all the angry thoughts I nursed about my husband and felt very ashamed. In spite of my good intentions, I hadn't made as much progress with Joe as I had hoped. It had been a long time since I'd been willing to look at the good in him. Somehow all my grievances seemed smaller stacked up against this one kind gesture.

All that next day, I thought about what it would be like having an elderly person in my home. Having cared for my mother, I had no illusions about what it would take. I found myself thinking, *It wouldn't be easy, but we could do it.* I was surprised that I wanted to do it. I knew that desire was outside of my nature. It just wasn't like me—the "me" who was jealous of her time, selfish with her resources, and stingy with her emotional reserves. All I knew was that my love for Papa compelled me to give whatever I could.

I joined Papa for his nightly stroll up and down the long hallway of his floor. At one end, a large glass window framed a red Texas sunset, and we stopped for a moment to watch it. I took his hand and kissed it. The arthritis in both his hands was getting worse. His fingers were twisting into odd shapes—especially his thumbs, which made it hard for him to perform simple daily tasks. He struggled to unlock his door and to open jars. Things he'd done easily before.

"Papa, I talked to Joe last night," I said, gently rubbing the knobby blue veins on his hand. "We wondered if you would consider coming to live with us."

I explained that we had a big house with a ground level basement we could easily turn into living quarters for him. "The boys would love having you around. We could make it work."

Papa pulled a white handkerchief from his pants pocket and dabbed at his eyes. "Thank you, hon," he said. "Thank you. I appreciate that more than you know, but I have to stay here. If I left, I wouldn't know nobody and nobody would know me. Besides, Marie has asked me several times if I was ready to move in with her, but I'm not. I want to keep on in my little apartment till the end if I'm able."

Papa was right about what his life would be like in another place. But I wondered if the day was coming when he would have no choice.

"Well then, Papa, you do what you think best," I said. "The offer is there if you want it."

But I knew then that he would never leave Texas. With every acre of cotton, wheat, and corn he'd planted over the years, he'd sown his soul. The people, the memories, the soil, the horses—all that was part of his life as a young man—were now so fused into his being that if parted, I doubted that Papa would physically survive.

I couldn't help but wonder, *What would it be like to have a place you knew you belonged? To have a home you loved so much you couldn't leave it without leaving yourself?*

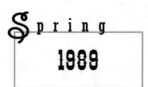

Spring
1989

Old Timer

Though six months had passed since our last visit, Papa and I picked up the same routine without missing a beat. Once again, we were scurrying to make it to the rec room in time for pool.

Because of our busy days and too many late nights talking, we were, as Papa said, "plumb wore out." We'd just pulled ourselves out of a deep afternoon slumber and barely had time to comb our hair.

I ran ahead to hurry along the elevator, then waited for my grandfather to catch up with me. "It's a pretty rough life we have," Papa announced on the way down. "Eating, sleeping, playing pool, and visiting. What more could you ask for?"

We burst out onto the first floor and nearly ran into Betty, the cleaning lady, on her way up. She escorted her ever-present buffer through the elevator doorway like a favored beau. Papa took my arm to steady himself.

As we started down the long hall, I heard a voice call, "In a hurry, Cowboy?"

I turned and nodded to Patsy. Papa carried on as though he didn't hear her.

Virgil was blustering around setting things up when we got there. The way his face turned all red when he saw me gave me the distinct feeling he didn't like me. He always acted nervous when I was around and, more often than not, would leave early if I was playing.

Of course, my pool game may have had something to do with that. True, I wasn't at his level, but, on most days, I didn't embarrass myself too badly. I usually played with Papa, and since he was one of the better players we were as likely to win as not. And every once in a while, I'd come up with a brilliant shot that made them think I had potential.

The boys were good about giving me pointers once they saw I was interested. Everybody but Virgil, that is. He had little patience with me.

"She's not gonna make that," he said to Boone as I lined up my shot. He was right. The cue ball sailed past its intended target but hit another of our balls, setting off a collision. When the commotion settled down, I'd pocketed two of ours.

"Look at that. Just look at that," Virgil said, shaking his head in disbelief.

"Hon, you did real good," Papa said winking at me.

The next ball stopped just short of the pocket.

"That's okay," Papa said. "You put it right where I can get it the next time around."

"Provided there is a next time," said Virgil. He was so outraged by my luck that he determined to clear the table. He almost did, too. But he scratched on the eight ball, ending the game. With that, he slammed his cue stick on the table and left in a huff.

"Guess Virgil's having a bad day," Papa said as he rolled the balls out of the pockets and onto the table for another game.

"For Virgil, every day's a bad day," Boone said as he racked. Then he nodded toward me. "Go ahead, you break."

I gave my cue stick to Papa—it was his good stick, the one he always let me use. "No thanks. I'm going to sit out this round, Boone. You and Papa play."

The room was quiet now. It was dinnertime—or suppertime, as Texans say. I poured a cup of coffee dregs from the pot stationed at the other end of the room, then pulled up a big, cushioned wicker chair for a bird's-eye view of the game. It was relaxing, watching Papa and Boone play. They seemed so easy together, laughing, talking, and teasing like boyhood chums.

It occurred to me that everything about Boone looked easy. White canvas sneakers. Gray cotton pants with elastic in the waist. He always wore a knit shirt. Usually striped and usually dirty. I found that funny since, of all the boys, he had best eyesight. He had on his hearing aid—that in itself was a sign of acceptance. When Boone wanted to be left alone, which was most of the time, he just left it off.

Suddenly he held out his stick to me and said, "Take my shot will you? I need to check something on my stove." He was back in a few minutes. "Did ya win yet?" he asked.

"No, but I got in the eleven." *Thankfully.*

"Much obliged. Dorothy's coming over for dinner tonight," he explained. "I didn't want the sauce to burn."

"No problem." But I could see it was a problem for Papa. He said nothing, but his mouth was drawn in a tight line. *What's he upset about?* I wondered.

As we ambled out to the parking lot later, I asked Papa why Boone's leaving bothered him.

"He's drinking again," he replied shaking his head. "Lately, every time we play he'll run into his room every little bit for a nip or two. I can smell it on him when he comes back."

"Have you talked to him about it?"

"Naw!" he said, looking at me as though I had taken leave of my senses. "There's no point in talkin' to a man who loves to drink. If it's what he's wantin' to do, ain't nobody gonna be able to stop him."

I was afraid Papa was right, but for Boone's sake as well as my grandfather's, I hoped Boone could hold things together.

Papa seemed physically stronger this visit. He was moving well, had good stamina. But I had noticed something that concerned me. He seemed withdrawn around everyone except the Midtown boys and me. Even at my aunt's house, he wasn't part of the activity. His great grandchildren, who adored him, teetered over to him offering hugs and kisses. He drank in their attention, but his interaction with the adults was minimal.

Since I wasn't with Papa every day, the change was more obvious to me than others. As we talked, I found myself repeating almost everything I said.

One night, after making up my bed on the sofa, I fixed my customary after dinner cup of decaf and, positioning a pillow against my back, snuggled into the corner of Mama's flowered sofa. Then I approached my grandfather with what I suspected.

"Papa, are you having trouble hearing?" I asked. Tears sprang to his eyes, and he looked away. "I haven't told nobody," he said quietly.

"Aunt Marie doesn't know?"

"No."

"Well, you need to tell her so she can have your hearing checked."

"I don't want Marie to have to worry about doing anything more for me," he retorted. "She does enough as it is. It would just mean a bunch of doctor appointments and money I don't have."

"But don't you see how much you're missing out on because you can't hear?"

"Yeah, I know it." He made little chewing motions with his mouth—a habit he'd developed from years of wearing false teeth. Often when he was buying time, he'd "chew his cud." After a moment he said, "You feel like a dummy. People is talkin' all around you. When they ask you a question, you don't even know what they've been talking about. They think you're a dumb guy. So, I just keep to myself and hope nobody talks to me."

"Papa," I said. "That kind of isolation isn't good for anyone. You keep that up and you won't live for long."

"It's not just the hearing," he said, shaking his head.

"Then what is it?"

"Nobody wants to hear what I have to say. I can still hear some. And I've gotten pretty good at reading lips, but when I try to talk nobody listens."

The last few times the family got together, I observed Papa watching our faces intently, straining to follow. His eyes would light up when something of interest came up, but before he could respond the moment was either gone or his words were drowned out by the general chaos of laugher and conversation. He wouldn't push to be heard. Instead he'd slump into his chair and stare at the floor, resigned to waiting out the night.

"I got lots of ideas about things," he continued. "I keep up with the news and sometimes when the kids are talkin' about something I'll have an opinion, something I want to contribute. But I don't get the chance."

"Papa, I understand more than you think. I know Joe and the kids love me, but they don't really care what I think or feel. Or maybe they do, but it doesn't feel like it to me. I'm just around or not around, and it doesn't seem to matter much either way."

"Yeah, that's it." His eyes widened in agreement.

That ache inside to know and be known. We both felt it.

I got up from the sofa and kissed Papa on the cheek. Then I knelt beside him and said, "I love you, Papa."

"I love you, too, hon. You'll never know what it means to have you come be with me like this. I get so lonely for somebody to be with. To talk to and eat with…"

We sat there for a while, holding hands. Tears in our eyes. Not tears of sadness, but of gratefulness—that somehow, across many years and miles, we had found each other. Papa began to pray, thanking God for His goodness and faithfulness to him even in his old age.

I wondered, *Does God see Papa as an aging cowboy? Or do eternal eyes see him with all the gifts and strength of his youth?* His uniqueness was woven into his being, and though the brilliance may have faded, the fabric was still there. Rich and overlayed with wisdom and character—if anything, more remarkable for its endurance. That was how I saw my grandfather, and it was why I treasured him.

Seeing Red

Papa wasn't always the man he would become. That shouldn't have surprised me, but it did. I think it's hard for most kids to think of their parents or grandparents as being in process. For me, Papa had been one-dimensional. He was a cowboy. A good cowboy. In a John Wayne movie, he'd have been one of the guys in a white hat who knew when to walk away and when to hold his ground. Wise. Shrewd. Tough. But kind to ladies and children. Always fair. And always right. Even the rumbles of his hard-living days fit into his cowboy image. I figured he just outgrew it and presto—like magic—turned into the icon I loved.

I'd heard that Papa had a fiery temper as a young man, but never having witnessed it first hand, I had a hard time believing it. Stories of Papa's wild side usually emerged in the context of other family members who had "gone bad." My grandfather had a nephew who ended up in the state penitentiary for killing a friend over a fifty-dollar pool game.

"Papa used to have a temper like that," someone said.

I should've put two and two together. After all, a man with his reputation for fighting must have had something fueling him. No doubt something about his upbringing contributed to it. Maybe it was all those boys in the house having to fight for what they wanted. Maybe because he was small he felt he had to prove himself. Or maybe he was just born with it.

Apart from genetics, it's hard to explain why one child is born into the world angry and another happy. I often wondered if being in a different family with different dynamics would diffuse the rage of an angry child before it caused irreparable harm. In any event, Papa was fortunate. Though he had many brushes with disaster, he learned to control his temper before there were serious consequences.

One such "brush" was a story that Mama never liked Papa to tell; she thought it put him in a bad light and glorified violence. Papa never showed any remorse over it either, which probably bothered her most. The story struck home with me because it epitomized a family trait that was a source of real trouble for Michael and me. When it happened, Papa was thirty-two—old enough to know better.

One morning, he hitched up a pair of bronco mules to take a wagon of wheat to the grain elevator. To weigh the grain, Papa was supposed to pull the team over the elevator to the flat ground beyond so that only the wagon remained on the elevator scale. However, before Papa could settle the team firmly on land, the man running the elevator started the lift. Papa yelled at the guy to stop, but it was too late. As the lift started, the mules' hind feet, which were still on the elevator, began to rise up with the wagon. The animals lurched forward to regain their footing but, in doing so, jerked the wagon and completely broke its coupling pole.

Papa was enraged. He would have to completely dismantle the whole front end of the wagon to fix it. He was looking at a day's labor, not to mention the expense of parts.

"Look what you did!" Papa yelled.

"What are you talkin' about? I didn't do nuthin'."

"You certainly did. You lifted up my mules' back feet—that's what startled 'em."

"Choate, you're a liar," growled the burly cowboy. "Them mules were plumb on the ground when I started that elevator."

Papa would have forgiven the man for his carelessness, but never for an attack on his character. He came around the wagon with fists flying. The grain operator, who was twice Papa's size, was more than happy to oblige him. But when the man picked up a 2 x 4 and cornered Papa between the wagon and the wall, Papa knew he was in trouble and started looking around for an equalizer.

He found it at his feet where a large hammer lay half-buried in grain on the floor. In one motion, Papa put his left arm up to protect himself and crouched down to grasp the hammer with his right hand. He ducked to the right as the 2 x 4 crashed beside him. Then, before the man knew what hit him, Papa landed a solid blow to the side of his head with the hammer.

"A couple days later, I saw that ol' boy in town," Papa chuckled, "and he was wearin' his hat all cocked off to one side. I could see a big, ugly knot right above his ear."

I asked Papa if he'd hit the man hard enough to hurt him or if he'd just wanted to scare him. He said, "No. I meant business. If you're gonna hit a man with a hammer, you'd better mean business."

He had a point, but I was appalled by his willingness to go to such an extreme over a relatively unimportant matter. I said, "Papa, you could have killed him. You had a wife and a baby. Didn't you think about what would happen to them if you went to jail or worse?"

"He called me a liar," Papa said simply. As far as he was concerned that explained it, and no more needed to be said on the subject.

But that, as I saw it, was the problem. Flying into a rage over every perceived injustice had the potential to be deadly. It was a tendency I recognized in myself and also in my son Michael. It wasn't just anger, it was a rage we felt justified in expressing because we were standing up for something that was right.

In sixth grade I stood in front of a scrawny kid with thick glasses who was surrounded by five or six bullies and announced, "If you're going to beat him up, you're going to have to beat me up first!" I wasn't more than 4'5" and seventy pounds myself, but the blood pounding in my ears drowned out all caution.

What saved me was the bullies' realization that if they fought me, they'd be the laughing stock of the school. There was no glory in beating up a girl. So the skinny kid and I both got off free. (Several years later, that kid filled out and morphed into a star football player who took his own revenge on those who had harassed him in his youth. It fit my sense of justice to a tee.)

But I wasn't always so lucky. One time my brother got in trouble for failing to return a library book on time. My parents took away his library card, which I thought unfair given the fact that we had no TV and books were our main source of entertainment. Edwin wasn't irresponsible—he'd just made a childish mistake. Of course, justice compelled me take some stand against his harsh punishment.

So, I took my own library card into the bathroom and burned it. Since the bathroom was located in the main hall, my parents smelled fire and came running. More punishment ensued—this time for me, and it was of a more physical nature than that meted out to my brother.

It was then I learned two things: taking a stand for a principle could be costly, and one action could trigger a set of events you didn't count on. I continued to rally to any cause I determined to be just, but from that point on I took my stands with a little more caution. With maturity, came the ability to discern which battles I could afford to fight, though even if I walked away, the injustice of it would burn inside me.

A lot of Papa's scrapes came from his inability to take this intermediary step of counting the cost, a weakness I saw in Michael, also. At age twelve, there had already been several episodes. For the most part, he was a kind, sensitive boy, but when he lost his temper he was like a bull that saw red. Whatever mechanism controlled rational thought clicked off, and he would physically and verbally attack whatever stood in his way.

I'd tried various forms of discipline with little success. The past few months, the fallout from his behavior—restrictions, loss of trust with friends and family—meant the weeks between blow-ups were miserable for him and the entire family. I was at a loss. Everything about my son was changing. His blonde hair had darkened into a highlighted brown. From an average built kid, he had lengthened into a tall and wiry, yet broad-shouldered, young man. But there was a change in his demeanor that frightened me. The rage within him was so strong it was almost palpable.

I'd never really understood Michael. I tried, but we seldom connected. As a baby, he was content to go anywhere, do anything, as long as he was with me. He clung to me with one arm around my neck like a monkey swinging from a tree. To identify us people would say, "You know, that little girl with that big baby." But Michael's big blue eyes took in everything and offered nothing.

As a toddler, when I hugged him he stood silently, as if waiting for it to be over. It seemed strange, but not wanting to intrude on his space, I left him to himself. Too late I realized what a mistake that was.

My younger son, David, was easier. He was born knowing how to delight his father and me with hugs, kisses, and amusing antics. His happy disposition and mediating personality was the oil that kept our family gears working.

This scenario was uncomfortably familiar. In my birth family, I had been Michael—the one unable to be myself around others. My little sister, Sharon, was the charmer. As a child, one of my first realizations was that cuteness was a wonderful gift to have. My second realization was that I didn't possess it. Instinctively, I knew it wasn't Sharon's fault that she did, but the unfairness of it smacked me in the face a hundred times a day.

I was not unloved, but I felt that who I was was not enough. I tried to be perfect even though it didn't leave me free to be myself, but I failed. So, I did the next best thing and tried to be good. Good, I discovered, only got you so far. The emotional rewards belonged to the person who could entice others into their world with the sheer force of their looks or personalities. This background gave me my first clue as to what was going on with Michael, though not in time to head trouble off at the pass.

Mike and Dave had always been loving brothers. Our frequent moves during their early years deepened their bond as they turned to each other for friendship and companionship. But Michael's rage was forcing a wedge between them. I sensed that his anger was not at his brother but at David's place in the family and the world. Everything was easy for David. School. People. Family. For Michael, it was all a struggle. It wasn't that he failed, but it took so much effort for him to do what came easily to his brother.

Years later, I recalled a time when I had been on the floor playing with the boys. David, only two, reached over and gave me a big squeeze and a kiss. I laughed, hugged him back, then happened to catch the look on four-year-old Michael's face. It was one of shock as if to say, "You mean, it's okay to do that?" Only later did it occur to me that it may have also meant, "Why are you one way with David and another way with me?"

I don't know why I didn't realize that Michael was processing some of the same conclusions I had reached as a child. That some people are born with gifts that will smooth life's way for them and others are not. The realization that you are a "have not" can be sobering.

The understanding that every person—no matter how gifted—has areas of lack that would qualify him or her as a "have not" was still years away for me. Even though a check told me something deep was stirring within Michael, the issue was unresolved in my own life, and I didn't put the pieces together.

Time revealed many things. I came to see how the fight for justice played into our world. Fairness wasn't a platitude for Michael and me. It was our only hope for leveling the playing field. In standing up for the underdog, we were standing up for ourselves.

That in itself may not have been so bad except we used causes as places to hide. They allowed us to be "right," while providing a shield against the pain that motivated us. Though I was grateful for the love of justice I'd inherited, and valued the compassion and passion it brought to my choices, my obsession with it was unhealthy.

The anger I saw in Michael scared me. Yet what scared me more was realizing it raged in me as well. I disguised it better, but what I had hidden so well from others and myself was exploding in my son. Desperate, I prayed that God would lead me to whatever resources I needed to figure out what was going on. I was hoping for a revelation that would change everything. What I got was the boot from our marriage counselor.

"Right now, you're too angry to address the issues in your marriage," he said. "I'd like to see you work with a woman I know who can help you get at core personal issues first."

I was incensed. I thought, *I've got a right to be angry! The past eighteen years, I've been the one willing to work on things, not Joe. Now I'm the stumbling block?* Yet the possibility that I could change my life apart from Joe appealed to me. So, I called the new therapist and, in our first visit, gave my assessment of my marriage. "Maybe a divorce is the best solution for all of us," I concluded.

I didn't believe in divorce. It ran against everything I believed. But the anger I saw in Michael and myself was a signal that, if nothing else, we could not go on as we were.

One day, it occurred to me that I could pull my robes of self-righteousness all I wanted, but, the fact was, it didn't matter if I was right or wrong. Even if justice as I envisioned it prevailed—if Joe did everything I thought he should do, the way I thought it should be done—the damage was done. There was too much anger. Too much resentment. Too much blaming. Too much distance. I had lived my life so long in the realm of principles and judgments that there was no longer any room for love.

"Life isn't fair" was an adage I simply could not accept. *It might be true, but it isn't right,* I told myself. At that point, it never occurred to me that life might not have to be fair to be good. But I did realize that my extreme insistence on justice had blighted my life. It sickened me now to realize I had chiseled that same message onto my son's heart.

Winter
1990

Three Amigos

I scanned the arrival gate in Dallas, looking for the shortest adult around. My sister, whom I failed to see working her way through the crowd, suddenly appeared at my side. "Hello!" she said slipping her arm around my waist and pulling me to her. My eyes teared as we hugged.

After four years of living in remote locations as missionaries, she and her family had recently moved to Lindale, a small Texas town two hours southeast of Dallas. It was hard to believe we could now reach each other by just an hour-and-a-half flight.

Sharon had olive skin, ash brown hair that shimmered silver highlights, and a full smile that lit up the world around her. She was one inch shorter than I, but she was four feet and eleven inches of dynamite. Like Papa and me, she never felt size was a detriment. She could out work, out play, out organize, and out argue just about anyone.

Sharon and I didn't really get to know each other until we were grown. The relationship I enjoy with her today exists simply because she refused to let me go.

Joe left for active duty in the army six months after we married. That fall, my mother died. Soon after, my brother Edwin moved away to go to college. That left Sharon and me.

I was surprised my fourteen-year-old sister wanted to spend time with me. She'd help me out with projects, errands, or anything else I needed. We laughed and cried our way through many weekends as we struggled to accept our mother's death, but it took me a while before I began to appreciate her.

It wasn't just that Sharon did things for me but that she did them with such kindness. And without expecting anything in return. Sometimes she would ask me to do something with her, but I seldom did. Still, she continued to give until she won me over.

Looking back, I'm ashamed of the way I took her for granted. I don't know how she was able to channel her grief into giving—whereas mine caused me to just hold tighter to myself. But then, Sharon always has possessed a measure of poise, maturity, and wisdom beyond her years.

I found it ironic that for so long I saw myself as a "have not," only to find that much of what I needed I had been given in my sister and my brother. Both gave to me freely.

Edwin had been my best friend my whole life. Just thirteen months younger than I, we felt like twins—though we looked nothing alike. I was fair while Edwin inherited the dark skin and black hair of our American Indian roots.

We did everything together and loved each other fiercely. Though I was as bossy as they came, I learned Edwin could only be pushed so far. He was laid back, had a great sense of humor, and thought I could do anything. He often let me take the lead, but when something came up he cared about, he took his stand. When that happened, you could forget about swaying him. He had a strong sense of what he wanted and how to get it.

I'm not sure when I realized that Edwin was not in the least compliant. Rather, he, like Sharon, had learned there were means of getting what you wanted that were much more effective than confrontation. How this major social skill escaped me, when both my siblings were so adept at it, amazed me. Maybe they learned from my example. At any rate, Edwin and I had a wonderful childhood. He was my fun, my intellectual sparring partner, and my encourager. I knew beyond a shadow of a doubt that he loved me. Sharon and I thought Edwin could do no wrong, and we looked to him as friend and protector.

One of my favorite memories is of Edwin rescuing Sharon from a killer chicken. Fuzzy was given as an Easter present to our next door neighbor Barbara, a girl my age. Before long though, Fuzzy, the adorable little chick, turned into a terror.

There was a six-foot high block wall between our houses where Fuzzy would perch waiting to attack us whenever we came into the yard. We loved to play on a little rope swing our dad had hung on the T-bar of the clothesline pole, but now we were petrified to go outside.

One day Edwin, who was ten, told Sharon to go out to the swing. "I'll take care of that chicken," he promised. Though not too keen on being used as bait, Sharon crouched in the swing, shaking from head to toe. Edwin, armed with a baseball bat, hid around the corner of the house. In the glow of territorial aggression, Fuzzy failed to sense the danger awaiting her and swooped down into our yard. Then she saw Ed. The big bird began shrieking wildly, but it was too late. Ed caught her in mid-flight. He took a mighty swing and down she went. Barbara, hearing the commotion, ran into the backyard screaming, "Fuzzy! Fuzzy!"

Ed calmly climbed up on the brick fence and dropped the chicken at Barbara's feet. Fuzzy landed with an awful thud. "The next time that chicken comes into our yard," he announced, "we're having white meat for dinner." Incredibly, Fuzzy wasn't dead, only stunned, and she never bothered us again after that.

Edwin was the kind of brother you could count on.

Now, I was looking forward to this weekend with him and Sharon. He was coming into Dallas from California, so my sister and I made our way down to the American Eagle terminal. Together we were flying into Wichita Falls to spend a few days with Papa.

Edwin met us at the escalator. Though my brother had been slight as a kid (weighing only eighty-six pounds his freshman year of high school), he was now almost six feet tall with a medium build. Gray was creeping into the edges of his dark hair, but his slanting, laughing eyes—so like my son David's—still exuded boyishness.

The three of us walked toward the gate, arm in arm, like the three musketeers. *All for one and one for all*, I thought. Over the years, we had each faced crises that had caused us to feel the loss of our mother again. Most had to do with the pain of watching our own children grow up without the benefit of her influence and knowing that all our lives had been profoundly diminished without the grace of her wisdom and caring.

Her death also denied us something else: the opportunity to challenge her. Children establish their identities by pushing against their parents, by striking out in areas beyond their parents' vision or approval. The years we would've spent grappling with independence in a mother/child relationship were lost to us. At the very point where we would've taken flight, we'd been grounded.

To this day I wonder, *Would my mother have supported us in our journey toward independence? What if we wanted to go in a direction she didn't approve of? Would she have let us go? Even helped us find our way? Would she have loved us no matter what?*

I want to say yes. But I can only attempt to answer those questions using the memories I have of her. To us, she was the ideal mom. We still view her with the rosy glasses of childhood. We never had the chance to appreciate the interplay of her strengths and weaknesses.

We are left with who we think she was. And we have what she built into us. But we never experienced going to head-to-head with the one who gave us birth. And we never had the opportunity of emerging from the struggle to find we could both not only survive but flourish.

Because our mother didn't survive, establishing independence and identity has been more complex for us. Delayed in some ways. Thwarted in others.

Ten years after my mother's death we finally recognized that while we couldn't go back in time to make up this loss, we could do something about it now. From that point on, we committed to "mother" each other as best we could. We agreed to give to each other in whatever way was needed, for the rest of our lives.

It was in this spirit that we planned this trip. Our grandfather had lost a daughter and we wanted him to know we would stand in her place. We were determined to love and care for Papa as my mother would have, had she lived.

Blood Kin

When the three of us came rolling into the parking lot of Midtown Manor in our rental car, Papa was waiting for us. He ushered us into the lobby as though we were the three kings from the Orient.

A sharp screeching noise startled me as I hugged Papa, and I saw he was sporting a new hearing aid. "Papa's coming in for a landing," I announced, moving back to restore quiet. "Where's the other one?" I asked, checking the opposite ear.

"I didn't want it," he said tersely. Then he drew his mouth into that tight line that signaled "end of discussion," so I let it drop.

Just then, the manager of Midtown Manor came to greet us. Mr. King was in his sixties himself, but he ran the place efficiently and fairly. He protected the residents from those who would prey on them. He enlisted their help in running the community. He found just the right niche for those who needed a place to belong. And he arranged a potpourri of social events to keep everyone active and involved.

In allowing the residents a say-so in how things were run, Mr. King headed off the discontent that usually characterized such places—and gave the residents a sense of dignity that was priceless.

"I understand you three kids sing," he said, shaking my hand. Somebody had gotten to him. It wasn't Papa we learned, but several of the residents who'd been members of the local Pentecostal churches we had sung in as children. "We were wondering if you would sing for us one night?"

He didn't have to twist our arms. Music always had been a strong bond between us, though we seldom had a chance to sing together any more. Having grown up singing in our father's church, we knew by heart the words to every verse of every great hymn of the faith. My dad also taught us a host of gospel and popular tunes.

Music was part of most everything we did as kids, even work. Edwin, always looking for some way to have fun, was usually the one to come up with some music game. As we washed dishes he'd say, "Let's see how many songs we can come up with that have the word 'heart' in it." And off we would go. "Until Then My Heart Will Go On Singing." "Let Me Call You Sweetheart." "Heart and Soul." The last one to come up with a title won. In addition to single words like "heart," we had an endless supply of categories. Names of towns. Names of states. Girl's names. Cars. Furniture.

We played "Name that Tune" long before it was a TV show. Sometimes singing the melody, other times just tapping out the rhythm to see who could recognize it first. And whenever one of us heard a pretty song, we'd teach it to each other then work out three part harmony. In our house, music took the space TV occupied in other homes. It was our entertainment, our way of relating. And we loved it.

But as we sat down later that afternoon to go through our repertoire, something happened we didn't expect. Like a middle-aged veteran who goes up in the attic to try on his old army uniform, we found a lot of things had changed. Our harmonies no longer "fit." Sharon's childhood soprano had mellowed into the alto range, which would have been fine except I, too, was an alto. And Edwin, who had sung tenor, now found his parts too high to sing comfortably.

All our arrangements needed revamping. However, it had been a long time since we'd worked on a project together, and we'd forgotten how strong-willed we were. I had a list of songs I thought we could adapt with just a little work. Sharon had hers. Edwin didn't want to work at all.

"I came here to visit with Papa," he said, "I don't want to spend all my time practicing."

"Well, it's too late now," I informed him. "The flyers are up and they're expecting us, so we might as well make the best of it."

His response was, "Then let's do a sing-along of the old hymns. They'd rather sing themselves than hear us anyway."

"But they did ask us to sing," Sharon reminded him.

Within minutes we reverted to the bickering of childhood.

I wondered what Papa thought of his three adult grandchildren arguing like six year-olds. The stubbornness should have come as no surprise though, since we got more than a little of it from him.

Whenever Papa made up his mind about something, it was set in stone. Like refusing a second hearing aid. "I don't want you spending your good money on an old man who may not last more than a few months anyway," he said. That was to become his catch phrase in the decade ahead, but it wasn't the whole story.

Papa was vain about his appearance. When tested for the hearing aid, his only question was, "Can I have the kind that fits inside my ear?" When told no, Papa refused to return to the clinic for several months. Finally, the isolation wore him down. "I hate havin' to wear that thing," he told Marie, "but I might as well accept it." It. Singular. There was no talking him into two. "One's just fine," he insisted. At least he could hear enough to interact with others again.

Still, that little flesh-colored piece of equipment aggravated him. Papa didn't like reminders that he was aging. The Sunday before, we'd all loaded up in the car and started for the church he now attended with my aunt. He didn't much care for the church, but he went on the general principle of honoring the Sabbath. He also liked the company and going out to eat afterwards. We were waiting at a light near the church when Papa said, "Hon, you'll need to turn right here."

I said, "Papa, I think we go through this intersection then it's about four more blocks on the left."

"No," he insisted. "You turn right and it's up the road on the left."

As the traffic light changed from red to green, the silence in the car was deafening. *Should I follow Papa's instructions or my own instincts?* If I did as he asked and he was wrong, he'd not only be humiliated but we'd all be late. Sick at heart, I drove through the intersection, praying the confusion was mine. But it wasn't. Papa's countenance fell as the big church came into view. He looked down at his hands and said, "Well, I guess I don't know my way around my own town any more."

I wanted to cry. We all knew that the incident signaled something important. Papa was no longer reliable. From now on, we would always wonder. Whether it was getting directions, confirming flight arrival times, or making arrangements for dinner, a third party would need to know also. Just to be sure.

Perhaps something like this had happened before, but this was the first time Edwin, Sharon, and I had witnessed it. It shook us up. We felt uncomfortable, as though we had seen Papa naked, and we were ashamed for him and ourselves.

We didn't speak of it again. Instead we moved into areas where Papa's mind roamed free and unerring. We filled the evenings listening to his adventures as a young man. For a while at least, the impairments of age had no place.

A frequent player in these memories was Papa's brother, Earl. They were close in age—number two and three of six boys. "Growing up, we was buddies," Papa said.

Those two were always up to some mischief. They had a nose for action of any kind—including gambling and fighting, of which they did more than their share. Even after both married, they remained close. Nobody thought anything could come between them. The event that finally destroyed their relationship was the last thing one would have expected: Papa got religion.

From the day Papa got saved, his friendship with Earl was doomed. That bothered me. *How could he let his brother go so easily?* I wondered. I couldn't imagine relinquishing my relationship with Edwin or Sharon without exhausting every possibility for reconciliation. But any anguish Papa felt about it, he kept to himself.

"Earl was having family trouble and he and his wife separated 'bout the time Mama and me got saved," he said.

So much for supporting each other in hard times, I thought. When I asked Papa about it, he said, "In those days, you didn't think about it like that. Earl wanted to live one way and I wanted to live another."

I later learned that my grandfather didn't abandon him entirely. More than once when Earl was on a drunken binge Papa went looking for him. He'd clean his brother up and bring him home. But Earl continued with his hard living and hard drinking until he died of emphysema at the age of sixty-three.

"He was buried in his Levis and a white shirt," Papa said. "Just like he wanted."

I was glad that Papa at least knew what his brother wanted. Their separation was something I couldn't understand until my own sons faced the demons of addiction. Then I could appreciate why Papa felt that the only way to stay clean was to stay away from temptation, even if that included your brother. Still, when I thought about what Papa and Earl had lost, I wondered if there could've been some middle ground.

Horse Trader

Before the gathering the next night, the four of us scurried around Papa's little apartment like performers dressing for a Broadway show. Sharon, Edwin and I were nervous—more than a little underprepared—but happy about singing together again.

By start time, the rec room was overflowing. Many people stood. Others brought chairs from adjoining rooms. At Edwin's insistence, we led the residents in a sing-along of old gospel tunes, with just a few of our songs interspersed in between. He was right, they loved it. And we loved visiting with them afterwards.

Conversations usually started with some connection. "We knew your Mama and Papa when they were out in Byers." Or, "We attended Southside Assembly with your granddaddy when he and Brother Parvin were on the deacon board." If they didn't know our family directly, they knew someone who did.

A lot of them remembered my mother and shared stories about how kind and shy she was. "So, you're Atha's children," they would say. "Yes," we would respond proudly. "We're Atha's children." There were few places left in the world where that meant anything to anyone but us, so we lingered until the very last person left, soaking up the last delicious drops of belonging.

We passed our new friends on our way to play pool the next day. Their faces lit up as we greeted them by name. Some trailed behind us to watch us play and, in between, we'd talk. Each one had a story. Where they grew up. How they came to Midtown Manor. What their children did, where they lived. Like us, they were reaching back, looking for ties to tether them to life.

Papa still played with the boys, but in the odd times the four of us would play. To keep the teams even, Papa and Ed split up and partnered with one of us girls. Sharon and I were streaky players, but we liked to win. It took a concerted effort on all our parts to keep the competition to a minimum.

Sharon racked the balls, and Papa gave Ed his stick to break. "That's a good cue stick you've got here, Papa," Ed observed.

"Yeah. It's a good one alright, considering I got it for free."

"Papa, have you been up to your old horse trading tricks again?" I asked.

He laughed, knowing exactly what I meant.

Papa had always dabbled in trading and that was where he made his real money. Even that sacred institution of the state of Texas recognized his ability. As an expert witness, he was often called upon to determine the value of a loss involving horses. When asked his official occupation, he proudly replied, "Horse trader."

Once he got the barn, Papa developed trading to a science. Well, it was more like a revolving door. As soon as a girl wanted to trade her horse, Papa would find one for her. Or, more commonly, Papa would buy horses he knew would appeal to his boarders then groom them for selling.

He had a knack for seeing potential in a horse. He'd take what others would call "old nags" then put blankets on them so they'd shed their old coats and grow new shiny ones. "I'd feed them good feed," he explained, "groom them, gentle them, and teach them manners. Then I could get twice what anyone else could for them." One reason was that he guaranteed the health and temperament of every horse he sold. In all the years he traded, only one man brought a horse back.

But Papa enjoyed bartering for its own sake. No wonder. He was good at it.

We didn't have to beg him to tell us about his new cue stick. Even at age eighty-six, recounting a successful trade was almost as rewarding as the trade itself.

Papa said one day he came across two quality cue sticks at a garage sale. He paid seven dollars total for them. The next day, he stashed one under his bed and took the other to the rec room to play with. Virgil spied it right away.

"I see you got yourself a new stick." Virgil said.

"Yep."

"Seems to suit you."

"Workin' pretty good so far," Papa said. "Wanna try it out?"

Virgil took the stick then proceeded to make some of the impossible shots for which he was known. Suddenly, Papa's shots got a little off, and Virgil took the game.

"Alva, I believe this is the best stick I ever played with," he said.

"It's a pretty good stick alright."

"I don't suppose you'd consider selling it to me now would ya?"

"That depends, I guess."

"On what?"

"On whether or not you'd give me seven dollars for it."

Virgil, one of the tightest men in the Manor, could hardly wait to pull a five and two ones from his wallet. "You better watch out," Virgil said with a grin as he handed the money to Papa, "you may never get another game off me without this stick."

"Guess I'll just have to try to find another one then," Papa lamented.

A smile tugged at my grandfather's mouth as he concluded the tale. "Of course, the next morning, I pulled the other stick out from under my bed and met Virgil in the rec room seven dollars richer."

Papa could trade just about anything and make a buck. He made his first trade as a seventeen-year-old kid. He owned a horse named Cap—a black, long-legged stallion he claimed was his all-time favorite horse.

"Today he'd be a racehorse," he said. "You had to be a good horseman to ride him. When you'd rein him in, he'd just tremble like he had a motor goin'. I raced him all the time—and won lots of money with him, too."

But one Sunday, as Papa rode into town, a man saw Cap and wanted him.

"You reckon that feller would sell that horse?" he asked a friend of Papa's later.

"Choate'd sell anything if the price was right," the friend replied. So the next day, the man rode sixteen miles to find Papa at the farm.

"I seen him comin'," Papa said, "and he was ridin' one of the most beautiful sorrels I've ever seen. She had a dark red coat with a light mane and tail that shimmered just like it was spun of copper. She was a beauty. But this guy only had eyes for Cap."

"How much you want for that horse?" the stranger asked.

Papa knew immediately that the sorrel was a better horse than Cap. The average price of a horse then was thirty-five dollars. Papa figured the sorrel was worth that and half again. Cap was flashy but he was high strung. He was no good for working or everyday riding. "I'll trade you even for that sorrel you're ridin," he said.

The man didn't bat an eye. "Sold."

Papa was right. The sorrel was a great horse and four weeks later he sold him for sixty dollars and a pair of silver-mounted spurs to a man who wanted him for his daughter.

"Didn't he think that was outrageous?" I asked.

"Yeah, he did. But I thought the horse was worth it, and in the end, I guess he did, too."

Now Papa was without a horse, so he bought a bay off his daddy for thirty-eight dollars. He hadn't had her a week when up came a friend of his, riding Cap.

"Where'd ya get that horse?" Papa asked him.

"The guy you sold him to couldn't handle him, so I bought him. But I'm here to see if you've got a nice gentle horse around. I'm tryin' to find one for a rich widow woman."

"How 'bout this here bay?" Papa asked.

The cowboy got off Cap and checked out the horse. "I think she'd fit the bill. How much you want for her?"

"Well, I'm kind of partial to ol' Cap," he said. "If you want this horse, I'll trade you even for him."

The cowboy thought about it a minute then handed Cap's reins to Papa.

"I figured that widow woman musta been really rich for him to give up Cap," Papa said. "But I didn't make out too bad myself. When it was all said and done, I had twenty-two dollars cash, a set of silver-mounted spurs, and my favorite horse back."

Summer
1990

Rattlesnakes

Though I'd been to Papa's five months earlier, summer found me packing again for Wichita Falls. By the time I caught the limo service in Stamford, I was willing the tires to carry me as fast as possible to La Guardia. I wanted to get away. *Just how long were you supposed to hang in before you called it quits?* I wondered. Yet something wouldn't allow me to let go. At first I thought it was God, but I was sensing a subtle change in the direction I was getting from Him in my quiet times.

Malachi 2:16 said God hated divorce. But what was becoming clear was that he also hated the way Joe, the boys, and I were living. Our lives weren't a testimony to our commitment to marriage; they were a sacrilege. As I asked myself the hard questions—What are you teaching your boys about what a marriage is like? …what a family is like? …about love and kindness? …about being a Christian?—I realized the futility of our situation.

In my mind I tried to visualize our family apart. For twenty years I'd sacrificed my own goals to keep the family working. Struggled to find some kind of peace in the midst of terrible loneliness. Tried to provide a safe place for the boys. And for what? To walk away?

I grieved over us. The boys loved their father. They loved me. In spite of the unresolved issues between Joe and me, we both were committed to our children. We did a lot with them separately and had a full cache of memories we treasured.

Every place we lived, Joe and the boys would find a secret hideaway. Often it was no more than a clump of trees or a boulder by the sea. But packing little boxes of raisins to snack on, they "hiked" to their special place on weekends in a ritual of male bonding.

When Joe was home, he put the boys to bed at night. Making a tent out of the blankets, he gathered them under the covers for scary action stories. They ended with Joe yelling "Ooga, ooga!" and tickling them into submission. Then he settled them down by reading aloud. *The Cat in the Hat* soon gave away to *The Lion, the Witch and the Wardrobe* as the years rolled by.

Most of my good times with the boys revolved around swimming, cooking, and shopping. Both boys could swim before they could walk. Being raised in southern California, Joe and I loved the water. So every vacation—every free moment—was spent at the beach or the pool. It was the one place I seemed able to relax and enjoy the boys.

Michael and David would ride on my back in the water. When they were older, we'd play tag, practice holding our breath, see who could dive the deepest. I never could get them to sing songs under water like Sharon, Ed, and I used to do by the hour, but they got to where they could beat me in any stroke. After swimming all day, they'd nose out of the water like little seals and run over to me, shivering, waiting to be embraced by my arms and a warm towel.

Therapy had given me a more realistic perspective about my relationship with the boys. True, the good times had been shrouded by depression, but I was beginning to give myself credit for the special times we had shared.

Every year before Christmas, I'd take each boy out of school for a day to do his holiday shopping. They also helped me bake for special occasions. Green and red popcorn balls for Christmas. A white cake with marshmallow frosting for David's birthday. Cheesecake for Daddy's. I have pictures of the boys' red and green smiles, colored by the sparkling candies we sprinkled on homemade rollout cookies. By the time he was seven, Mike was a good little baker. In time, so was David.

But now, the activities they once begged for no longer interested them. Little league gave us a bond for a while. I loved sports and loved watching the boys play. My best Mother's Day ever was a doubleheader that lasted the whole afternoon. But as the boys approached adolescence, I realized with panic that I had little they wanted.

Our relationship consisted primarily of discipline. They were mad at me. I was mad at them. And I was at a loss for how to deal with them. Not only was my relationship with Joe falling apart, I was losing the boys as well. It wasn't just age. Years of inconsistent discipline, combined with the animosity Joe and I felt toward each other, were catching up to us. I saw disaster coming and felt powerless to stop it.

No wonder I ran to Texas. For a few days I could get away from daily failure. And I felt wanted. I don't know who was lonelier then, Papa or I. But we thrived on what we gave each other.

This visit had been particularly good. With his hearing aid, Papa felt part of the world again, and he had more stamina than he'd had for a while.

We went to Piccadilly every day for lunch. One afternoon, after sharing a peach cobbler and lingering over a second cup of coffee, Papa said, "Would you like to ride over to the barn?"

I hadn't been there since we had taken the boys riding two years earlier. Neither had Papa.

"Is it still open?"

"Nah. Nobody's been boarding in there for over a year. They had different ones try to make a go of it and they couldn't."

"Guess they need you to show them how, Papa."

"Yeah, guess so," he smiled. "I heard they're fixin' to build out there. I'd like to go see it again before they do."

"Build what?" I asked.

"Oh, houses or somethin'. Ev'ry so many years they try to do something with that land, but the creek keeps overflowing. They keep saying they can fix it, but I don't think they ever will."

The bridge was torn out where they were widening the creek, but we were still able to get in by the old road.

"You want to go in?" Papa asked.

"Sure," I said, "but there's a padlock on the gate."

Papa was ahead of me. I got the feeling he'd already thought this through. "We can get in. We can climb over the fence."

"Okay," I laughed. "I can if you can."

My grandfather, at eighty-seven, climbed over the fence with the excitement of a schoolboy playing hooky for the day. I had on a dress, so I crawled underneath. We were both giddy with the joy of adventure.

Papa started toward the worn path leading to the barn. It was so badly overgrown that there was barely room for us to walk. Then I remembered that my sister had encountered a poisonous snake along this road. I stopped, suddenly aware of a very disturbing sound.

"Papa," I asked, "do rattlers sound like Rainbird sprinklers?" I asked.

"Well, yeah. Guess they do," he replied. "With all this grass growed up out here, these fields are probably full of them. 'Course it's katydids makin' most the racket."

Katydids I could handle, but rattlers? The blood rushed to my head in a surge of panic. This place was not safe. I must've been crazy to bring Papa here. What would I do if one of us were bitten? If Papa were bitten, I could run for help. If I were bitten, I'd have to get help myself. But how? Weren't you supposed to lie still to slow the circulation of poison in the bloodstream? I played out various scenarios. They weren't pleasant, but the process enabled me to put one foot in front of the other until we reached the barn.

Papa opened the big, dilapidated door and I walked into the cavernous hall. As my eyes adjusted to the dirty dusk inside, I glimpsed a moving shadow toward the back of the barn.

"Papa…" I called. No answer. "Papa!" I turned just as he caught up with me. At the same time, a large, sable horse came thundering out of an open stall.

I screamed as he bore down on us. *We're dead*, I thought. I could see the headlines: *Outlaw horse kills man and granddaughter.*

But suddenly Papa jumped in front of me. He swept his cowboy hat off his head and began waving his arms in big, forceful circles. "Git outta here! Go on!" he yelled with authority. "Git."

The horse dug in his back hooves and skidded to a stop. With a snort he turned about-face and ran back to his stall as fast as he could.

"If you act smarter than a horse," Papa said, "it'll never occur to him he's bigger than you are." I guess that horse must've thought Papa was pretty smart because he didn't so much as stick his nose out of his stall the rest of the time we were there.

Still a little bit jumpy, I crooked my arm through Papa's and let him lead me down memory lane. It smelled like horse manure, not flowers, but to Papa, nothing was sweeter than the smell of the barn anyway. He checked out the tack room. The stalls. Most were in bad repair. I saw him wince then choose the happier world of memories.

"Mama and I had some pretty good times out here," he said. "And I had more than my share of good horses."

Every horse Papa got, he renamed. "By the time I got finished with him, he'd practically be a different horse anyway," Papa claimed. Mama used to tease him about the names he chose for them. "I don't know where he gets them!" she'd say if she thought one was silly. There was Shorty, Hot Shot, Coyote, Rex, Holiday, Kid, Badger, Bugger. Mama made him rename Bugger.

Papa and I laughed as we strolled down the barn. The tops of the double Dutch doors in back were open, giving a view clear to the outside. We walked slowly toward them, then rested our elbows on the ledge and looked out over the wild pasture.

Papa's shoulders sagged. He told me how he'd repaired the barn's basic structure. Fixed up the tack room. Rebuilt the stalls. Put in the arena. Tended the garden.

He surveyed the land surrounding the barn, narrowing his eyes as they passed over overgrown fields and broken-down fences.

"This is the last time I'll come out here," he said.

I patted his arm. "It's hard seeing things change."

"It says in Isaiah, 'All flesh is grass...but the word of the Lord stands forever.' That's just the way it is when it gets down to it. Nothin' lasts except the Lord."

I said nothing but thought of the people I loved who had died—of those I thought would care for me who'd let me down. Life had not turned out like I expected, and I felt crushed by responsibilities I was unequipped to handle. Maybe Papa was right. There was no security apart from God.

I became aware once again of the cacophony just outside the barn. For a few minutes I'd forgotten the snake-filled grass. Fear jumped in my throat reminding me that there was no way out except the way we'd come.

By the time we got back to the car, I was shaking. Clouds began moving in and with the day's adventure ended, the dread of parting started to descend on us.

"Sure am gonna miss you, hon," Papa said at lunch the next day. We were at Luby's. I had an early afternoon flight so there wasn't time for Piccadilly. "Luby's is good, too," Papa said, "and I don't want you to leave without a good dinner." But I was too upset to eat much.

Leaving Papa was part of it. Going home was the other. I was afraid to go back. Every bit as afraid as I had been to walk through the snakes at the barn.

My spiritual journey didn't seem to be making much impact on my family situation, and I felt like I was walking a tightrope without a net. Before long, decisions would have to be made that I didn't want to make. Fear gripped me as I tried to envision myself in an unknown future. I knew I was headed for a dark time where not even Papa could help me.

Leaning on the Everlasting Arms

Folding a tiny pillow under my head, I snuggled against the window and allowed my thoughts to drift. It was hard for me to reconcile the turmoil I lived in daily with the peace Christ promised. I didn't know what to do with the reality that for whatever reason, God didn't seem to be "working" for me. Yet the spiritual experiences and teachings of my heritage were like a life preserver that encircled me as I treaded churning waters. Deep down, my gut told me there was something of value there. Something worth sorting out and holding to.

As a child, I loved church. And I especially loved going with Mama and Papa. Their services were more than a little lively. I listened in awe as people spoke in "tongues"—an unknown spiritual language commonly heard in Pentecostal services. I waited in anticipation for an interpretation. These interpretations sandwiched between heartfelt "Thus sayeth the Lords" put the listener on notice, just in case he or she was tempted to doubt the message.

The music—the heart of the service—was very different from the classical and traditional heritage bequeathed to the church by men like John Wesley and Martin Luther. Pentecostal music often had an upbeat tempo and it came from the heart. What it lacked in sophistication it gained in passion. People like Elvis Presley and Jerry Lee Lewis, who came from

Assembly of God backgrounds like my grandparents, later cashed in on the passion part and mostly left religion behind.

In those days, a service would never be confined to a single hour. Sometimes the preacher would forgo preaching and let people sing and dance all night until, by the time things died down, all the kids were asleep on the church benches and had to be carried out in their parents' arms.

Every church service began with a rousing rendition of "Leaning on the Everlasting Arms": "What a fellowship, what a joy divine, leaning on the everlasting arms…" People got out of their pews and shook hands with everyone to let them know they were welcome. Their broad smiles and handshakes offered a warmth that I accepted at face value.

After a few announcements, the serious singing began. As "I'll Fly Away" and "I'm So Glad Jesus Lifted Me" filled the rafters, the men, women, and children began clapping, raising hands, shouting, crying. "He will fill your heart today with overflowing," they sang. "As the Lord commanded you, bring your vessels, not a few. He will fill your heart today with over-flowing with the Holy Ghost and power."

Soon one person then another would move out into the aisle and begin dancing. I was mesmerized. I envied their freedom, though, even as a kid, I was unsure about whether or not the Holy Spirit was responsible for it all. People didn't seem so much like they were "taken over" as responding to something that made them happy. Had it not been for what happened to my grandmother, I would have rejected the whole thing lock, stock, and barrel. But instead, I looked for what was real, like my grandparents taught me to do.

Early on, they taught me the importance of "discerning the spirits." Papa said, "There's a lot of hollerin' and carryin' on in these services. Some of it has to do with true worship and repentance and some of it don't." As Papa put it, there were people who were willing to be "fools for Christ's sake," and then there were "just fools." There were women who found a way to get the attention in church that they'd never been able to get anywhere else. There were men who had never held a serious position in their lives who suddenly found themselves deacons and reveled in their newfound importance.

And Mama and Papa were the first to recognize the charlatans of their day. The preachers who were too lazy to do anything else. The ones who loved to talk but had nothing to say. The ones who got high from the power of swaying the emotions of people. The crooks. But my grandparents never stood up against them. They maintained, "We're not going to lift our hand against the Lord's anointed." They had a healthy respect for God's ways not being our ways, and felt their best bet was to mind their own business and tend to their own spiritual journeys.

But it grieved them to see how people misused and abused God's name. Once, after a two-hour service with more announcements than worship, Mama said, "Sure seems like you have to put up with an awful lot of palaver to get to a little bit of truth."

I remember thinking, *Palaver? Where'd she learn a word like that?* She and Papa both amazed me with the vocabulary they would come up with—often right in the middle of some sentence with an improperly conjugated verb.

I looked up the word. It meant "idle chatter, especially prolonged." Given that "palaver" was an accurate description of what we'd just sat through, I wondered what made them hang in there. But Papa said, "There's nothin' anybody in or out of the church could ever do that could turn me against the Lord, not after what He did for me."

Papa was saved in Hobart, Oklahoma, under the preaching of Sister Hartwell in what was called the "Valentine Revival." Yes, the Mrs. did the preaching. I found it ironic that the one place equality of the sexes existed from the beginning was in the Pentecostal movement. They took literally the Bible's injunction that in Christ there was neither Jew nor Greek, slave nor free, male nor female. It would take forty years for our culture to catch onto what these people took for granted, and many institutions debate it still. But Papa had a convincing perspective: "It'd be pretty hard for me to come down on a woman who wanted to preach—bein's as I was saved under one."

Woman or no, Papa's conversion was not an easy one. One day he noticed a feeling of heaviness in his chest. It kept getting worse, crushing him like a sack of stones. He became so obsessed with his health he lost all interest in everything. At first he thought he was physically sick, but as the weeks went by, he realized it was more than that.

"I'm heartsick," he told Cora.

"About what?" she asked.

He couldn't say. Their new baby, Marie, was just three weeks old. They were deeply in love. But Papa was inconsolable.

"It feels like God's hand is heavy on me," he said, "and if I don't get right with Him, I'm gonna die." Papa had never gone to church so he hadn't a clue as to what was happening to him. Mama had gone to church all her life but she'd never heard about anything that affected people like this, so she too was at a loss.

One afternoon when Papa was out in the field, that dark cloud gripped him again. He ran into the nearby brush and, throwing himself across the stump of a mesquite tree, cried out for a God he didn't know how to find. Two hours later, he got up, still oppressed by his unseen burden, walked back to the house, and told Mama he was going to see his daddy.

Papa's voice trembled with emotion as he related what happened next.

We'd been living in Seminole with Cora's folks where I'd work in the oil fields when there was work. But I had quit my job because the Lord had been dealing with me so much. I didn't know it was the Lord. I just knew there was somethin' the matter with me.

When I got to my daddy's, he saw I was needin' a change. Poppa was share cropping there in Hobart, Oklahoma, and they furnished everything. The croppers did all the work and got about half of whatever they made, so we figured we could get by. Earl was at home, and Poppa told me and Earl to go get Cora and Marie and bring them to Hobart. So we did.

Comin' back, we was drivin' out to Poppa's and there was a car turned off the highway behind us. It was 'bout half a mile up before we turned off the road into Poppa's gate. We was surprised when the car followed us in. We knew all the cars in the area and theirs wasn't familiar, so we knew they was strangers. But we didn't pay them no mind once we pulled up near the house 'cause all our family came runnin' out. They hadn't seen Marie yet, so they was all makin' over the grandbaby and all. So this family in this other car, they sat there a little while, then they got out of the car and were fussin' over the baby, too.

Finally, we got around to introducin' ourselves. Their name was Hartwell. After things settled down a bit, they said, "We're ministers, and if it's okay, we'd like to sing a few songs for you."

Well, we loved music so we invited them in and they sang some lively tunes. Good ol' gospel tunes we'd never heard before. Their boy played the guitar and sang, too. Then Sister Hartwell said, "We're fixin' to put up a tent tomorrow in Colbert for a revival meetin' and we wondered if we could get some help?" Nobody said nothin'. Then after a minute I said, "I'll help you put your tent up."

Well, I surprised everyone 'cause they knew me. I had never offered to do nothin' like that before. That just shows you how desperate I was. I hadn't had such feelings in all my life. It was—I can't explain it…the conviction of the Holy Ghost can make you so miserable.

I still thought I was gonna die, and I wanted to accept the Lord first. So I was wantin' to go to church. That's why I told them I'd help them. We went over there the next day—Earl and me—and we got the tent up. But that night there come a storm as rough as I'd ever seen, and it just tore that tent to strings. I'll tell you, I thought, That's it. So much for religion. *I didn't know enough to know that I could just kneel down before the Lord and pray through. I didn't know that. I thought I had to have somebody to help me. So I was really low.*

But the next day, Sister Hartwell come back up there. And that was the Lord, because we didn't have the gas money to drive into Colbert again and see her. Well, there was a vacant schoolhouse about a mile north of Poppa's house and she says, "We've secured this here vacant schoolhouse, and we're going to start the revival Sunday night. We'd like ya'll to come." So, I told them okay, we'd attend the meetin'.

I don't guess Cora knew what to think about me sayin' that because—I don't tell this often—but I'd gamble, drink, fight, and do a lot of things. Nobody else didn't know what to think about it either, especially Poppa and them.

Now, Cora belonged to the Methodist church, but she lived a better life than a lot of Pentecostal people. She was for anything that would change me. But one thing she never done was try to change me herself. She never did tell me one time that I better not drink any more, that I better not gamble. She knew that if she woulda tried to make me turn, it wouldn't work. Either she was smart enough, or else she loved me enough that she just wouldn't fuss over it.

So, we walked and carried the baby a mile up the road. And my brother and sister, Lois and Royce, and Momma got to goin' with us some. I think it was the second night I went to the altar and I prayed till one o'clock in the morning. And I didn't feel a thing 'cept I thought I was going to die if I didn't touch the Lord. But nothin' happened, so I got up and we went on home.

The next night, I went back to the altar again and stayed that night until everybody was worn out. Now, my Momma was Church of Christ, and she thought I was overdoing the thing—I was praying so hard. She went and sat on the altar and said, "Now son, you've confessed your sins. That's all you can do. You're saved, now just get up and go on." But I didn't pay no attention to her. I just kept bombarding heaven till the Lord come down and finally it happened. It was like somebody just lifted that ton of bricks off my back.

Up until that time, there was any amount of people I didn't like. It wasn't my nature to like people. I was ashamed of it, but I had an awful disposition. But when I got up from that altar, I couldn't think of one person I didn't like. And I'd think about people that I used to just lay awake to hate and I couldn't see a thing wrong with 'em. I loved 'em. From that day till this, I haven't changed. It's been that real to me.

It was such a change in my life that we went back the next night, and, after the preachin', Cora just got up and fell at the altar. And wasn't but a little bit and she went to speakin' in tongues. And we didn't know a thing about the Holy Ghost. We didn't know you was supposed to git the Holy Ghost. But she was so clean that when she fell at the altar, the Lord just baptized her and she went to speakin' in other tongues and danced—I wish you coulda seen her dance. She could dance faster than anybody when she danced under the power. And she shouted all over that place.

This was so opposite to our natures, but the Lord says you're not the same. "Old things have passed away and all things have become new." That's what happened in my life. It was a real born-again experience. If God hadn't given me a real born-again experience, I wouldn't have accepted it because if I hadn't gotten something real, I wouldn't have settled for it. He knew I needed to have something I knew I had.

There are people who accept the Lord and go about their lives like nothin' happened. That's something I don't understand. Guess the Lord will tell me about it by and by. I used to swear. I used awful language. I'd swear with nearly every breath. I'd swear at the table and nearly everywhere else. But from that day on, I never swore again.

Poppa said, "It won't last. He won't live it. I know him and it won't last." Well, I proved to him that it did last. I proved it to the family. I seen every one in my family except Earl, pray through. Even Poppa. I saw him pray through.

Holy Ghost

The genuineness of my grandfather's walk with the Lord challenged me to examine my own. There was little room for the miraculous in my faith. It was intellectual, well-grounded, but had nothing of the power Papa experienced.

My grandparents claimed it was the Holy Spirit who changed their hearts. I knew the term well. Holy Spirit. Holy Ghost. A passionate belief in the miraculous work of the third person of the Trinity was what set apart those in the Pentecostal movement from the rest of the religious community. And after their conversion, my grandparents were unabashed Pentecostals.

The Pentecostal movement packed almost as much wallop in Hobart and Colbert as it did in Jerusalem on the original Day of Pentecost. There were healings and many unusual events like my grandmother's experience. But the real miracles were found in the transformation of men like my Papa. As the result, there were many conversions.

But the Pentecostals caused division in many communities. Not only did their lively worship challenge the stoic style of traditional religion, they held to a standard of "holiness" many found offensive.

It didn't start out as a mandate. On their own, people started making changes on the outside that reflected that the cleaning up the Holy Spirit had been doing on the inside. But like so many other causes that begin with the purest of motives, a simple passion for obedience quickly turned into stifling legalism.

The word "Pentecostal" was enough to let everybody in town know exactly where you stood. You didn't drink, dance, or gamble. The girls didn't wear makeup. Or wear pants like a man. The women wore their hair long and the men kept theirs short.

Pentecostals were considered fanatics. "Holy rollers" they were called, because when "slain in the Spirit," they would fall to the ground. It wasn't hard to imagine why someone might think twice about being associated with the movement, but for people who were desperate—as most were during the Depression—the power of the Holy Spirit seemed the last hope.

A spiritual heritage that recognized and sought after the Holy Spirit was something I received from both sides of my family. My father was an Assembly of God minister. He eventually left the denomination because his broader view of some biblical issues left him out of sync with the powers that be. Also, his love of critical thinking and education made him suspect among the uneducated populace that birthed the movement.

But my father's parents were also saved during the early days of Pentecost. The result was that my grandfather Westbrook, who did his share of wild living, broke free of that lifestyle. For him it was a long process, not an immediate deliverance like Papa Choate, but in time, it was just as effective.

My family's spiritual history kept me grounded as I sorted out my faith. Some of the counselors I worked with blamed my Pentecostal roots for everything negative in my life, but I never accepted that.

I often had to make a case that all religious convictions are not repressive. There were enough destructive dynamics and attitudes still entrenched in me and my family to explain our idiosyncrasies without laying the blame at God's door. If anything, it seemed it was those things not yet exposed to God's healing that troubled us.

I certainly didn't have all the pieces put together, but I sensed that whatever ability we had to fight the shadows came from God's presence in our lives. After all, there was no denying that things definitely took a turn for the better in our family once the Lord entered the picture.

Because of the changes in my grandparents' lives, their children were spared the devastation of any number of vices that abounded on both sides. Others could call our faith bondage, but for those of us who benefited from the change, it was freedom.

So now, two generations later, I found myself wondering if God still worked in the same way. *Could He still change hearts?* One thing I did know:

whatever it was that transformed Papa's life was what I needed. Nothing less than that kind of power could change my home, my marriage, and me. I was too stubborn and too angry to simply mellow out in the course of time. Even though I was already a Christian, I recognized I needed my heart "fixed." The question was, how?

My grandparents' conversions had been marked by a dramatic display of the Holy Spirit—a display that served as a sign of God's presence in their community. It was Mama's baptism in the Holy Spirit that broke through the spiritual barriers in Hobart and Colbert. As she began to speak in tongues and dance in the Spirit, people flooded the altars. Papa said, "Cora was so quiet and shy that everybody knew it just had to be the Lord."

But it was the inner work of the Holy Spirit in their hearts and lives for which I hungered. Not flash. Not a temporary wonder. But the kind of power that could take an ornery cowboy and turn him into a gentle man and a passionate preacher for the rest of his years. That's not to say Papa didn't struggle to live a Christian life. He battled his temper. He had a tendency to isolate himself from those who didn't see things as he did. He had his blind spots, but from the night Papa knelt at the altar, the direction of his life was forever changed.

And when my grandparents talked about the Holy Ghost, they weren't referring to some emotional outburst. They were talking about a person. They depended on the Holy Spirit for friendship. For nurturing. For direction. For accountability. They believed the Holy Spirit was God's presence on earth. To be with Him, to learn whatever He wanted to teach them, was the whole point of their lives. They gave Him permission to show them when they were wrong, to challenge their motives, thoughts, and actions as they moved through every single day.

My grandparents' understanding of the role of the Holy Spirit did not come from Bible school or from listening to the great preachers of their day. Before the era of television, such opportunities didn't even exist. Their theology was forged solely on what God revealed to them in Bible study and prayer. They didn't accept anything they heard—even from the pulpit—at face value. What didn't agree with God's Word was discarded.

However, both Mama and Papa were very liberal in their view of Scripture. "There's lots of things nobody's gonna figure out this side of heaven," Papa said, "so I'm more than a little leery of anybody who thinks they know it all."

I once asked Papa what he thought about predestination. The Assembly of God view is Armenian—that salvation is a matter of free will. You're saved when you choose Christ but can lose your salvation if you don't watch your step. That was my tradition, but over the years, I'd belonged to churches that held dear every variation of that theme possible. Some taught "once saved always saved." The Calvinists held that only certain ones were predestined for salvation. The rest were just out of luck.

I struggled to find the truth in these views but found I could make columns, line up supporting Scriptures, and make a case for every single one of them. My salvation seemed assured in any event. As a five year old, I went forward in response to an altar call my father made in a Sunday night service. It was a child's decision, but one I clung to over the years—making me, I assumed, one of the chosen. But since that view precluded any sense of hope or justice for those who weren't "chosen," I remained in the free will camp.

However, my years of wandering in a spiritual wilderness had given me a different perspective. There were times when I knew I was not where I needed to be. When I chose what was wrong over what was right. Times when I did what was right on the outside, while rebelling with everything I had on the inside. I was miserable, but at my core, I knew that I belonged to God.

A lot of Pentecostal teaching was hell, fire, and brimstone, but I took my lead from my grandparents, who never focused on eternal damnation. It was love that drew them to God. Likewise, it wasn't fear of hell that compelled me to search for Him. It was the ache inside. But that ache had God's shape, and somewhere inside me, as if encoded into my DNA, I was now sensing that knowing Him, really knowing Him, was possible.

As for any confusion I had about the conflicts of certain theological points, Papa put my mind at ease. "I'm not sure about this predestination business," he said. "I think God is so big that He's probably got it worked out so that both sides have part of it right. If we could puzzle it all out here, then we'd be as smart as God, so I don't spend too much time worrying about it. I will say, that the older I get and the more I see how merciful God is, I'm thinking it's a lot harder to get unsaved than I used to."

"You mean 'once saved always saved'?" I asked. He thought a minute then, his eyes twinkling, added, "Maybe, but I don't think I'd tell the grandkids that."

I laughed then shook my head as I realized the implication of his words. Papa was still rethinking his theology, still open to discovering the new facets of age-old truths. Papa believed in a God who never changed. Yet, because He was continually revealing more of His infinite truth to a finite creation, God could never be put in a box or confined to just one puny viewpoint.

My grandparents felt that one was obligated to try to figure things out, but the process should foster humility, not arrogance. Convictions must be held to, but always with a heart open to deeper revelation.

Once when I asked my grandmother about some thorny theological issue, she pointed me to Philippians 2:12. "It says to work out your own salvation with fear and trembling. I can tell you my understanding of it based on what I see in God's Word, but nothing takes the place of discovering God's truth for yourself."

Mama and Papa spent hours in deep theological discussions doing just that. Not arguing, but sorting out. And they rejoiced when they found something new—even if it shook the foundations of a tradition they'd long held.

In a very systematic way, they fine-tuned their theology. Their example convinced me that theology is not something to be left to divinity professors. In fact, every living person has a theology and lives out his life according to what he believes about God—be it good or bad, true or false.

"Developing one's theology," I once heard someone say, "is like constructing a jacket. You work on it. You tailor it through the years according to your understanding of right and wrong. Then when hard times come, you go to the closet and pull out that jacket. Only then will you discover how well it fits."

The idea is, those who have taken time to search out truth will have a theology in place that will give them comfort and dignity in difficult circumstances. Those who have not, face life and death with whatever garment they have sewn, no matter how threadbare or ill-constructed. The jacket can and should be retailored along the way, but the person who's given thought to life's hard questions would certainly be ahead of the game.

I was engaged in that process—a process I observed my grandparents participating in often. Having listened to many of their discussions—as well thought out as treatises written by the apostle Paul—I assumed my grandparents had a respectable level of education. I clearly recall the day I realized I was mistaken.

One afternoon, I heard Mama reading the newspaper out loud to Papa. She stumbled over the words. Papa helped her with the ones she couldn't get until, together, they caught the sense of what they were reading. I was shocked to realize that between them, they could muster no more than a third or fourth grade reading proficiency. *How could that be?* I wondered. For years I'd heard both of them read the complex, poetic language of the King James Bible with a fluency an orator would envy.

The only explanation was either they had memorized the passages through years of reading and rereading, or they had received a supernatural ability to comprehend God's Word. I thought of what Mama told me, that the Holy Spirit would teach us all we needed to know, and wondered if I was, indeed, witnessing a miracle.

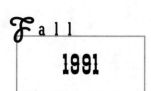

Fall
1991

Hard Times

By the time I came to Papa in the fall of 1991, I was hungry to know how the Holy Spirit worked in someone's life. Papa believed God meets us by working through the circumstances, events, and relationships of our lives. Yet those defining experiences and the understanding of their spiritual significance are sometimes years apart. I understood this as I listened to my grandfather's story.

Looking back, Papa could see how God used hard times to make him aware of his need for Him. But in the early 1920s, as economic forces destroyed all that his family owned, God seemed nowhere to be found.

Thomas, Papa's father, was heavily in debt from two previous crop failures and unable to make the lease payments on the farmland after the price of cotton fell. The Choates gambled. And they lost. Within weeks the bank took back their teams of mules and horses, and McCormick Deering came for their tractor. Thomas and his family went from prosperity to homelessness overnight.

"We gotta do something," Thomas explained when they could no longer stay on the land. So, accompanied by Cora's father, Thomas headed out east to Wister, Oklahoma, then toward the piney country of Arkansas. They traveled throughout the Talihina, Poteau area and came across property along a creek. It ran between Winding Stair and Buffalo Mountain in Le Fleur County, Oklahoma.

"It was Cora's daddy, who gave us the idea of running a sawmill," Papa said.

No one else had a better idea, so they did what many families did during that time: sold much of what they owned and pooled their resources.

Mr. White told Poppa he thought we could make money at a sawmill, even with things so cheap. So, we leased one saw mill and sublet another. Our family and the Whites moved down there in 1926. That was before Cora and I got married.

We got set up and started milling. We cut big stacks of lumber on both sides of the creek till it looked like a little town. After about three months, we thought things was gonna get better so Cora and I married. But it all went from bad to worse.

The price of lumber went down till it wouldn't pay to put it under the saw. You couldn't even sell it 'cause it wouldn't pay to haul it into town. The sawmill couldn't pay the hands. All the hands could get was just meals. And I was workin' there as one of the hands. We had all that lumber, and they'd let us get groceries on it. That's all they could give us. Couldn't pay us no money.

Well, after six months I could see things wasn't gonna work out. One day I got up early and told Cora to wash up my clothes. I said, "I'm leaving in the morning and goin' West to find something to do."

That next day, I told Poppa I was leaving. He was just sick about it. We was all disheartened and discouraged.

"Don't go yet," Poppa said. "Give me a little bit to see what we can do."

He called the family together to take stock of everything we owned. We had two wagons but no teams; we'd owed some on the teams after the crop failures so the bank had taken the teams. But we had pretty good furniture for them days. We had an organ. My Momma had a big range stove that was really something. Took three men to carry it. Poppa had a blacksmith shop. Momma had a horse and buggy, and Pernie had a model-T—a good one.

After talking it over, Poppa said, "You boys get out there and trade these houses and lumber. Just trade everything we've got for some teams to pull these wagons. We can make some over jets for the wagons then we'll all just head out."

We went to work making two long wagon beds and putting over jets on 'em. The wagon beds were about three or four feet and we attached wagon bows to 'em. Them bows had metal loops on the ends that you could nail to the wagon. Next, we got some ducking—sheeting or canvas is what it was—and put it over the bows. That's what they called an over jet. When we was done, we had us a couple of covered wagons, but we still didn't have nothin' to pull 'em.

So, Pernie traded his car for a pair o' little mules. Then we traded two houses, the horse and buggy, the furniture and everything we had there—the blacksmith shop and all—for a pair of horses. Now we had a team of mules and a team of horses, our harnesses, and our wagons.

We loaded everything we could put in the wagons and drove off. I'm tellin' you, it was a sad day. We left lumber stacked as high as a man all the way down the creek.

The Whites went their own way, but the Choates traveled in those wagons for eighteen days seeking work and food. They drove from town to town through the triangle of land where Texas, Oklahoma, and Arkansas meet. They came up with nothing. Provisions dwindled. Finally, Thomas and his three sons, Alva, Earl, and Pernie, accepted reality: split up or starve. So—with many tears—brothers, sisters, parents, and children parted ways.

Papa said, "Me and Cora wound up at Hobart, Oklahoma, and picked cotton in the fall, but when the cotton run out, there was no work of any kind. You talk about hard times, them was hard times. You couldn't get anything to do."

The terror of not being able to provide for his family created the first chink of vulnerability in Papa's self-sufficiency. It took another year, but the Great Depression finally brought my grandfather to his knees. Papa fell under conviction as the Holy Spirit began to reveal the arrogance with which he'd lived his life.

"I always thought I could do anything and was ready to whup anybody who said I couldn't," he said. "The day I realized that if it weren't for the Lord I wouldn't even have the breath I draw, well, that was a heavy day."

Without a doubt, those years of economic hardship were the most difficult of Papa's life. Until now. I couldn't help but wonder which he found more difficult: the fear of being without basic food and shelter, or the fear of being alone.

I knew something of the latter, but Papa knew both. He'd survived the physical hardship of the Great Depression, but the emotional battle brought on by aging was getting the best of him.

With each visit, I noticed an increasing desperateness for my attention. Papa seemed less interested in socializing and was jealous of anyone I wanted to see.

I couldn't blame him. Though the hearing aid had greatly improved Papa's ability to track what was going on around him, it had no power to change how others viewed him. In a group of younger people, he became invisible. It wasn't that he didn't try; he was simply ignored. It was as though being old precluded the possibility that he might have something interesting to say. People treated him as a relic to be cared for, rather than a person capable of interaction.

Only a very few—my aunt and a couple of family members—related to Papa in a meaningful way. My sister, who was now living four hours away, stayed with him once a month. Yet, even these one-on-one visits failed to stave off his loneliness and depression.

I did what I could when we were together. We walked arm in arm. Held hands over pie and coffee. I touched his face after prayers each night and wondered how many of his days went by without a single touch. One day I played connect-the-dots on his arm, tracing one age spot to another. He laughed.

"Papa," I said, "I like to touch you as much as I can when I'm here to make up for all the time I can't be near you."

He smiled and put his hand over mine, "That's okay," he said. "Papa don't mind."

The truth was, Karen didn't mind either.

I had a privileged position in Papa's life. Now it was I who nurtured him, feeding his sagging spirit with my words and presence. But, though our roles were reversing, Papa was not a burden. The more I gave to him, the more I received. And loving him was giving me the confidence that I had something worthwhile inside to claim for me and my children.

It had been over two years since I had decided to give God an honest chance—a major shift in direction. It wasn't the dramatic breakthrough I had hoped for, but there'd been changes.

Though still tallying the pros and cons of divorce, I felt my spirit gaining strength. The depression was lifting. It seemed the further I traveled on my spiritual journey and the more I took responsibility for choices that were mine, the less power depression held over me.

One day I was doing dishes at the kitchen sink when a melody came to me. It was taken from Philippians 1:6 "He who has begun a good work in you will complete it…" As I sang I felt enfolded by a feeling I couldn't quite identify. It wasn't happiness. Or joy. But it was something good. Then it came to me. Hope. Hope not based on any circumstance, but on God's commitment to me. It was just what I needed because I was being forced to make the choice I'd put off for so long.

Joe's company was moving to Atlanta. If I intended to leave, this was the time to do it. Or if I chose to stay, it could be a new beginning. More and more I sensed God saying something I couldn't believe: the choice was up to me.

The message was clear: *No matter what you choose, I will go with you. Both roads will be hard, but the choice is yours.*

Until now, I'd thought to divorce or not divorce was a choice between good and evil. God's way or my way. Maybe I was wrong.

I had always believed that God had a "perfect will" for me—a plan that only I could thwart. I didn't see myself as having many choices. Instead, I waited for specific direction and was puzzled, then enraged, if no answer came.

My question flew directly to Him. *But aren't there times when You do want me to follow a particular course of action?*

Yes, I sensed Him saying, *and when that happens, don't you think I'd communicate it clearly so you could obey?*

Slowly, the truth dawned on me. God's will was for me to love Him. Beyond that, there might be any number of ways the other pieces of the puzzle could fit together.

With this insight, I suddenly felt released from my marriage vows. I understood that this liberty in no way diminished God's commitment to the marriage covenant, but it was the first time I realized He cared about how I felt. That toughing it out wasn't what He was after. He saw the pain I lived with every day and was saying, *Okay. Enough.*

That little revelation knocked the pins right out from under me.

Moral Fiber

Without "God's will" to hide behind, I was forced to examine my personal responsibility in my marriage. What were my moral obligations to Joe and to my children? And how could I take action when a move in any direction would hurt someone?

I already knew integrity could be costly. The way Papa lost his job on the Blackwell Ranch imprinted that lesson deeply into my memory from an early age.

Papa was sick about being fired because, in 1939, jobs were still hard to come by. It happened about a year after old man Blackwell died. Papa had continued working the farm for his son, Brice Blackwell II.

One day I was riding with Brice and his wife, Wanda, in their pickup when Blackwell says to me, "Mr. Choate, I'm gonna need the boys to start working on Sundays."

"That won't accomplish nothing," I told him.

"Brice, he's right," Wanda agreed. "The boys need a day off to rest."

Blackwell just got a hard look on his face and pointed over toward a sandy patch of land. "I want you to have the boys plant cotton over there this Sunday."

I said, "Now, Mr. Blackwell, you know I don't work on Sunday, and I don't think the boys should either. But I'll tell them if you make me."

"Do it," he said.

So, I told the boys to plant the cotton on Sunday.

We had a great big, four-row plow and must have planted over a hundred acres that day. But that night a big rain came and washed away all the seed. That soil was sandy though. I knew it would dry out real quick, so I told Blackwell, "It's Okay. I'll have the boys plant again Wednesday."

But he said, "No. Wait till Sunday, then plant it." So we did. Then that night there was another rainstorm that washed that seed away. I figured we'd plant again the next Wednesday but Blackwell stopped us. "Better hold off till Sunday," he said.

That time, the cotton took, but by now the season was so late that instead of growing cotton balls, the plants shot up high as a man's head. It was leafy on top so that the poison used for pest control couldn't get underneath the top layer. The entire crop got eaten by insects.

When harvest time came around, Blackwell came out to the barn and asked me when I was going to pick the cotton on the sand.

I said, "We're not gonna pick it."

"Why not?" he asked

"There's no cotton to pick."

Blackwell narrowed his eyes then he threw open the door to his pickup truck. "Git in," he said, "and we'll just see."

He looked for himself. He walked down row by row, but there wasn't a single boll worth pickin'. So we got back in the truck. I figured that was it for me 'cause Blackwell was already mad at me. That spring he'd nearly drowned trying to herd some cattle across the creek during a storm, and I guess he thought I didn't do enough to help him. Anyway, after checking out the cotton, he was fumin'. Didn't say a word till we got back to the barn. I told him I'd see him the next day but he said, "Mr. Choate, I think I'll be needing someone else to do your job. I don't think you have my best interest at heart."

It would have been easy for Papa to compromise his beliefs, especially since his relationship with his boss was already tenuous. But my grandfather had a commitment to honor the Sabbath, and he did what he thought was right even though it cost him.

I admired that kind of integrity, and it weighed in heavily as I considered how my choices would impact the future of my family.

Drought

After returning from supper one evening, Papa instructed me to drive my car into Midtown Manor's back parking lot as though it were the first time I'd been there. He made sure the visitor pass was visible in the windshield. Then reminded me to park on the street-side of the parking lot where he felt it was safer. I noticed the more fragile Papa became, the more important routine seemed to him.

Papa leaned heavily on my arm as we negotiated the uphill tilt of the sidewalk at the back entrance. The walkway pooled into a large semicircular cement patio near the door, making it easy to load and unload both passengers and groceries from the car.

Patsy, in her wheelchair, was parked at the edge of the patio tending to a beautiful flower garden. Given the year-round dramatic changes of climate and the poor soil conditions, maintaining a garden was no easy task. Rich, farm bottomland this was not. Here, even if you watered, the sun baked the dirt into hard clods almost as fast as you could till it.

I had noticed this little garden wonderland each time we came in, flourishing in defiance of sun, heat, cold, and wind. I should've known it was a labor of love. It blossomed thanks to Patsy's effort and joy. We stopped a moment to chat as Papa fumbled to find the right key to unlock the door.

"Patsy, I have to hand it to you, working in this heat," I said.

"Oh, I don't even notice it once I get busy," she replied. "Besides, it'll be cooling off soon." She reached across and nipped a shriveled leaf and bud off one of the rose bushes.

Just then a car pulled up. A fiftyish-looking woman got out and helped an elderly lady into a wheelchair. I didn't know either of them. Neither did Papa. They greeted Patsy warmly while Papa and I waited for an introduction.

"I'm sorry, Cowboy, I didn't realize you two hadn't met," Patsy said after an awkward silence. "Gladys, this is Alva Choate."

Gladys nodded toward Papa. "Gladys Snyder," she said, smiling.

Papa nodded back. "Nice to meet ya."

"I'm Evelyn, Gladys's daughter," said the younger woman.

Patsy continued, "And this is Alva's granddaughter from back East."

As we shook hands Gladys told us she'd only been at Midtown Manor a couple weeks. Papa made it a point to find out which apartment she'd moved into. I knew why. He had no designs on the woman; he just wanted to know who was missing.

It was happening more and more. People who had been there for years were now suddenly gone. The turnover was disturbing because it seldom meant good news. Usually someone had fallen, or died, or, worse, had to move in with their kids.

The women would talk about it loudly and in detail. I could hear them in the rec room while we were playing pool. The men seldom mentioned it, but they listened in on the women folk without saying a word and dug out what they could indirectly, as Papa had just done. Sometimes Papa and Boone would share what they knew between them.

The spirits of those who left hung around like a cloud until it happened to someone else. The lingering, unasked question was, "Will I be next?"

Gladys and Evelyn waited patiently behind us while Papa tried to unlock the door. After several attempts, the key finally turned. Using his body weight, Papa wedged the door open until we all passed through, then he closed it tightly after us. We said our "good evenings" at the elevator door.

"Guess ol' Mrs. Harding died," Papa said as we began our ascent to the sixth floor. I surmised Mrs. Harding's apartment was the one Gladys now occupied.

"I knew she was doin' poorly."

Left unsaid was the fact that Papa hadn't heard it before now. It meant he wasn't getting out of his apartment much, and I suspected he was having trouble hearing again. Pool with the boys was his only outing unless Sharon or I came. Marie also came and took him to the grocery store once a week. Other than that, he might as well have been under house arrest. It wasn't that he didn't have opportunities; he just wouldn't take them.

It was hard seeing my grandfather, who'd always embraced change, now shy away from it. Anything different, anything new, was an all-too-present reminder of other changes he did not want to face.

Like Boone's new girlfriend. Papa was definitely not happy about that. The previous afternoon when the boys gathered to play, a large, gray-haired woman plopped herself down on one of the folding chairs near the table. I expected Boone to throw her a dirty look since he had no patience with onlookers, especially women, but he didn't. I introduced myself to her.

"I'm Agnes," she replied tersely and returned her gaze to the pool table. Boone looked up but didn't acknowledge her.

Then I caught the look on Papa's face. The drawn mouth. Intense eyes that telegraphed displeasure. I put the pieces together—Agnes must be with Boone. Boone and Papa used to get together for dinner every once in a while, but as soon as Boone would take up with a lady, Papa was out of there.

The comfortable world Papa enjoyed at Midtown Manor centered on Boone—and Agnes was a threat. She and another good buddy of Boone's: Jack Daniels. Papa understood how fragile his world was. He was fighting to establish some constancy, and it angered him that Boone was willing to throw it away.

"Women and booze," Papa said shaking his head. "He can't seem to be without either one."

The drinking had caused problems a few times, and there'd been some talk of asking him to leave. However with the female occupants outnumbering the males two to one, and Boone willing to do his part to befriend a lonely woman, most residents weren't inclined to hold him to the letter of the law.

Still, it upset Papa to think about losing his friend to a woman or the bottle. For him, when Boone left, it would all go. The camaraderie. The fun. The subtle distinction that made Midtown Manor a senior citizens' apartment building, not an old folks' home. He knew Boone was skating on thin ice, but there wasn't one single thing he could do about it.

And that was the problem. The number of things beyond Papa's control was increasing. Twisted fingers. Swollen feet. Dimming eyesight. Against his will, his body was changing. His mind was changing. His life was changing. But one of the greatest changes I noted was his response to these things.

It was most evident in his battle to be seen and heard. Before, he fought. Now, he accepted it meekly. That disturbed me. I knew Papa. It signaled he was giving up.

I could almost hear him replaying the losses of his lifetime in his mind. The farm. His wife. The barn. His horses. And now, he saw himself disappearing little by little.

It was getting more and more difficult for Papa to find the humor in life, to enjoy the flowers in the garden. He didn't have the energy to nurture what was best about him anymore. And he lacked the will to prune away tendencies that diminished his world.

Though Papa had always adapted to difficult situations, never before had circumstances struck at the core of his identity. Even through the years he worked off the range—doing things for which he had no passion—his confidence remained unshaken. This insecurity was new to him.

I sensed he still had another round or two in him. Fire still burned in his eyes when he talked about things he loved. Yet he seemed to need the mirror of another soul to believe that he existed. That he was worth fighting for.

The past five years, Papa had been my mirror. In his eyes I had not only seen myself as loved by him, but loved by God. Now, I realized, it was my turn to return the favor.

Movin' On

I didn't tell Papa what was going on in my family. Too much was up in the air. In the meantime, I didn't want him to worry. He was so observant that I'm sure he knew something was up, but he never pressed me. I kept him busy telling me all the stories of his relationship with Mama. Perhaps because I longed for a happy ending somewhere, I couldn't get enough of them.

The next morning, Papa showered as I fixed breakfast. I cooked and cleaned up now—it took all the energy Papa had to dress for the day. I set out plates of eggs, sausage, and biscuits on the table then returned to the kitchen to get our coffee. Just as I rounded the corner, my grandfather emerged from the bathroom. The fresh scent of soap and aftershave followed him.

Papa walked carefully toward the table wearing his every day slacks and a flimsy white strap T-shirt. "I think I'll wait till after breakfast to put on my shirt," he said. "More drops in my lap than makes it to my mouth these days."

I assured Papa that was fine. But it did seem strange to see my grandfather, a man who had always insisted on certain civilities and manners, come to the table without a proper shirt.

Papa sat down heavily and took several quick, deep breaths. Then he took my hand and offered thanks. He seemed so tired I wondered if he'd be up to my questions, but just the thought of my grandmother seemed to rejuvenate him.

Though he and Mama were crazy over heels in love with each other, it didn't put food on the table. They were certain as soon as Papa landed a steady job, all their troubles would be over. "I was going every day huntin' jobs," he said.

'Course I'd worked on ranches all my life and thought I could do anything with livestock anyone else could do. And I just about could .

One day this fella told me, "I know where you can get a job if you can handle the man's stock. His name is Lee Brazil. He's got some real bad stock, and he's needin' somebody to help him."

Well, Brazil had the good fortune to be farming wheat instead of cotton, and since the bottom hadn't fallen out of wheat yet, he was one of the few people able to hire any hands. But he had outlaw stock—mules that was wild and mean. They'd run off, kick you, bite you, and everything else. He couldn't get his crop in 'cause he was always chasing them mules. They'd get into his neighbors' crops and all, and the neighbors had threatened to kill 'em if Brazil didn't keep them off their land.

Well, I headed down there the next morning, 'bout four miles. Brazil was out in the field when I got there. I went out to where he was and introduced myself—told him I was lookin' for a job and heard he might need a man. Brazil was a man of few words so he just said, "Yup. I'll give you a job if you can handle my stock."

I told him, "I'll be right down."

We didn't have nothing to move—only some clothes and a little cookin' outfit. I rented a little ol' one room house 'bout a quarter of a mile from this guy. Paid four dollars a month for it. No runnin' water unless you ran and got it. It had a cook stove and bed stand on it, and that was about it.

Cora and I stayed there 'bout six months, then we got a chance to move into a nice house. The man whose land joined Brazil's had a great big, nine-room house on it but he lived in town. He told me if I moved into his house, I could have it free of rent. It was the same distance from where I worked, so of course I said yes.

We went into town to buy some things for the house. We bought a feather bed, and I got Cora a new red dress—it was real pretty. I give ten dollars for it. That dress would cost you fifty dollars or more now.

We got a bill of groceries that woulda lasted us two or three weeks—a twenty-five-pound sack of flour and the like.

My daddy had taken us into town in his wagon, so after we come back and put our stuff in the house Poppa said, "Why don't you come spend the night with us? I'll bring you back tomorrow."

So, that's what we did. The next evening he brought us back, and as soon as we opened the door we knew somethin' was wrong. Took a minute for us to figure it out 'cause we just couldn't believe it.

Someone had broken into our house and didn't leave one thing. They got our new mattress. They got our groceries. They stripped cloths off the tables. They took our dishes. They got Cora's new dress. They just cleaned the house like you'd moved out.

I couldn't explain how we felt. We didn't have enough to stay over, so we had to go back to Poppa's to spend the night. Cora didn't say anything, just did a lot of bawling. The next day, Poppa and Momma gave us enough to camp with, and we went home so I could work. There was nothin' else we could do.

I worked for Lee Brazil 'bout a year. Started out making six dollars a week. Finally got a fifty cent a day raise. That was nine dollars a week—more than most people made. But I started out at six. Them was rough days. You can tell the kids about it, but you can't make them understand it. We didn't get a complete housekeeping setup for a long time. At six dollars a week, it took a long time to get built back up again.

That was the year Marie was born—1929. Cora wanted to be near her momma when the baby was born, so we moved to Maud, Oklahoma, that fall. I got a job in Seminole working in the oil fields.

Soon after that was when I ended up going to see my daddy in Hobart and gettin' saved. But I couldn't stay there for long without a job, so I went back to workin' the oil fields in Seminole. Working when they had work. The next year, Atha was born out there in the country near Maud, Oklahoma. We wasn't in Maud, but that was the closest town to us. In those days, babies was born at home, so a lot of the particulars didn't get recorded right. But Atha's birth certificate said Maud, so I guess it was Maud.

But I always was hopin' to get back workin' with livestock. One day, my brother, Pernie, who was living in Byers, said he'd heard one of the ranchers was hiring. So I went to see him. Turns out he needed a farm hand, and I got the job. I moved the family back to Texas and worked for John Adair three years.

Starting Over

Papa never seemed to mind moving. I guess when you don't have much but the clothes on your back it's easier. As often said of those times, life was harder but it was also simpler. By comparison, the move I was considering was monumental.

The transfer to Atlanta was imminent, yet I was paralyzed. Since coming home from Papa's, every waking moment taunted me with indecision and confusion.

A verse that seemed highlighted from my quiet time was Psalm 51:6: "You desire truth in the inward parts, and in the hidden part You will make me to know wisdom." It hardly seemed to answer the question I began every day by asking: Should I go or stay? A small, still voice inside me said, *Maybe you're asking the wrong question.*

So, I read the verse again and asked, *What's the point here?* Truth. Integrity. What did I know about either one of them?

I considered myself the world's greatest hypocrite. Going to church. Teaching my children the godly principles with which I'd grown up. Yet I was so lost myself. *How can I say I love God and not be able to show His love to the family He has given me?* Perhaps fear—not commitment—kept me in place. Maybe I was just using Joe to keep my world in tact.

As I examined my heart, integrity seemed as far removed from me as the Pacific Ocean. The idea of truth frustrated me even more.

Jesus said, "The truth will set you free." But, though I considered myself His, I was not free. I felt like Lazarus who, after being resurrected, was found by his friends in grave clothes bound as tight as a mummy.

Truth, as I understood it, was a set of rules, like the Ten Commandments—God's standard of behaving and interacting with Him and other people. Yet the Bible says we are born with a sin nature, and not one person can live without breaking His law. No one. Given my own inclination to sin, I had no trouble accepting that as fact. But the bottom line was, if freedom came from keeping the law, there was no hope.

God, do you stack the deck against us then punish us for not being perfect? I wondered.

Then, I remembered a verse I'd known for years, John 14:6. "I am the way, the truth, and the life…" *The truth was not rules. The truth was Jesus.* And He claimed to be not only truth, but life.

The implications of this for me dawned slowly. *I'd invested my time in the wrong place. My projections, strategies, and pro and con lists only fostered confusion. But if truth and freedom were found in the person of Jesus Christ, my energy would be best spent focusing on Him. Until I understood the truth about Him, I had little basis to understand the truth about myself or my marriage.*

As I thought about knowing God, I could see, as Papa claimed, that the circumstances of my life were pushing me in His direction. But though I believed in a personal God, I had difficulty envisioning Jesus Christ as someone with whom I could interact. The Holy Spirit, whom I expected to be more mystical and undefined, seemed easier. But one of the roles of the Holy Spirit, I learned, was to lead me to the truth.

Speaking of the Holy Spirit, Jesus said, "…when He, the Spirit of truth, has come, He will guide you into all truth" (John 16:13).

Alright, then what was the truth about Christ? That seemed a good place to start. He was fully God. Fully man. He lived perfectly because the love and knowledge of God resided in Him perfectly.

It occurred to me that if Jesus knew every fact of science and every event past, present, and future, then would He not also know the reality of every heart and every relationship? If so, perhaps He could reveal things to me I'd never considered.

It was hard to believe that by allowing the Holy Spirit to lead me to Christ, I would find the truth I needed to live my life. But lacking any brilliant ideas of my own, I decided to give it a shot.

Over the next few weeks, I spent time every day being with Jesus. Not studying the Bible. Not reading books. Not making requests. There were other times for that. With quiet music playing, I simply sat on my living room sofa with a cup of coffee and asked Him to join me.

I acknowledged that He was not only all-powerful and all-knowing, but good. I thanked Him for being my God and loving me even though I didn't know how to love Him. And I listened. Sometimes I was enveloped with a sense of well-being. Usually, nothing remarkable happened, but there would be hope—even a hint of joy—in that day. Once I felt so over-whelmed by his love, I crumbled to the floor and cried. There seemed no need for resolutions or answers. It was enough to be with Him.

Soon, I began to notice that new thoughts came unsolicited to my mind. Not in response to any question, but out of the blue. Sometimes it was a different perspective on something with which I had struggled, or some nagging thought. For instance, I had this uneasy feeling that I was mistaken about what fueled the internal pressure I felt to leave my marriage.

Our problems were real enough, but it occurred to me that maybe I didn't really want solutions. Maybe I just wanted out. The chance to try things on my own. One counselor had pointed out that when Joe tried to offer me the intimacy I said I wanted, I found another issue to blow up.

"If Joe does move toward you," he said, "then we're going to find out what you're really made of."

That set off alarms. Had I been playing games all these years? Was it possible that Joe couldn't win because I didn't want him to? That was a sobering thought.

I wasn't sure what to do with these impressions. So I placed them on a back shelf of my mind, tucking them away like you would hide a key you knew was important but couldn't quite remember what it was to.

I felt "stuck." The issues seemed too tangled for me to unravel. I knew something had to change. So one day, frustrated by my inability to see any future as things were, I made my choice. I would leave.

Joe had been reaching for me, and, as the counselor suspected, it scared me to death. I couldn't be a person of integrity and not honestly engage, but to engage meant to trust Joe. I just didn't think I could do that.

So together, Joe and I told the boys that we were going to separate. Michael showed nothing. David cried until his eyes were swollen shut. The next morning, I kissed Michael and sent him off to school like I did every morning. I thought he was "handling" it. David begged to stay home and I let him.

He crawled in my king size bed and surrounded on all sides by used tissues, asked me once again to explain the unexplainable.

"Your daddy is a good man," I said, "and I care very much for him, but sometimes things happen you can't get over. It's hurting us and it's hurting you—for your dad and me to be in the same house but so distant from each other. It's better for us to separate and see how we feel about living apart."

"But you told me that when you get married it's forever," he cried.

"Yes, and when we got married, that's what we intended. But sometimes things just don't work out."

David narrowed his eyes and, with vehemence I'd never before heard, retorted, "Well, you should've thought about that before you had children!"

I didn't know what to say. There was no way to justify the gap between the ideal and reality to an eleven-year-old boy. So, I went forward with what I felt I had to do.

I expected to be overwhelmed with remorse and guilt once we talked to the boys. Instead I was overjoyed. I felt I was right where I needed to be, even though it flew in the face of everything I believed about marriage and commitment.

Freedom is within my grasp, I thought. *That's why I'm so euphoric.* Later, I realized that wasn't it at all. Rather, having a true choice about my life removed the stifling pressure. I no longer felt trapped. That allowed me to look objectively at my situation without being defensive.

So confident did I feel, that I found myself willing to explore the ideas about truth that had challenged me a few weeks earlier. Mentally, I reached back and pulled out the key I'd hidden. With it, I opened my heart to possibilities I had previously refused to consider.

In my evaluation process the past few years, I'd owned some painful truths about myself—like my inflexibility and need to be right that often got in the way of genuine relationship. It built barriers no one, including Joe, could overcome. But for the first time, I saw this realization had implications.

What if my reason for leaving Joe was based on a lie? That my unhappiness wasn't about him, but me? Was it possible I had made Joe and our marriage a scapegoat for my own issues? If so, the freedom I was seeking was not going to be found either running to or from my marriage.

That put a different spin on everything. I envisioned myself two years down the road. Could I make it? Yes, I could. Could I be happy? Well, I thought so—eventually. But was it my first choice?

I took a long hard look at myself and what I truly valued. My children. My family. Joe. Somewhere deep inside, I knew all that we'd meant to each other—all that we'd built together—counted for something.

After all, I was not in an abusive situation where leaving was necessary to protect my children or me. I wasn't doing all the work and getting no response. It may have been true in the past, but recently Joe had proven willing to do whatever was needed to get us on track. I wasn't sure if I trusted it, but I'd seen changes in his priorities. A softness in the shell that gave me hope.

The realization formed deep within me. Quiet but certain. My first choice was for us to stay together. Not because we were bound by the strangling cords of empty wedding vows, but because our marriage held the possibility for what I longed for most. A home. A place of belonging. I wanted that for my children and me, and no one was better equipped to build that home with me than Joe.

I saw that all things being equal, the person with whom you've shared years and children is likely your best bet for long-term peace and happiness. Perhaps that's why God gave such weight to the vows of marriage—to protect those it embraced. God was not just protecting my children by assuring them a two-parent home; He was also protecting me from my own impulsiveness and blindness. He was giving us all every chance to work it out.

The marriage covenant is God's gift to every man and woman who choose a life together. In time, I understood that. It took me longer to realize that at the core of that sacramental relationship were two people God loved enough to die for.

Yes, He valued our wedding vows. But He loved me.

I now knew that if I left my husband, God would not waiver in His commitment to me, but neither could He spare me the pain of ripping apart a family that had been together for twenty-one years.

That moment's revelation changed everything. The next day, I told Joe I was willing to move to Atlanta if he still wanted me to. He welcomed me back with a trusting kindness I didn't deserve.

I wish I could say an incredible peace then obscured all doubts, but it didn't. Instead, the reality that there were no guarantees hit me full force.

Like many new beginnings, this one was sown with tears. There were the gut-wrenching goodbyes to my friends in Connecticut. The isolation of a new place. And there was no safety net. No support system, church, or even a friendly face at the grocery store. Just me, alone with a family that wasn't working yet, clinging to a commitment on God's part that the truth would, indeed, set me free.

I felt sick, physically sick, thinking about all the work that lay ahead. The parting words from my counselor were, "It's not enough just to be there—you have to make it better." That was true, yet I knew good intentions alone couldn't change me. That would take a miracle. All I could do was cooperate with the process. I could honestly try. And ask God to help me deal with all the garbage in my own heart as it surfaced. I recognized the step for what it was—a conscious choice of faith. It was something I wanted to do whether it succeeded or failed. But I knew it wouldn't be easy. And it wasn't.

After the move, the idealism of my choice quickly faded. Instead, I was filled with deep sorrow. When grief overwhelmed me, all that kept me from bolting was the confidence that God was with me. I felt like someone I loved dearly had died.

I broke down and cried uncontrollably when I realized that was exactly what had happened. I had died. It was my own death I mourned. With the move, I had given up my hope for any future, for any love, for any happiness that I could envision on my own. Unless God came through with a new life for me, I was gone.

Everything was on the line and I prayed desperately that my faith was not in vain. That, somehow, I could both give away my life and also find it.

Arizona

Many of life's troubles are of our own making. I learned that from Papa. Though he and Mama had been through difficult times, he admitted that some experiences were harder than they needed to be because of poor judgment and pride. To my grandmother's dismay, Papa would often put himself at risk with little consideration for the consequences. What finally cured him of his recklessness was Arizona.

It was January 1940. Papa had just lost his job at the Blackwell ranch. Then a letter from Earl started him thinking outside the borders of Texas.

"Earl had been out in Yuma, Arizona, 'bout six months and wrote back that he was driving a caterpillar and gettin' good money for it," Papa said. "That sounded good to me. I'd done just about everything I knew to do where I was, so I figured, why not give it a try?" Mama, however, was adamantly opposed.

"At least we've got family here," she said.

"Earl is family," Papa replied.

Mama didn't argue. Earl hadn't exactly been stable, and Papa knew it. If things didn't work out, they'd be on their own in the middle of nowhere. However, Mama's point was even if things did work out, they'd *still* be on their own in the middle of nowhere—and that's not where she wanted to be.

Though known for his stubbornness, Mama was the one person to whom Papa usually listened. Not this time. He was determined to go and go they did, over Mama's strong objections. The family packed up, sold what they couldn't carry, and headed West.

Papa said, "We hadn't been in Yuma but a couple weeks when I realized I'd made a big mistake. There were no jobs there either. Anybody who could drive a caterpillar already was. I worked in the lettuce fields some. Drove tractors whenever somebody was sick or somethin'. But after six months, nothing steady came through, and the family was in a bad way."

Then Mama had a gall bladder attack. "She needs an operation," the doctor said. But, of course, there was no money for that. So, Mama played her trump card. She said, "Alva, if I'm gonna die, I want to die in Texas." That's all it took. The next day, Papa bundled her up, and the family headed back for home.

Deep down, Papa feared she wouldn't make the trip. Yuma was as far southwest as you could get in Arizona without infringing on Mexico. And by now it was summertime. Without air conditioning, the heat was unbearable. But they drove at night across the deserts of Arizona and New Mexico until they crossed into Texas. Shortly thereafter, Mama realized she was no longer in pain.

With her symptoms gone, it seemed a miraculous healing. My grandparents took it as a sign from God, and in their exhilaration, both of them swore they'd never move out of Texas again.

It goes to show you can keep from making a lot of wrong choices just by knowing where you belong. It was a lesson Papa learned the hard way, and one I hoped to learn from his experience.

It had been over a year since I had visited my grandfather. Though I'd wanted to come, I was needed at home. Things were improving between Joe and me, but the boys weren't doing well—especially Michael, who'd just started eighth grade. He was withdrawn. Failing academically. And enraged. Sadly, his brother had become the target for his anger.

David, crushed at having lost his best friend, was grief-stricken.

Michael underwent extensive evaluation and was diagnosed with ADHD and several other learning disabilities. "Because your son is bright, he's been able to compensate to this point," the psychologist told us. "But now his compensatory strategies are no longer working. He's panicked."

Mike felt stupid. Desperate to keep teachers, peers, and us from discovering how much he missed, he acted out. Causing problems at home and school took the focus off schoolwork.

The move had taken Mike out of the familiar environment he'd learned to negotiate. When he was in control, he couldn't be exposed. But now, in a new place, he was lost. We learned that junior high is usually when kids like Michael can no longer fake their way through school—the subject matter simply becomes too demanding. "This issue would have come to the forefront with Michael even if you hadn't moved" we were told, but there was no doubt we'd exacerbated the problem.

We knew ADHD and learning disabilities weren't the only problems. Family dynamics, Michael's innate personality, and years of turmoil and inconsistency in our home all played a part. It wasn't hard to understand why he was angry. The question was, what could be done about it?

A flurry of professional assessments and recommendations over the next year did little to diffuse Mike's rage. We saw him try. We saw him fail. We saw him destroying every relationship he valued and hate himself for it. But when he refused to participate in any kind of family or personal counseling, we enrolled him in a small private high school—a boarding school claiming to specialize in helping kids like him. We weren't sure if it was the right step, but being out of options at home, it seemed better than doing nothing.

We dreaded telling Michael, knowing that, no matter how we phrased it, it would feel like abandonment to him. Joe and I went together to his room to talk with him.

I knocked quietly on the door. "Come in," he said.

He was hanging up his clothes. He turned around, surprised to see us both. His eyes darted from one of us to the other. "What's up?" he asked.

Joe cleared his throat then said, "As you know, we talked earlier this summer about the need for our family to have some rules we all abide by..."

"Yeah, I know," Mike interrupted, "I signed the contract."

"Then you know one of the main conditions you agreed to was being respectful. No swearing. No verbal or physical abuse. But, Mike, it's still a problem."

Michael looked down at the floor. There'd been a blow-up the day before, so he didn't try to deny it. His face clouded. Joe turned away.

"Mike," I broke in, "we said if it continued, you couldn't stay here. We see you're trying, but, for whatever reason, we're not able to help you get a handle on your anger. We've decided a boarding school equipped to deal with issues like yours might help." My voice cracked as I fought for control. "And maybe taking a break from us will give you the opportunity to figure out what's really going on. We're in a destructive cycle here, and it's hurting all of us."

Even as I said the words, I wondered how I would find the strength to take my son to a place where no one knew him—and leave him. Now almost six feet tall and as thin as the wire hanger on which he was hanging his shirt, he looked vulnerable and afraid.

Tears welled up in Michael's eyes. None of us could speak. Finally, Michael hardened his gaze and said, "Fine. I'll go, but only if it's a school in Connecticut." Home. He wanted to go home. Back to the last place he felt he belonged. He was too young to know that home isn't home when the people you love aren't there anymore. Still, I could understand his desire. I felt that way about Texas. It's as though the land itself holds some promise of getting back what's been lost along the way. If being in Connecticut eased the transition for him, then I was all for it.

The school we were considering happened to be in Connecticut—just two hours from where we'd lived. We found it on our own by going to the library, after all other leads failed. We consulted with every psychiatrist and counselor we'd worked with the past couple of years. No one was able to help direct us toward anything other than hospital facilities.

Too late we would discover that a good educational consultant rather than the medical community would have been more help. Perhaps, with some guidance, we'd have realized the school we selected didn't have their act together. The kids had too much time alone. They weren't adequately supervised. And discipline was sporadic and arbitrary—the last thing an ADHD kid requiring structure needed.

Still, for the most part, Michael did well there. He made good friends. Smaller classroom size helped tremendously, as did personalized attention from the faculty. And his relationship with us improved dramatically.

But after being there one year, Michael discovered something that would alter his life forever. Magic potions that buffered the pain and isolation he'd felt all his life—alcohol and drugs. He embraced them both like a drowning man grabbing a lifeline.

Whether or not Mike would've made that discovery under any circumstances, we'll never know. But from the moment he began using, everything changed. It took us a while to realize just how much. But on that summer evening when we told Michael he'd be going away, we thought we'd made the best choice for him and for us.

David was quiet about the decision. He was torn because he loved his brother and wanted him near, but he was also tired of being the brunt of

Michael's anger. I'd seen him hardening to protect himself from the pain of rejection. His eyes seldom laughed anymore.

Though there were glaring issues with both kids that needed attention, I felt ill-equipped to address them. I thought perhaps boarding school for Mike would offer another perspective, another structure, that might help us all. My own background left me without the tools I needed. Mike's weaknesses were mine, and so were many of his issues. I was still emotionally unsettled, struggling with my place in our home. I'd also accepted that my days as the disciplinarian in the home were numbered.

Unfortunately, Joe's effectiveness was also limited. His poor relationship with his father left him at a loss to know how to draw boundaries. His dad had died of a heart attack the year before. When the policeman came to our door in Connecticut to notify Joe of the death, as "next-of-kin," the phrase seemed sadly ironic. The last time Joe had spoken to his father, he was sixteen. There'd been an argument over Joe's driver's license, and his dad had refused to let it go.

Belittling and hateful words. Silence. It was the only discipline Joe had ever known. He couldn't envision any other kind. To him, discipline meant inflicting on Michael and David the kind of pain he had endured, and he simply could not do it. Instead, he vowed nothing would come between him and his sons.

Joe couldn't stand for the boys to be angry with him. So he placated, bribed, dismissed, did whatever he had to do to avoid conflict, even though that undermined my attempts to discipline. I compensated by being overly strict and harsh, something our counselor pointed out was as detrimental to the boys as their dad's permissiveness. The tension not only caused problems between Joe and me, but we woke up one day to realize that, for fifteen years, we had inadvertently trained our boys to be experts in the skill of playing one parent against the other.

But just as we were beginning to understand our roles in this dynamic, we were sabotaged on another front. Joe became very ill.

I came in one evening to find him on the bed holding his stomach protectively.

"Another bad day?" I asked. He shook his head yes.

"The prednisone isn't working," he replied weakly. He laid back and closed his eyes to hold back tears. Though he'd suffered with bouts of colitis for over twenty years, in the past six months it had become debilitating. Joe stood with me in the decision to get help for Mike, but now he didn't have the strength to be involved in the daily scrimmages.

Little stabs of panic warned me something big was going on. Things were blowing apart everywhere, but I calmed myself with the assurance that we were all in it together for the long haul.

I took comfort from my grandparents' experience, noting that once they made up their minds to get home, it didn't take long to get there. That's what I hoped for with my family—that once we got our direction set, we'd quickly move out of this desert season of our lives.

It had been happening for me personally. The catalyst was a panic attack.

I'd struggled with these attacks since moving to Georgia. One morning after getting David off for school, the fear gripped my throat. *You can't make it here,* my thoughts screamed. *Nothing's changed. You'll die if you stay.* But a verse I memorized as a child came to me—Joshua 1:9. I began to say it out loud.

"Have I not commanded you? Be strong and of good courage; do not be afraid nor be dismayed, for the Lord your God is with you wherever you go."

I repeated the verse again. And again. The words calmed my spirit, then came a very simple but profound realization: *I have been at this place before. Not just once or twice, but hundreds of times. This place where I have been afraid, and asked for God's help, and He has spoken to me.* I would take comfort from His words for a short time, then retreat back into my fear—only to go through the same struggle all over again.

I saw before me a clear choice: to believe God and to accept His peace in what was happening with Joe and the boys, or to live in constant fear. My history had been to vacillate between the two. To surrender then rebel. To give God my fear then take it back.

I blamed God for hiding when I was searching so desperately for Him. But now I could see how I had dictated the terms of our relationship. I was amazed at God's patience—that, without wrath, He simply let me wander until I wore myself out. The high price I'd paid, in terms of my own peace of mind, had been unnecessary.

Like the children of Israel who wandered in the desert for forty years—on what should have been a four-day journey—I agonized for two decades in a spiritual limbo largely of my own making. Going in circles. Fighting the same battles over and over again with God, with Joe, with myself until I was just sick of it. Sick enough to finally make a life choice. If I were going to trust God, there would be no more going back. I would trust regardless of whether circumstances were victorious or crushing.

I sensed the Holy Spirit asking me if I was now ready to allow Him to take over. Completely. From my heart I said, "Yes. I give you permission to do whatever is needed in me and my family to make us whole." It wasn't a hypothetical prayer. I felt hard times were coming, and I didn't want to face what lay ahead without God's help.

Off the Range

I settled into a holding pattern with the family. Mike was in boarding school. Dave's new passion—bass guitar—kept him busy. Joe had surgery followed by a long recovery, but he was improving.

My job was to be there. To fill in wherever needed as caregiver, chauffeur, nurse, counselor, cook. It was rewarding to meet the needs of my family, but I struggled with the big picture. In many ways, I felt on the shelf.

As I was giving myself more and more to a loving relationship with God, He was affirming the gifts He had given me. Creativity. The ability to communicate. Even my intensity. But since my calling at the moment was to nurture my family, there didn't seem to be time or place for my gifts. That confused me. If indeed the way to find one's life was to lose it, then serving my family and expressing my own uniqueness through my God-given gifts had to be related. But I couldn't see it.

Long ago, I accepted that my route to personal fulfillment would not be a direct one. I learned this more out of frustration than anything else. I knew what all the books and programs advocated. *Set goals. Break them down into doable components and you can accomplish anything. Whether a sales quota, a spiritual or personal growth goal, or a new car, what you want is within your grasp!*

All I can say is, though this method has proven valuable for many people, it never worked for me. Instead, I followed a pattern that began in my youth. An emergency demanding all my time and attention would hit the very moment I was to begin my well-planned regime. It was usually a personal crisis—sick mother, sick children, sick husband—something I knew I was to give priority, but it still blew a hole in the bottom of the boat.

I felt like one of those cows my grandfather and his roping horse would cut out from the herd and bring in from the pasture.

"Once a good workhorse zeroed in on a particular animal," Papa claimed, "that was the last step that cow took in its own direction. My horse would keep hedging her in until she made her way to where I wanted her to be."

I identified with the cow. No matter which direction I started in, something formidable stepped right in front of me to block me. It happened to me so many times that I finally realized it was no quirk of fate. Somebody was trying to tell me something.

That "someone" was the Holy Spirit. By now I recognized the internal check that signaled me to pay attention. Lately He'd been paging me loud and clear. I tested the water from time to time—a music group, teaching a class, charity work, writing—yet through the daily demands of my family, the same message kept coming through. Not this way. Not now.

I thought often of Papa's barren years when I chafed under my own.

Papa was disillusioned after he got fired from the Blackwell ranch. He didn't regret his decision not to work on Sundays, but losing his job took the wind out of his sails. That's when he moved to Arizona. The disappointment made him vulnerable to doing something he never would have done otherwise.

When he came back from Arizona, Papa realized there was little chance of making a living on the range. Though the economy settled down, the lifestyle he loved was fading. Cowboys were becoming relics. The real work on ranches was done by machinery. Livestock was handled with cattle prods. Roping was a forgotten art form.

So Papa reconciled himself to reality and spent the next two decades wandering in various trades. Those years weren't his brightest.

I worked for the county from '43 to '49. I was supposed to be a bridge man, but I done whatever needed to be done. I drove tractors. Caterpillars. I drove anything that needed drivin' or shoveled anything that needed shovelin'. But a cousin of mine named Watts owned

a car dealership. He knew my heart was botherin' me so he said he'd give me a job as parts manager. I took it on the spot and that was the end of my county work. I worked at the Jeep dealership for ten years.

Just about lost that job before I got started though. One day my boss came and wanted me to lie to the customers about the cost of certain parts. I said, "No, I'm not gonna do that. It's cheatin'."

He got all huffy and said, "Your job is to tell the customer whatever I tell you to tell them!"

But I wouldn't give in. I said, "If I'll cheat for you, I'll cheat against you."

He got real quiet thinkin' about that, and I guess it made sense to him. I didn't lose my job anyway.

I stayed on at the Jeep dealership till Watts sold out. Then I drove a cattle truck for four years. I liked it alright, but I had to be gone too much and leave Mama by herself. We didn't care much for bein' apart, so that's when I went to workin' for myself doin' carpentry work. Now, I'm no carpenter, so I don't know how I got by with it. But I was honest and nobody complained.

At first I did it on the side when I wasn't drivin' the truck. I'd take any kind of odd job I thought I could do—like that roofing job where I cut the head off that lady's big ol' flower. Then I got hired by Faith Apartments to be their maintenance man and I quit drivin' altogether.

During the years he worked off the range, there were few opportunities for Papa to utilize his natural abilities. But he did his best; he was grateful to be working and happy he could fulfill his responsibilities. That's when Papa proved himself to be a man of integrity and character. He did what was needful with no guarantee things would turn in his favor.

Papa was sixty by then and had given up hope of working with live-stock again. But just when it seemed his dream of cowboy life was gone forever, he was offered the job at the barn—an opportunity for which he wouldn't even have known to ask.

The sweet irony of it was, all he'd learned working in the business world and all the odd jobs he had done over the years provided him with the experience he needed to succeed at the barn.

My grandmother once told me, "God doesn't waste anything. If our lives are completely His, He takes every experience, every good and bad thing that comes into our lives, and uses it all to bring us into the abundant life He promised."

She reminded me that King David in the Bible spent years as a shepherd before reigning over the nation of Israel. It proved to be the perfect preparation for his royal calling. The Psalms reveal that David's compassionate heart was shaped by his days in the fields caring for helpless sheep. Because of his life experience, David didn't rule God's people with an iron first, he shepherded them.

This perspective helped me cope with the incongruities of my life. What I was giving my family was important. I enjoyed nurturing them, but I sensed this wasn't the entire story. There was something ahead that would demand all the resources and gifts God had given me.

I made a choice to believe that all I was experiencing—even the despair, the boredom, the impatience—was somehow being woven into the fabric of my life. It all had purpose, even if I couldn't see it.

Determined to continue to give myself joyfully to my first calling of wife and mother, I set aside my own agenda. If something came along that I was interested in, I tried it, but at the first sign of conflict, I opted for my first priority.

During this time I was offered a tremendous opportunity. A church asked me to handle their public relations for a large capital funds campaign. I turned it down. But Joe asked me to rethink my decision. "I can tell you have a passion for this project," he said. "Are you sure you wouldn't like to give it a shot?" After further prayer, I accepted.

The project was demanding. Stretching. But also exhilarating. And not one time did I have to make a choice between a family crisis or my job. I was learning that when something was right for me, it was right for my family. God made a way for me to do it. But if I tried to do something that wasn't best for me, life was miserable for everyone.

Instead of being frustrated when obstacles thwarted my plans, I began to accept these blocks as guidance. From a position of trust, I began to get a tiny glimpse of what God's desire was for me during this season. With growing conviction, I sensed that God was trying to give me a gift. Time. Time for reflection. Time to sort out what was going on in my household. Time to experience and recognize His guidance. Time to gather strength for what lay ahead.

Summer
1993

Happy Birthday

Fifteen of us stood under Midtown Manor's impressive portico, and surrounded Papa like wagons around a campfire. For the first time ever, my brother, sister, and I, along with all our families, were together in Texas. Joe insisted on renting a luxury car that would be comfortable for Papa, so we all oohed and aahed as Michael eased a big black Cadillac up to the entrance. Someone opened the door and Papa slid into the front seat like a wealthy New Yorker.

An excellent driver, Mike was thrilled to be Papa's official chauffeur. It wasn't until we returned the vehicle to the rental agency that someone noticed the rental agreement prohibited anyone under the age of twenty-five from driving. But, at the week's end, there had been no mishaps—so at least along with being ignorant we were also lucky.

Mike had been home all summer. We continued to go through predictable cycles: four to six weeks of model behavior followed by a catastrophic blow-up. But he was trying and was on medication for ADHD, which helped. Still, we all walked on eggshells.

On this trip, Michael let his guard down. He soaked up the love and acceptance of our extended family like a thirsty sponge.

The occasion of our visit was Papa's ninetieth birthday. My aunt and her family decorated the rec room at Midtown Manor in a cowboy theme, arranged for food, and invited everyone in the whole building. We came to join them in a musical tribute to our grandfather. Between us there were enough singers, pianists, guitar pickers, and bass players to make music for hours.

Papa sat up front in a big cushioned chair. He scanned the audience as if he were on the platform of a country church, waiting to preach. We sang, bantered back and forth, and told stories while Papa laughed and cried.

At the end, we asked everyone to join us in singing a song that had been my grandmother's favorite: "What A Day That Will Be."

There is coming a day when no heartaches shall come,
No more clouds in the sky, no more tears to dim the eye;
All is peace for evermore on that happy golden shore—
What a day, glorious day, that will be.

What a day that will be when my Jesus I shall see,
And I look upon His face—the One who saved me by His grace;
When He takes me by the hand, and leads me through the Promised Land,
What a day, glorious day, that will be.

The last chorus ended amidst sniffles and tears. Papa stood up slowly. With one hand he leaned heavily on the table beside him, and with the other he wiped his face with his ever-present white kerchief. Taking his time, he folded the handkerchief and put it back in his pants' pocket. As he looked at all of us standing together in his honor, you could almost see the words forming in his mind.

His eyes began to twinkle. "If Mr. King had known how rich I was," he said nodding toward the manager of Midtown Manor, "he'd have gone up on my rent a long time ago." The place broke into applause, and with that, Papa sat down.

Everyone swarmed around him as the party broke into gentle chaos. It was time for cake, ice cream, and mingling. The night just seemed to go together like some kind of gourmet dessert where all the flavors mix together creating something you can't quite define except to say, "It's delicious!"

Good Eye

Papa's little apartment couldn't begin to hold us all, so two of us took turns staying with him at night. The rest of us stayed at the Holiday Inn. Though the hotel was where we hung out, Papa was less than enthusiastic about joining us there. Too much noise. He didn't think he could hear. But not wanting to miss out on anything, he finally agreed to come.

The Holiday Inn stood between Midtown Manor and the highway. Though the distance between the back doors of the hotel and Midtown wasn't much further apart than the house had been to the barn, Papa couldn't walk it. He'd be "tuckered out" for the day. So instead, Mike picked him up in the Caddy.

No sooner did the rest of us start across the street than heavy rain drops began to splat in quarter-size dollops on our summer clothes. The hot wind kicked up as we hurried, knocking us against each other—hair and clothing whipping one way and then the other.

Michael parked under the large overhang at the hotel's entrance, ahead of us. Slowly, Papa extricated himself from the car, then struggled to keep his balance against the wind. He leaned against the car to steady himself. Pulling his cowboy hat down in front and tucking his chin into the collar of his jacket, he made an efficient wind buffer for himself before taking Edwin's arm and walking into the hotel.

By the time we gathered in the lobby, Papa was the only one who didn't look like something the cat drug in.

The storm ended as quickly as it began (Papa said it would), and before we knew it, the kids changed into swimsuits and were jumping into the king-sized pool. Papa couldn't hear above the squeals and laughter of the children's games, but neither could we. We were all content to watch them play and lose ourselves to memories of our own.

They're growing up so fast. Wasn't it just yesterday that Edwin, Sharon, and I played this way? In the rush of years, how had there been time for four generations? Perhaps the greater wonder was how we managed to stay connected.

Much of the credit had to go to my grandparents. Their commitment to God, each other, and us shielded us much like Papa's cowboy hat and jacket protected him from the afternoon's summer storm. By holding to faith and each other, we knew it was possible to come through turbulent times relatively unscathed when others were blown apart.

Only time would tell how successfully we would integrate those values into our own families, but one thing Papa consistently preached was that the odds of building a good family increased considerably when you started with quality.

My grandfather had an eye for a good woman, a fine horse, and an honest man. Though he spent most of his life poor, he could spot quality a mile off. "If you start with quality, most anything else can be fixed," he said. He proved his theory with horses.

People get rid of horses when they can't handle 'em. The horse will rear up when they try to mount him or somethin' like that. So that's what I'd have to break him of.

Some of my best bargains were horses that were as beautiful as could be, but they was wild. A few times I bought a high strung horse then, after I trained him, sold the same horse back to same guy for a lot more than I paid him for him.

Papa knew that it was the temperament of a horse that ultimately made it desirable or not. That, and training. Properly trained, a horse could be worth two or three times standard market value.

Once a man killed two of his neighbor's horses that wandered onto his property. They belonged to two little girls, and when their daddy sued the man, Papa was brought into court to estimate their value.

"They weren't no count as horses," Papa said. "They was just little Shetlands, but they was pets."

On the open market they would've only been worth $35 but Papa valued them at what he could have sold them for—$100 and $125 respectively. The prosecution said nobody could get that much for a Shetland. "Well, I can," he replied, producing bills of sale showing he'd sold several Shetlands for that amount.

Papa claimed that most everything he learned about life, he learned from horses. My grandmother wouldn't have wanted that analogy carried too far, but she possessed two characteristics he placed a premium on: quality and good temperament. To Papa's credit, he put the same effort into nurturing the woman he loved as he did his horses.

Papa attributed the success of their fifty-some-year partnership to Mama's kind and gentle spirit. "She was turned real good that way," Papa said in what sounded very much like horse terms. But he was right. My grandmother was a beautiful woman with a shy humility that endeared her to everyone who knew her.

She could get out of sorts though. I remember one spring she was absolutely crotchety. She was all over Papa for everything from how he ran their errands to how he drove his truck. Papa just laid low until she got over it.

He once told Joe, "Things go a lot better if I just let Mama have her say. Afterward, I go out to the barn and think about it. If things need to be different, I can see to it later—if it comes to that. But lots of times, her talkin' about it is enough."

Long before popular psychologists identified intrinsic differences in the sexes, Papa knew when he was out of his element. Like most women, Mama lived in a very intuitive, verbal world. She may have been quiet, but she was also direct. If Papa didn't know how to respond, he said nothing and let her think he'd gotten the picture until he actually *did* get the picture. They usually ended up on the same page. And Mama didn't push him often.

You could say my grandparents became very adept at handling each other. They forged their relationship with give and take, guided by respect and caring. The idea of equality of rights and responsibilities (the model for most marriages in my generation) was foreign to them. They relied implicitly on one thing: character.

Whenever talk turned to Mama, Papa was quick to point out the importance of marrying a quality person. Most the great-grandkids were teenagers now and interested in the opposite sex, so he took the opportunity to plant a few seeds.

"With Mama," he said by way of example, "I never had to worry about her doin' the right thing because she had character. I never was good enough for her, but I was smart enough to know a good thing when I seen it. I was just lucky she felt the same way about me."

When I married Joe at nineteen, I didn't know as much as I thought I did. But I was certain of one thing: he was a quality person. He was honest, hardworking, and loyal. For years my anger discounted these things, but ultimately, his character was why I stayed.

During the worst of my depression in Connecticut, I was non-functioning. For several months I didn't fix meals, do the laundry, or clean the house. I was a zombie who slept every chance I could and tried not to cry when the kids were around. Joe, who'd never been involved with the day-to-day activities of running the household, moved silently into place.

I seldom had anything good or kind to say. Certainly not to him. Even the pain in his eyes made me angry. Bewildered by the change in me and devastated by my desire to end the marriage, he began his own spiritual journey in earnest. I told him, "I'm happy for you, but I want nothing to do with it. It's too late."

He didn't push me but, from time to time, attempted to make his case. One evening he came to our room and sat beside me on the bed.

Looking me straight in the eye he said, "Karen, I know you're sick of our life together. I know I've let you down by not being there and not seeing how lonely you've been. But I swear to you, I didn't see it. I'll work at being more open and do whatever it takes to…"

"And I'm supposed to believe you," I retorted. Then I started with my usual litany of grievances.

He didn't try to talk over me. He just waited until I stopped.

"I know there's no reason for you to believe me, but I am committed to you and the boys. I know you want another life, and if you had it to do over, you'd choose someone different than me."

I didn't refute him. I did want the exact opposite of what I had. At least he understood that.

"I'm not a flashy kind of guy," he continued, "and I can't make myself be something I'm not, so I can't give you excitement or whatever it is you're looking for. But I do have something good to offer."

Tears filled his eyes. "I can promise you loyalty...stability...commitment. I can provide for you, financially. And I do love you. I haven't done a very good job of showing it, but I can learn if you'll give me a chance."

He saw me stiffen and looked away. "I know. You've heard it before."

He moved closer and took my hand. This time, it was I who looked away.

"Most the things I'm talking about sound pretty boring," he said, "but in the long run, they're values you can trust. Things you can build a life on."

I gulped down the lump in my throat. I didn't doubt his sincerity, but the distance between us was something we couldn't pretend wasn't there. I shook my head and said, "Joe, I'm just so lonely..."

He smiled sadly. "And I'm lonely, too."

That response I didn't expect. Joe, lonely? The Joe who, for most of our married life, practically winced every time the kids or I spoke to him? I stood there with my mouth open for a moment then asked, "Well, then, if we're both lonely, what's the problem?"

We actually laughed at the irony of it. The two of us, living under the same roof. Sleeping side by side in the same bed. Wanting the same thing and dying for the lack of it.

Joe gave me a lot to think about in that conversation. He's not a lawyer for no reason. Even though I'd given him a hard time, I couldn't deny what he'd been doing to keep our family together the past few months. He had no understanding of clinical depression, yet he never berated me for not doing my part. He simply did my part and his, too. Working. Cooking. Cleaning. Caring. And waiting.

He'd gone to counseling himself and held on. For me. For the boys. For our family. He held on when I couldn't. He held on when it looked like nothing he could do would turn things around. But the simple fact that he was there—loving our family through the daily acts of caring for Michael, David, and me—touched me. Eventually, this commitment convinced me that what Joe had to offer was, indeed, too precious to walk away from.

But simply staying together and the work of becoming "one" were two different things. Though we had been in Atlanta almost two years, we were still struggling to overcome old patterns and behaviors. We had both looked forward to this trip to Texas, hoping that the ties holding our extended family together would embrace us, too, and pull us tight until our own bonds strengthened.

Mating Season

"Sharon, would you mind combin' down the back of my hair?" Papa asked. My sister tried to get the wisps of dark hair to stay down at the crown. Papa still had a full head of hair; it had turned a dusky charcoal but was curly and had a number of troublesome cowlicks.

It had always been Mama's job to wet down the comb and make one more pass at taming the back. Now, whenever Sharon or I was around he'd ask us to do the honors. After Mama died, Papa told us that he dreamed over and over again that he was dressing to go somewhere. Then Mama would come into the room to comb the back of his hair.

We were happy to do it in her place, even though we didn't have much success. I guess it made him feel cared for. I doubt anything short of Butch Wax could've made a long-term difference. As long as his hair was wet, he looked as dapper as the next guy. And most the time he had on a cowboy hat so you didn't notice much.

Papa was particular about his appearance. He'd sooner die than step outside without everything in place. He might eat breakfast in a strap T-shirt, but he looked like a million bucks when he walked out the door. The ironing board was always set up in his room so he could press his trousers before putting them on. I never once saw him in a wrinkled shirt. You'd think he had a girlfriend the way he dressed up all the time, but we knew better.

Papa was as much in love with Mama now as the day he married her. Today we would say they were soul mates. I always thought that kind of closeness came from sharing many of the same passions, but in their case that wasn't true. Their love of God and family was the fabric that kept them together. Outside of that, each was content to simply accommodate what was important to the other. What gave them oneness was the genuine appreciation of who the other was.

The biggest gap in their relationship was that Mama had no interest whatsoever in animals. She did love one large watchdog they owned, a cream-colored mixed breed named Missy. She never admitted it except to say, "Missy's a good dog." But she fed her choice scraps off the back porch when she thought no one was looking.

Mama came from farming, not ranching stock. She spooked easily and had a fear of animals, which she never overcame. The only time you'd catch Mama at the barn was when Papa wandered too far from the tack room to hear the phone. If someone needed him, then Mama would tie a silk scarf around her head and set out to find him.

Mama never went to the barn without a scarf. The large folded triangle she knotted tightly under her chin, served two purposes: It kept the smell of the barn out of her hair, and it kept the wind from ruining the results of her weekly trip to the hairdresser.

It's been noted that Texas has two kids of women. "Big hair" and "big mamma." Mama leaned toward "big hair." It was teased lightly on top then pulled into a French roll at the nape of her neck. In her sixties, she was silver-haired, but she had beautiful skin—in spite of the years she'd spent outside in cotton fields and gardens. The big bonnet she'd worn to protect her face from the sun did its job well.

My grandmother lived a simple life, a life close to God and His earth. Yet she was a deep, multi-faceted person. A thinker. Wise. Both self-assured and humble. But the quality that endeared her most to Papa was her quiet spirit. There was a peace about her that enveloped everyone around her. I first noticed it in the weeks before my mother died.

We had called my grandparents when my mother's condition became critical. We expected Mama to be on the next plane, but instead she said, "I'll call you back as soon as I can come." We didn't hear from her until the next evening.

Only later did I learn why she delayed.

"I was so upset myself that I knew I wouldn't be any good to Atha or any of you until I got this settled between God and me."

After the phone call, she spent the next twenty-four hours praying until her grief was bathed in God's comfort. And when she came to us, it was not with a mother's despair, but God's peace. I didn't recognize it as such because she didn't try to preach to or even talk to us about it then. She was simply there to hold us. To cry with us. To fix meals. To listen. Her presence was worth a thousand sermons.

Papa fully appreciated what it meant to have someone like her at his side. As he retold the stories of their years together, it was clear Mama was the anchor. For more than fifty years, his life had been graced by the love and faith of my grandmother. Because for him that bond would never be broken—even after she died—he never once considered remarrying. However, we discovered he was under considerable pressure to do so.

After playing pool one morning, several of us—with kids in tow—made our way up to Papa's apartment. We had plans for a frosty Dr. Pepper before meeting the others for lunch. We started down Papa's hallway, when a large woman came out from her apartment. She sauntered toward us, taking her half out of the middle. The kids flattened up against the wall on either side to make room for her. The rest of us rearranged ourselves into a single-file formation as we wished her good morning. All she got from Papa was a quick nod and a thin-lipped scowl.

Papa fumbled with the lock then pushed the door open for us. Once inside, he closed the door quickly behind us and breathed a sigh of relief. "That's one woman I don't care too much for bein' around," he told us.

He said he'd come home one day to find a note under his door. It was a hand-written letter making a case for why Papa should remarry. It was one of several installments delivered unsigned. "But I got a pretty good idea it was her that sent 'em," he said.

She and couple o' ladies are always tryin' to prove that it's okay for me to marry again. They send me all the Bible verses and such. 'Course I know that as far as the Bible's concerned, there's no problem. And it's fine with me if other people want to do that, but it's not for me. There's a bunch down there that just sits around gabbin' all the time about everybody else's business. They think I need a wife. But they can think again. I'm not interested.

You should see what some of these folks go through trying to get together with each other. There was this one fellow, Frank. Him and his wife was friends of ours years ago. Well, he moved in here not too long ago after his wife died. I was real happy about that 'cause he's a good boy, a real clean-living fellow—somebody I thought I might enjoy spending time with.

But word had gotten around he was comin' and there was this lady living here, Muriel Watkins, who set her sights on him. Frank and me both knew her from before. Her husband died, oh, musta been a couple years before she moved in.

Far as I knew, she didn't smoke before, but after she moved here, she started hanging out with that group down in the rec room. She'd sit down there with them by the hour, lightin' up one cigarette after the other. But she knew Frank wouldn't have nothin' to do with any woman who smoked tobacco, so, the next thing you know, she's up and quit. Overnight.

By the time Frank got here, you woulda never known a cigarette had touched her lips. At least that's what he thought 'cause he took up with her right away, and they've been together every since. Muriel wants to get married but Frank ain't ever gonna get married. He's too cheap. They'd lose one of their social security checks.

That's the main reason more folks around here don't get married. You get cut way down on your social security. Some of 'em wouldn't want to get married anyway—like Boone. He's not interested in mar-ryin' nobody, but still them ladies is fallin' all over themselves to get next in line.

Boone was a one-woman-at-a-time kind of guy though. He didn't want life to get too complicated. But when one girlfriend fell by the way, he was never long in getting another.

"You shoulda seen the last one he had," Papa said. "Now she was an ugly woman. Hard to look at. She was that bad." He shook his head in won-derment. "I just can't see somebody being willin' to settle for just about anything," he said, "but some people do."

Before coming to Midtown Manor, Papa never would have begrudged a man finding a woman, but things were different for him now. There weren't a lot of guys Papa cared to be friends with, and he resented that the ones he did like kept getting snagged by the ladies. Once they did, that was it for Papa. He wasn't interested in being a third wheel, even if invited.

So, he just sat back. Observed. And shook his head at what he saw.

Papa could have developed a small group of friends who got together with no strings attached. It would've meant companionship. Someone to eat dinner with every once in a while. But Papa wanted no mistake about his position.

He expressed his point of view to us succinctly: "I'm ninety years old and had fifty years of a pretty nigh perfect marriage," he said, "so why would I want to go and mess things up now?"

We couldn't argue with him.

The Tie That Binds

The family was still together on the weekend. When Sunday rolled around, we decided to hold our own service rather than drag our cumbersome group into an unknown church. We tried unsuccessfully to plan a simple praise and worship service. Oddly enough, the fly in the ointment was music. We were five families, all active in different churches, yet we couldn't find three choruses we all knew.

Instead we reverted to the heritage we shared—gospel music and hymns. These songs expressed faith in the language into which we were born. Many were no longer popular or praised, but they were our mother tongue.

As we all gathered in my aunt's living room, I sensed it was important for my children to hear these songs. They have little interest in them now, but someday, when they embark on their own spiritual journey, perhaps the memory of them will guide them home. Or at least start them in the right direction.

The gathering of the clan to celebrate Papa's birthday was a monumental time of family bonding. We had only to look around the room to be reminded of God's goodness in giving us to each other. I was very aware that without Papa's example of faith and perseverance, it was unlikely I would've been in that room with my own family in tact.

We took turns telling our individual "Papa" stories—sharing the moments, the acts, the words of his life that most impacted ours. Then Papa took our gifts and offered them back to God. "If it wasn't for the Lord," he said, "there wouldn't be any reason for you all to be sayin' the things you're sayin'." Once again he told us the story of his conversion, then he preached as good a sermon as you'd hear in any church.

At times, we stopped him to ask questions, probing for details that would embed the people, places, and events into our minds.

One thing we all noticed was that Papa had absolutely no trouble hearing us. Even with his hearing aid, he'd been struggling again. He could get by, but we were back to repeating things several times. Yet whenever talk turned to the things of God, Papa came to attention. He could hear. He could remember Scripture and references. His mind cleared. His body seemed to bypass its limitations when the conversation turned to spiritual things.

After Papa delivered our Sunday sermon, we gathered around him. As we touched him, praying words of blessing over him, we sensed God's presence strongly in the room. As we had no set agenda, what happened next took place without forethought. We began to give thanks. We acknowledged God's greatness and His place in our lives. Then we began to pray for each other.

Because our families were close, we were aware of the many burdens we carried. Emotional. Relational. Physical. Financial. We'd tried to put these concerns out of our minds as much as possible over the weekend, but now we realized we had the opportunity to lay them before God and each other as a family.

To my surprise, Joe spoke first. Fighting tears, he shared honestly about the severity of his illness. His suffering. The fear. He'd had surgery to remove his colon several months before, but he was not doing well. He asked if we would lay hands on him as we had Papa.

After him, several others came forward. Vulnerable and humble. From this openness came brokenness and gratitude. God's presence flowed over us like fragrant oil, and we knew this was truly a holy moment.

The Holy Spirit touched us profoundly that day. That we had been privileged to experience Him together was an act of grace that brought joy and an incredible sense of peace. We accepted it and marveled that God had given us so much. Like Papa, we discovered we were rich. Very rich.

We departed for our many corners of the world, determined to hold to the comfort of God's presence. Sadly, for Papa that consolation was short-lived. When we left, he fell apart.

I received a phone call from him late one night two weeks later. He was hysterical. "Something happened to me when you all were here," he cried. "I didn't treat you right. I just wished I would have died before you came because I'm so ashamed of how I acted."

"Papa, what are you talking about? You were wonderful to us."

"No. I didn't get to spend any time with the great-grandkids. I didn't mean to hurt their feelings. You all did so much for me, and I didn't do nothin' for you."

"Papa, I haven't heard anyone say you hurt their feelings, and all the kids had a wonderful time. We didn't come expecting anything from you— we just wanted to be together and we were."

I talked until I was blue in the face, but my assurances fell on deaf ears.

"I don't even know how I could call myself a Christian when I treated y'all so bad," he said. "Hon, I'm sorry." Then he cried so hard he couldn't talk. The realization that Papa was not rational dawned slowly.

I calmed him as much as possible, then asked, "Papa, have you talked to Marie about this?" He had not.

"Then let me see if I can reach her now and one of us will call you right back, okay?"

I don't think he heard me, but I lost no time in getting my aunt on the phone. She was shocked.

"I just saw Papa yesterday and he seemed fine," she said.

"Well, he's in some sort of crisis now. It may be depression or the emotional rebound from all the activity of his birthday, but he's in trouble."

Aunt Marie immediately went over to check on him. Then the next day, she took him to the doctor who put him on antidepressants. It took a few weeks, but Papa finally settled down.

In retrospect, we should have known a visit like ours would be stressful. The shock of being inundated with people and showered with constant activity and attention, only to be left alone again, was too much for Papa. We felt bad for not being more sensitive to him, but we were learning.

I thought back to when my children were babies. When I tried to discover what upset them, what hurt them, what reached them, words were of little help. What counted was my presence. One on one. To know what they felt, I needed to hear their cries, look into their eyes, and see the subtle shifts of their bodies to find the pain. Only then could I comfort them. I wondered if that wasn't what Papa needed now. I realized that if I hoped to reach my grandfather in any meaningful way, I would need to learn the lessons of "presence" once again.

Winter
1994

Medicine Man

I walked the now familiar corridor of 3-south at Atlanta's Saint Joseph's hospital and entered my husband's room. He looked weak but, as usual, was clean-shaven and smelled wonderful. I kissed him tenderly.

"You doing okay?" I asked.

He smiled, but his eyes brimmed with tears. "Alright, considering." He sat up and carefully moved all the IVs and wires as he scooted to one side of the bed. He was making room for me. I kicked off my shoes and crawled in, nestling myself against him. We pulled up the white cotton hospital blankets and, for the next forty minutes, slept soundly.

It was the best rest either of us got these days. I came to the hospital each day after getting David off to school and returned home at 3:00 P.M. The afternoons and evenings were filled driving David to music lessons and band practices, as well as catching up on chores, paperwork, and bills.

Though Mike was away at school, he frequently had long breaks. When home, he and Dave hung around with a group of kids that didn't impress me much, but at least the two of them were back to being best buddies. That helped. I was too tired to deal with feuding siblings on top of everything else.

We were making some strides as a family. Going back to Texas did a lot for Joe, the boys, and me. It rooted us. It reminded us that we belonged together. Now that Joe was ill, I treasured that time even more.

Since the summer of Papa's ninetieth birthday party, Joe had faced repeated complications, the result of scar tissue from his first surgery. There'd been multiple surgeries to remove blockages. Lengthy recovery periods. Months of intravenous fluids at home and in the hospital. Yet as soon as he went on a regular diet, the cycle would begin all over again.

The bottom line was, Joe was unable to eat. He looked like a skeleton with a too-large head and eyes sunken deeply into dark sockets. He was literally starving to death. We were taking it one day at a time, hoping the next surgery or the next procedure would work, but we were running out of options.

Edwin came back during Joe's next hospitalization and helped with the boys and daily hospital schedule. I cried when he left, dreading managing alone again. But my brother's companionship had given me just enough relief to keep going.

Joe's illness had been a wake-up call for both us. The very real possibility of losing each other was beginning to do something we had been unable to do on our own: break down the distance and bitterness between us.

We snuggled in the hospital bed and talked hour after hour about where we'd missed the mark. How we hurt each other with words and actions that we now regretted. How we failed to hold a consistent standard for our boys. But we also spoke of our desire for a new start.

We both sensed that building a new foundation likely meant tearing down the old one first. We recognized that the process had begun with Joe's illness. All the things he relied on in the past—work, position, and money—were threatened now. For once, there was nothing I could do to fix anything. We were both helpless. Joe was too sick—and I was spread too thin—to meet all the demands made of us.

We felt like we were stranded at sea in a small boat with a hole in the bottom. What surprised us was how glad we were to be in that boat together. We felt God's peace in spite of our circumstances.

For some time, Joe and I had been on separate spiritual journeys, but now we were beginning to pray together. Not just "God bless our family" kind of prayers, but honest petitions for God's work in our lives.

With the growing closeness Joe and I were finding, I found myself feeling joyful. Even happy. It seemed ironic considering the stress we were under. But we were learning that with God, things often seem to be the opposite of how we think they should be. We didn't analyze our feelings too closely; we just enjoyed the comfort of being together and waited.

Papa and I kept in touch by phone. He loved Joe as if he were his own and was worried about him.

"Joe will be coming home in the next few days," I informed him. "They're going to try six weeks of at-home IV feedings again. That should give his system a chance to heal." That was the plan, but the flatness in my voice reflected my lack of hope. We had no reason to think this approach would be any more successful this time than the last.

"Well, you tell Joseph I'm prayin' for him, hon," Papa said. "I don't know why he's been so good to me, but there's nobody in this world that's done more for me than he has." Like a father who tells each boy, "You're my favorite son," Papa expressed his gratitude to his kids and grandkids with hyperbole. I had to smile. It still felt great to be appreciated.

Several weeks later, I returned home from grocery shopping to find Joe waiting for me at the door. "You need to call your aunt right away," he told me. "Something's wrong with Papa."

"Papa's in the hospital," Aunt Marie said on the phone. "The night watchman at Midtown Manor called me late last night to come get him. They found him wandering the halls in his underwear. He was saying words but they weren't making any sense and well…" she hesitated, "Papa just isn't himself." We both were quiet. The fear hung between us that Papa might be losing it in a big way.

The doctors suspected the beginning of dementia or perhaps a small stroke, but tests proved that the most likely culprit was medication. Like many elderly people, Papa had been adding to his daily regiment of drugs. He was taking something for his heart, depression, blood pressure, arthritis, digestion, and prostate, plus an assortment of home remedies. The interaction of some drugs and the long-term effects of others, combined with Papa's irregular manner of taking them, affected his mental state.

After a complete evaluation, his doctor determined several medications were no longer needed. The interaction issues were resolved. But Papa needed supervision taking his meds. On his own, he often missed doses. If he realized that he'd forgotten, he'd double up then get reactions from overdosing. Also, Papa's eyesight had deteriorated. He couldn't read the bottles even with a magnifying glass, so sometimes he took the wrong medication by mistake.

My aunt began to monitor his meds using a daily pillbox. The system would help for a while, but we saw the handwriting on the wall.

"Papa doesn't want to leave Midtown Manor," Aunt Marie told me. "So, I'll do all I can to keep him there as long as I can." I heard the pain in her voice. The day-to-day burden of taking care of Papa was hers. It would have been easier to just close up shop and move him into a nursing facility, but I loved her for her willingness to wait and see how it played out.

"Will he be okay there by himself when he comes home from the hospital?" I asked. She said she'd stay with him for a few days then see what happened.

But Joe had another idea. "Why don't you go back for a week? I'll be okay at home alone for part of the day," he insisted. "Mike's here to drive Dave to practices and both boys will be here in evenings to help out."

So I booked a flight, grateful for the opportunity to see Papa.

He'd been out of the hospital a few days when I arrived and, to my amazement, was as sharp as ever. The drug-induced fog was completely gone.

I looked around his apartment to see how well he'd been doing on his own. It wasn't as clean as other times—especially the bathroom and kitchen—but I chalked it up to his being sick and made a mental note to arrange for someone to come and help him once a week.

Papa looked a little ragged. He no longer wore cowboy boots. "My arth-a-ritis is just too bad all the time now," he said matter-of-factly, though I detected an edge of anger in his voice. Instead, he wore black, thick-soled walking shoes with thin white cotton socks, cut at the top to allow for the swelling in his legs.

Before his hospitalization, Papa walked the hallways of the sixth floor every day for exercise. He hadn't exercised since returning home, and even though he looked forward to getting out when I came, it didn't seem likely. But he surprised me.

"You up to eating out?" he asked soon after I settled in.

"I am, Papa, but wouldn't you rather I fix something here? I thought I'd go to the grocery store and pick up some things for the week. I don't mind cooking."

"Well, I mind you having to cook," he said. "And besides, I'd like to get out of here."

I laughed. "Fine then. Let's go."

He stood up slowly from his chair then turned around to get his keys from the table. He took a couple of steps then froze. It took me a minute to realize he was toppling backwards. I grabbed his arm then moved behind him, steadying him until he was able to right himself. While he stood quietly for a moment regaining his equilibrium, I tried to calm my pounding heart.

Papa, however, acted as though nothing had happened. He picked up his keys and fumbled around trying to find the key to the apartment. He couldn't. With an angry grunt, he handed the key case to me. "I can't see which one it is, so I might as well give up," he said.

Once we maneuvered our way outside, I locked the door behind us. Papa moved slowly down the long hallway, leaning heavily on my arm.

"Papa, did you want to go to Luby's?" I asked. At this rate, I didn't think he could manage the walk from the mall parking lot to the restaurant. He answered me with silence. Obviously, he didn't much care for that idea, so I tried another one.

"Then what about Pat's? A good hamburger sounds great to me."

"Can't," he said tersely. "Pat's is closed."

Papa stared down at the ground as though absorbed in the task of walking. Then I heard him breathe in sharply several times and realized he was holding back tears. We both understood his favorite restaurant wasn't the only thing shutting down.

Drugstore Cowboy

The September 25, 1994, edition of the *Wichita Falls Sunday Time Records News* simply stated that after twenty-five years at Fourth and Burnett, Pat's Drive-Inn "finally succumbed to make way for the multipurpose events center." I thought "succumbed" an interesting choice of words.

The residents were glad that the crime-filled shanties would be razed, but it hadn't occurred to them that the only restaurant within walking distance of their homes would also be swept away.

The next day, Papa and I stood with several other residents in the atrium balcony of the sixth floor and watched the bulldozers do their job. It would take weeks to clear out all the buildings. The demolition had begun. The complex would eventually include not only a convention center but also a fifty-thousand-square-foot livestock barn and seating for twelve hundred rodeo fans.

Ida held on to her cotton candy hair with one hand as she leaned over the rail to get a better look down the street. "Guess you can't stop progress," she said wistfully.

Deets sat on one of the sofas shaking his head. "Well, there's plenty of progress goin' on around here," he said. "Ever since they built them falls, it's been one thing after another."

With the falls, the city staked its claim to the modern world. Papa wasn't too impressed with the fifty-four-foot man-made waterfalls because, in his opinion, the water was too muddy to be beautiful. But mud was beside the point.

The city was named after an Indian camp that settled near a small waterfall along the Wichita River. When a flood swept away the waterfalls, the singular identifying feature of the town washed away with it. A hundred years after the flood, the loss apparently still bothered someone; in the 1980s the city determined to rebuild the falls near its original location.

It proved a good move. Set in Lucy Park, not five minutes from Midtown's back door, the falls have become one of the city's few tourist attractions. It's also a favorite site for weddings, special events, and photo opportunities. And for those who walk and picnic in the park's 170-acre recreational area, the cascade of water is a refreshing sight on a sweltering Texas day.

The falls also seem an appropriate symbol for the area since an ample water supply was a major contributing factor to its development as a city. As early as 1860, settlers began to farm the prairie grasslands, thus establishing an agricultural community that would have been impossible under more arid conditions.

Then on July 29, 1918, the Fowler well struck oil. That well—located in Burkburnett, just fifteen miles north of Wichita Falls—ignited a frenzied quest for oil that changed the area's economic base overnight. Within a decade, Wichita Falls grew from a little town of ten thousand to a major city of over more than forty-three thousand.

In 1940, just as oil money began to wane, good fortune smiled on the city again when it was selected to house Sheppard Air Force Base. The foundation of the economy shifted once more, this time to the military. But the city's farming and ranching roots remained entrenched in its culture.

Even today there are old-timers who farmed the land with a story or two to tell. And there are enough people roaming the malls in boots and cowboy hats to keep the mystique of cowboy life alive.

Papa thought western clothes were the most beautiful style of dress there could be. He'd smile at the mere sight of a man or woman wearing a good pair of boots and a quality cowboy hat. But Papa had little use for drugstore cowboys—men who tried to pass themselves off as cowboys but in their entire lives had never worked even a day on a ranch. But what aggravated him most were city slickers.

"All these doctors from Houston or Dallas come out here and buy land. Then they go around talkin' about how they're gonna spend the weekends 'on the ranch.'" Papa would shake his head in disgust. "Maybe they haven't got but two or three hundred acres."

Three hundred acres may not be enough to make a decent ranch in Texas, but after living in Connecticut—where in the 1980s a third of an acre building lot went for a quarter of a million dollars—it sounded like a lot of land to me.

I'm convinced that a major factor in Texans' pride of "bigness," as well as their fierce commitment to independence, comes from the expanse of its land. Driving on Highway 287 from Dallas to Wichita Falls, I'm overwhelmed by the miles and miles of raw land bordering the highway. That kind of openness tends to make one think big and free.

The Blackwell ranch, where Papa was foreman, was a big ranch—even by Texas standards. But while Papa had the utmost respect for the man who hired him, he didn't consider Blackwell's sons cowboys. Sometime that caused problems.

One day Papa brought the cows into the wheat field to graze, as he often did, but then a big storm blew in.

"It commenced to rainin' real hard," Papa said, "so I had to get the cattle out of the field before they spooked and trampled the wheat."

He was leaving the barn with his hired hand when the phone rang. It was one of Blackwell's son, Brice II, checking up on things.

He said, "Now, Mr. Choate, you'll be needin' to git the cattle out of the wheat field, so I'm driving in from town to give you a hand."

Papa said, "That's okay, Mr. Blackwell. Jim and me was headed out there right now. We can handle it."

"No, I want to come out. I got some slickers for us, and it'll go faster."

Papa knew it was no use trying to talk him out of coming, but he wasn't happy about it. Brice Blackwell II was a drugstore cowboy, and Papa claimed, "Blackwell on a horse was downright dangerous." Now he would have to give Blackwell his best workhorse, Prince, and Papa would be left to work two hundred head of cattle with a sorry, no-sense paint pony he'd taken as part of a trade.

"I didn't even think enough of him to give him a name," Papa said, "but the boys all called him Loco." And when it came to usefulness on the range, Loco and Blackwell were pretty much on a par.

Over an hour went by as Papa and Jim waited for Blackwell to drive in from the city.

"We coulda had the job done by now," Jim complained as the rain gathered more fury. "He just wants to go back into town and brag to his buddies 'bout workin' on the ranch."

"Well, he's the boss," Papa said, "so I guess he can do that if he wants to."

Finally, Blackwell came careening onto the muddy flat in front of the barn in his big fancy Cadillac like he was the U.S. Calvary. He looked like a dandy. New Tony Lama boots, a black felt Stetson hat.

"You boys ready?" he asked as he handed each of them a bright yellow slicker.

"I don't think I'll be needin' this," Papa said. "I ain't use to workin' in rain gear."

"Don't be silly, we'll get soaked out there without it." Blackwell pulled his on, and, reluctantly, Papa and Jim followed suit.

"Here, you'll be needin' my horse," Papa said, handing Prince's reins to Blackwell. Papa then attempted to mount Loco, but the yellow slicker spooked the horse.

"Whoa! Whoa! Settle down!" he ordered. Loco sensed Papa's aggravation and was taking advantage of the situation. It took some coaxing, but finally Papa mounted Loco and led the way out to the wheat field.

By now it had been raining hard for hours, and it had already been a very wet spring. Papa noticed on the way out that the creek, which ran in the bottom of a ten-foot gully, had overflowed it banks. Now you couldn't even tell where the drop off was.

The three men struggled to round up the cattle and get them out of the pasture, but many of the cows had babies who were reluctant to cross the swift water. Blackwell was in the way, and Loco was so skittish Papa could barely control him. What should've been a relatively simple job was turning into a fiasco, and Papa was getting angrier by the minute.

Finally, he dismounted Loco and began pushing the calves into the swollen river one by one. Then Papa mounted Loco again and started off to drive the remaining stragglers into the creek.

"Follow me!" Blackwell yelled once he saw where Papa was headed. He spurred Prince ahead of him to take the lead.

"Blackwell!" Papa shouted through the storm. His boss passed him by running Prince through the knee-deep water at the river's edge. Papa tried to warn him that the drop off was inches to his right. But Blackwell didn't hear, and, right then and there—being about as put out as he'd ever been in his life—Papa decided it wouldn't hurt Blackwell to learn a lesson.

Blackwell looked back over his shoulder and gave Papa a nod as if to say, "I'm in charge, let's go." But his proud look changed to terror as Prince stumbled off the edge of the gully into the deep waters. The Stetson tumbled downstream as horse and rider dropped completely out of sight. Not a ripple broke the flow of the river for what seemed like an eternity. Papa panicked as he realized what he'd done. He had allowed his boss, not to mention a prize cow horse, to walk into a very dangerous situation.

Papa scanned the river again just as Prince burst out of the water, nose first, on the opposite bank. The horse managed to get his front legs on the dirt rim, but his hindquarters remained under water. A few moments later, Blackwell bobbed up right in between his legs, sputtering and choking. Any other horse would have pawed him down, but being the great animal he was, Prince waited patiently while Blackwell clawed his way onto the bank.

"My boots! My boots!" Blackwell cried. "They're ruined."

Papa shook his head. It was coming back to him now why he'd let the man ride off the precipice in the first place. "Come on, Blackwell," Papa said as he led him over to Prince, who now stood quietly by the bank. They rode back to the barn in silence.

Once in the tack room, Blackwell sat on a bench and started to pull off his boots.

"I wouldn't do that if I was you," Papa said. "You take those off now and you won't get them on again until they're dry."

"But that could take hours, and I can't ride with soaking wet feet!" Blackwell exclaimed. "What else can I do?"

Papa measured his words slowly. "Well, Mr. Blackwell. I guess if I was you, I'd head back into town and get me some dry clothes."

Red began to creep up the back of Mr. Blackwell's neck as he realized he'd been played for a fool. He looked hard at Papa. "Well, I reckon that's what I'll do then." Blackwell then turned on his wet heel, got into his Cadillac, and hightailed it back into town.

"I guess it was the orneriest thing I ever done after I became a Christian, and it was foolish of me 'cause he coulda drowned," Papa said. His voice sounded penitent, but the twinkle in his eye gave him away. "He never did care for me much after that," he said.

Spring Cleaning

I laughed at Papa's drugstore cowboy story, but the truth was, I saw myself in Blackwell. The blustering pride. The know-it-all attitude. But also the desire to do something that mattered to you only to discover you weren't very good at it. The hardest part was knowing that, in the attempt, you'd put yourself and others at risk. As Joe and I began a sorting process, our ineptness became apparent. Figuring out what needed to change—and how to change it—exposed giant gaps in our parenting.

We'd been in therapy to gain some understanding of our family system. We felt the old adage, "All you can do is your best," didn't cut it when your best wasn't enough. Our choice was either to learn and grow or hurt our children. Our boys, losing the battle with peer pressure, drugs, and alcohol, motivated us. We weren't giving up without a fight.

It was scary letting go of the old ways of doing things, but there was also the hope that things could change. We wanted to salvage the good in our family and discard the patterns that were hurting us, but it was a laborious and time-consuming task.

A situation with Papa offered me a much needed break. My sister called to say Papa's apartment needed a major cleaning. Even with a weekly housekeeper and my aunt's help, the grime was winning out. Sharon cleaned when she was there, but this was beyond maintenance.

She asked if I would help her take care of it. I never thought I would see the day I'd welcome the task of spring cleaning, but tackling a problem with a tangible solution was just what I needed.

However, the logistics proved more challenging than expected. Sharon said, "I don't think Papa will let us do the work ourselves. He has a fit every time I try to do anything."

One night a few weeks earlier, Sharon waited until he went to bed then scoured the bathroom. She ran the shower to disguise her activities, but nothing got by Papa.

The next morning he stayed in bed a little longer than usual. When he heard Sharon stir, he got up, showered and shaved in his sparkling clean bathroom. Twenty minutes later Papa came out enveloped in a cloud of steam and talc.

"How ya' doin' this morning?" he asked Sharon, who was folding the blankets that made up her bed.

"Great!" she said, then looked at the clock. "But it's late! Let me start breakfast—you must be starving."

Papa walked unevenly to his easy chair and sat down. "Well, I thought I'd let you sleep in a bit," he sighed, catching his breath. "I figured you'd be tired after workin' all night."

There was no way Papa would let us give his place the kind of cleaning it needed. He couldn't stand to see us to do housework for him, and he was jealous of anything that took away time we could be spending together.

Broaching the subject wouldn't be easy either. He'd always been so proud of his home. No matter how we phrased it, he was going to be offended that we thought his apartment wasn't clean. But it wasn't. He couldn't see the dirt. He couldn't smell bathroom odors. And he was physically unable to get in and clean where needed.

So, it was with some trepidation that we lined up a cleaning service to do a major overhaul. As we expected, Papa was steamed. "I don't want to spend our time and money cleaning house," he insisted. "It's fine like it is."

We could see the wheels spinning behind his piercing eyes. He did not like this. Besides the insult to his housekeeping, the thought of upheaval and having strangers delve into the nooks and crannies of his home upset him.

"Papa, this needs to be done while we're here to oversee it," Sharon insisted. "Aunt Marie has to work so it's a help to her if we do it." It was borderline manipulation, but we were willing to use every method of persuasion possible.

"Papa, you don't have to worry about anything," I assured him. "None of us will lift a finger. A crew will come in and be out in a day. No problem."

He drew his mouth into a straight line, fuming silently for a few moments, then said, "Well, go ahead. You girls go and do whatever you want to do."

We hugged and kissed him like children who'd been promised a trip to Disneyland and assured him he would be delighted with the end result. The plan was for Sharon to start walking Papa to the car before the cleaners came. I wanted to give them instructions away from Papa's watchful eyes and big ears that had suddenly become extraordinarily keen.

But the cleaners came early. And Papa wasn't about to leave before giving everybody and everything the once-over.

"Besides a general cleaning, the walls need to be scrubbed thoroughly—especially in the kitchen," I told the strong looking middle-aged woman in charge. I showed her the layers of grease on the walls and above his stove and cook top. "The burners. The oven. The cabinets. It all needs to be gone over."

They were also to strip and wax the floors. Shampoo the carpet. Disinfect the bathroom. As we closed the door behind us, we thought we were set. But Papa said, "There not gonna do the walls are they?"

"Yes, they're going to do everything," I said.

He turned around 180 degrees and said, "Excuse me. I'll join you in just a minute—I forgot my hat."

He went back into the apartment and came back a few moments later, hat in hand. Sharon and I looked at each other.

"You two go ahead," I said. "I think I'll make a quick trip to the bathroom before we take off." My sister, taking Papa firmly by the arm, continued toward the elevator. When I returned to the apartment, the crew was already busy at work.

"Before we go, I want to make sure you don't have any questions about what we want done," I said smiling brightly.

"Yes, ma'am," said the woman in charge. She showed me her worksheet notes. "Got it all here."

"Including the walls?"

A puzzled look crossed her face. "The walls? Your granddaddy just told us not to bother with the walls."

Just as we suspected. I couldn't think of a single reason why Papa wouldn't want the walls washed—unless he was worried the solvents might wear down the paint he'd so carefully preserved over the years.

We were stumped about how his apartment had gotten so dirty in the first place. What in Papa's lifestyle had changed in the past six months to account for grease buildup on every inch of the floor and walls? Whatever the cause, a thorough scrubbing was called for.

I caught up with Sharon and Papa in the parking lot. Sharon pulled an envelope from her purse that held a check from one of our cousins. "Papa, Linda sent money to buy a new bedspread and throw covers for your chair and sofa. What do you say we do a little shopping?"

"Might as well," he said dryly, "can't go home." So we headed to Sike's.

Right away Papa spied a western-style dark turquoise and black bedspread. The matching soft blankets would serve well as throw covers on his flowered chair and sofa, too. The purchases lifted Papa's spirits so he was in a good mood by the time we hit Piccadilly for lunch.

I was surprised when he ordered a fried salmon patty instead of his usual chicken fried steak. "Papa, I don't think I've ever seen you order fish in a restaurant before," I remarked.

"Well, I don't much like fish. But when I started having all this trouble, the doctor said to cut out the beef and eat more fish. And I've been doin' what he says. I've even been frying up some of that frozen fish at home, and it's not too bad. Either that or I'm gettin' use to it."

We didn't have the heart to tell him that deep-fried anything wouldn't be on any doctor's approved diet. Later, when we passed this news along to Aunt Marie she said, "Well, I've been wondering what he's been cooking to go through the Crisco oil the way he does. Every time he gives me a shopping list, he's got oil on it. I've been asking him what he was using it for, and he says, 'just for cookin'.' "

Papa had been using one large bottle a week to fry first his sausage, then his fish. No wonder every surface of his home was covered in grease.

With that mystery solved, we returned to his apartment late that afternoon anticipating the fresh scent of cleanliness. Instead, a man cleaning the floor greeted us. "I was just getting started," he informed us as we crowded into the entry.

"I thought they said it was okay to come back after 4:00…"

"We thought we'd be finished by then," he said, "but the crew boss had to leave early. We were short people, so it took longer."

They took a few shortcuts as well, I noted. I checked out the kitchen. The appliances. The floors. They'd been wiped down, but not cleaned. The grease and deep level grime remained. I called the company and explained the situation.

"We'll get another full crew out there tomorrow," they assured me, and, true to their word, they did. But the job ended up being a lot more involved that any of us anticipated.

The upshot was, the cleaning, which we had promised Papa would be over in one quick day, took three days. We became like birds with no place to land from 10:00 A.M. to 4:00 P.M. every day. We hovered over Sike's Mall. Restaurants. Coffee shops. I was sure Papa wanted to tan our hides, but instead he teased us about dragging a ninety-one-year-old man all over town for days on end.

"That spring cleanin' is a big job," he conceded.

I agreed. By now I had accepted that few things respond to a quick fix.

Sing-along

The fourth day of my visit, Sharon, Papa, and I headed down to the rec hall to watch the boys play pool. We took a few minutes to greet everyone in the foyer. Patsy, flushed from working in the garden, wheeled over offering a smile. Ida pursed her lips in a quick hello. Deets stood up to greet us. The skin peeling off his freckled nose told me he'd spent some time out in the sun. "Good to see you again," he said, shaking my hand firmly.

Mr. King came from the office. "Well, hello there, Alva! Still hanging out with the pretty ladies?" he teased.

"One of the advantages of bein' related," Papa retorted. "Don't know how someone like me got such great lookin' granddaughters."

"We were just wonderin' the same thing," said Deets.

I laughed, amazed at how sharp and witty so many of the people here were. But Mr. King had something specific on his mind. "Speaking of pretty ladies, are y'all up to puttin' on a sing-along for us tonight?" he asked Sharon and me. It had been a standing invitation since Papa's birthday party.

By now the residents knew us well. We knew them not only by name, but also by illness, personal tragedy, and little quirks. There was only one real problem in the group. It had to do with Boone and a woman named Shirley: they disliked each other intensely.

Shirley loved to play the piano but nearly drove everybody crazy playing all hours of the day and night. Boone's apartment was located directly across the hallway from the rec room, so he heard more than most. And he missed no opportunity to express his disdain.

That day, as Sharon and I walked arm in arm with Papa toward the rec hall, the staccato of piano trills warned us that Shirley was on the bench.

"Boone isn't gonna like that," Papa commented. "He hates her playin' any time—but especially when we is playin' pool."

We greeted the group seated around the donut and coffee table and nodded at Shirley who beamed at having an expanded audience. The boys waited at the back while Papa retrieved his stick from the closet.

We got hugs from Boone and Walter. Virgil turned beet red and busied himself racking balls so he wouldn't be drawn into the festivities. Shirley finished her song then ran toward me with music in tow. Boone saw her, curled his lip, and shook his fist at her. She threw him a haughty look but took my hand, ignoring him.

"Come here," she said, pulling me toward the piano. "I was wondering if you could show me how to play this?" She held out the sheet music.

"I'd rather not play while the boys are playing pool," I said.

"They're always playin'," she sniffed. "If it was up to them, nobody'd get to do nothin' in here. They think they own the place. I think they just don't like no women around."

There was some truth to that. There was one woman—a mouthy, gnarly chain- smoker who knew her way around a pool hall—who pushed the point. She hung around the back, smoking and hacking nonstop, hoping to get in a game. The boys let her play a few times when someone had to leave early, but most times they ignored her. She could beat them, and that didn't go over too well. Though even if she hadn't, it wouldn't have made a difference. They were never going to let her be one of the boys.

Later, when due to illnesses the boys had trouble keeping their group going, I wondered if they wished they'd been a little more flexible in their criteria, but I doubt it. She stopped coming around once the government passed a law forbidding smoking in public areas. The law pretty much broke up the socializing in the rec room, too. Donuts and coffee alone weren't enough to keep the fabric of the community together.

But that morning, Boone's scowls sent Shirley home, and the boys enjoyed their games without piano accompaniment. Afterwards, Papa, Sharon, and I lunched at Piccadilly then returned to the rec hall to prepare for the sing-along.

No sooner had we started practicing when Boone appeared.

My first thought was, Oh no, he's upset about the piano! But he surprised us. "Y'all mind if I sing with you some?" he asked. We welcomed him, and for the next thirty minutes he sang every song he could think of. He was amazingly mellow. If he didn't know the words, he'd smile sweetly at us, then close his eyes and rock with the music.

Papa didn't sing at all. He just sat quietly in a big padded chair looking at Boone with narrowed eyes.

Boone was on a roll. "How 'bout 'The Battle Hymn of the Republic'? Can you play that one?" he asked.

As I began to play, Boone planted his feet, threw back his head and from memory sang every verse with the gusto and drama of an opera star. Afterwards he patted Sharon and me on the shoulders. "I thank you, girls. I really enjoyed that, and I'll look forward to seeing you tonight for sure." With that he turned on his heel and left just as abruptly as he appeared.

We gathered up our things, feeling pretty good about making Boone's day. Back in the apartment, I commented on Boone's enthusiasm. "Papa, I had no idea Boone loved music so much."

"Boone's always liked singing," he said.

"Yeah, but I don't think I've ever seen him so happy."

Papa shook his head. "He wasn't happy. He was drunk!" he informed me.

Sharon and I looked at each other. "Drunk?"

We were so naive it was pathetic, but it made sense. Boone had been so much warmer than usual. Outgoing. Friendly. His behavior certainly had not been typical "Boone."

"He'll be drinking the rest of the afternoon now," Papa said. "Once he gets started that's it."

That burst our bubble, but we were hopeful the night's music would speak to him.

"Boone's not goin' nowheres tonight," Papa said, and he was right.

Boone didn't make it, but the rest of Midtown Manor turned out in force. Fifteen minutes before start time every seat was filled, with many standing along the back and side aisles. The kitchen door opening to the rec room revealed carts laden with bowls of ice cream ready to roll the moment the singing ended. Coffee brewed in two, thirty-cup percolators, and a festive spirit electrified the whole place. You would've thought Elvis was coming.

Sharon and I distributed the Methodist and Baptist hymnals and took requests from both. A bit of diplomacy was required to keep various denominational factions happy. Thankfully, a few songs overlapped. "In the

Garden." "How Great Thou Art." But on the whole, the Methodists tended toward the great hymns of the church, while the Baptists and Pentecostals wanted the old gospel songs. Most of the residents were pretty tolerant as long as their favorite was in the mix somewhere.

Something sweet always happened as we sang these songs. Music has a way of attaching itself to the important events of our lives so that even a phrase of a melody can flood the mind with memories.

I can never hear "Precious Memories" or "Zion's Hill" without thinking of my grandmother and granddad Westbrook. I see them standing stiffly, side by side, in formal contrast to the easy Texas twang of their voices.

"Standing on the Promises" makes me think of my mother. Shortly before she died, I came home and heard her playing that song on the piano. I was surprised because, at the time, she was seldom out of bed. I wondered why that particular song had drawn her. It had a clunky tune, wasn't likely to be considered good music by anyone's standards, and she had never mentioned it as a favorite.

Knowing she was shy about playing in front of anyone, I entered the room softly. At the piano, wearing her white quilted robe, she looked like an angel. I closed my eyes and listened as she sang in a weak voice:

Standing on the promises I cannot fall,
Listening every moment to the Spirit's call,
Resting in my Savior, as my all in all,
Standing on the promises of God
Standing…Standing…Standing on the promises of God my Savior…
Standing…Standing…I'm standing on the promises of God.

Then she saw me and stopped, embarrassed. She said, "I always thought this was a nothing-kind-of song, but now I understand why it would mean something to someone."

This song was important to my mother's journey. But not until I became a wife and mother myself did I fully appreciate it as an expression of her faith. It couldn't have been easy to accept that her time was up before the age of forty. *What must it have been like to release a husband and children into a world without her care?* I wondered. In the end she was content to stand on the promises of God—for herself and for us.

As I heard this song sung by the dear people of Midtown Manor, I was deeply moved. And there were many such songs. Each with a memory and a story. Each a call to faith and hope.

When the sing-along ended, we lingered to enjoy melted ice cream, hot coffee, and each other's company. No one seemed surprised to find that God had given comfort and strength to us through these songs and the promises they celebrated.

Flowers of the Grass

Several weeks after returning home, Papa called to give me the news: "Mr. King has cancer," he said.

"Will he keep working?" I asked.

"No. He's already gone. Left the first of the month."

His leaving was a serious blow to the heart and soul of Midtown Manor. The loss hit Papa hard. Sensing it, my sister went to see him the following week. As the elevator made the slow climb to the sixth floor, Sharon rubbed her hand lightly up and down Papa's back.

"How you doing, Papa?" she asked.

"Not so good."

"No? Why, what's the matter?"

He shrugged his shoulders. "Just old age."

"Well, when did that happen?" she teased, but Papa wasn't game.

"Don't know. It's been comin' on a long time. Guess it's about time I check outta this place anyway. Way things are goin' it won't be too long."

It took some coaxing to get to the bottom of it, but Sharon learned that the doctor had found a lump in Papa's throat during his last exam. Papa refused treatment.

"At my age, there just ain't no point. I don't know if it's somethin' bad or not but I'm not interested in having any more surgery."

We agreed with my aunt, who felt this was Papa's choice to make. After a while the lump went away, so it didn't matter; the real concern was my grandfather's depression.

Papa depended on his faith to keep going. He went to church with my aunt when he was able, but electronic music wreaked havoc with his hearing aid. He didn't know the songs or the people, so he gained little from the services. His failing eyesight made it hard to read his Bible, and though he had stored a wealth of scripture to memory, the effort of retrieving it exhausted him. And he couldn't pray for extended times like he used to.

"I can't even concentrate enough to remember all the kids' names any more," he said sadly. "I don't know why the Lord just don't take me."

When we were with him, we read the Bible to him and tried to engage him in discussions of spiritual things. But that, too, was becoming difficult. His throat seemed constantly irritated. When he tried to talk or pray out loud, he was racked by coughing spasms.

After several tries, he'd shake his head and wave us off with the back of his hand. That was it for him. Frustrating. Everyday life was becoming more and more frustrating. The only things he looked forward to were visits with family, eating out, and playing pool with the boys. It was pool that got Papa out twice a day. Other than that, he sat in his big blue easy chair, alone.

Sharon called me from Papa's apartment one morning while he was dressing. "We're going down to play pool in just a minute so I don't have long," she said, "but I wanted to let you know how Papa is doing."

She said he was depressed but fighting it. "He's really slowed down," she said. "I don't know how someone can move so slow and still stay upright; but if he can go at his own pace, he does okay. His stamina's pretty good considering."

The previous morning, they had played pool for over two hours with Walter and Boone.

"Virgil played with us the first day I came, but I think I scared him off," she said. "After we'd finished playing, I went over to him and gave him a hug. He got real still, and I saw he had tears in his eyes. So I patted his arm, and all of a sudden he ran from the room like a bat out of hell. I didn't know what got into him."

"That's the last you'll see of Virgil for a few days," Papa predicted. Sharon said every time she walked into the room, Virgil would turn all red and bolt.

"Don't pay him no mind," Papa said. "He just has a hard time bein' around women." Someone told Papa that Virgil married once but came home one day to find his house deserted. His bride ran off and left no forwarding address. Virgil never got over it.

Poor guy, I thought. Getting old was a tough journey for anyone; I couldn't imagine doing it alone. But having felt the rejection of my children, I could understand how that pain could cause someone to opt out of life. There were many times I wished I could run away and turn my back on my kids, but I couldn't.

As I looked at my children, I grieved for what I saw. It seemed like only yesterday all it took to make their eyes shine was a pile of blankets made into a fort on a rainy day. Today, their eyes were heavy-lidded. Blurred by pot and whatever else they were taking.

Though I had confronted them numerous times with my suspicions of drug use, they double-teamed me, telling me I was crazy. Paranoid.

"Everything would be okay if you'd just let it go," they insisted.

Without proof, Joe and I were reluctant to pursue it. But the look in their eyes, the smell on their clothes, their hostility toward us, the changes in their behavior, all made me uneasy. David had dropped out of his band. Mike, who'd been very interested in sports, did little but sleep then fight me to stay out all night.

Still, I hadn't caught them in the act, so I began to wonder if they were right. Maybe my fear was projecting all this onto them. Maybe it was my problem. I didn't know what to do, so I asked God to show me the truth. If I was wrong—and I hoped I was—then I had a lot of personal work to do. But if I wasn't, then my boys needed serious help.

Soon after, in April of 1995, I had a dream about Michael. In the dream, I had left Mike home with a friend, and when I returned, he'd destroyed the walls in his room. He'd pulled off the wallboard in places. Gouged and stripped it in others. He'd painted graffiti everywhere until the room was defaced from one end to the other.

I awoke angry and disturbed, but before I could clear my head, the thought came to my mind: *This is a warning.*

I'm a prolific dreamer, and my family respects that important things are sometimes revealed to me through dreams. I once dreamed of a company transfer weeks before it came to pass. After that, Joe was a believer. But usually my dreams don't foretell events so much as help me sort out feelings and give perspective to issues with which I'm dealing. I don't make decisions based on my dreams alone, but I do pay attention to them.

In the Bible God used dreams to communicate with people, so I leave myself open to that possibility. It's not hard for me to believe that, because of my stubbornness, God's best chance of getting through to me is when I'm asleep. When I have dreams, I record them, tuck them away, and see if they confirm something else going on in my life.

I knew this dream was significant because its details and power haunted me long after I was awake. Knowing that other people in your dreams are most often representations of parts of yourself, I grappled with whether or not the dream was about Michael or me. But my first thought—that the dream was a warning for Michael—kept flashing in my mind like a neon sign.

Mike got up late that morning. I found him in the kitchen staring inside the refrigerator.

"Would you like me to fix breakfast?" I asked.

"No," he said rubbing his stomach. "My stomach's all upset."

It usually was. I came up beside him, and gently rubbed his bony back through his T-shirt.

"I don't know what's wrong with me," he said. "I feel like I'm starving to death, but when I try to eat, I feel sick. My whole body clock is off."

I could think of a few contributing factors for that, but I decided to keep my mouth shut.

"Mike, I had a dream about you last night," I said.

He froze and turned to look at me. "Yeah? What was it?"

As I relayed the dream to him, I could see the wheels turning.

"Think it means something?" he asked.

"Yes, hon, I do. I think it's a warning."

"About what?"

"You. It may be picture of what you're doing to yourself. If the walls in the room are you, then the defacing of the room could be the self-destructive things you're doing. I don't know for sure, but that's my gut feeling about it."

His eyes pierced mine in rapt attention.

"I have an opinion about it if you want to hear it," I continued.

He nodded yes.

"Until now, you've had a covering that's been yours because, as a family, we're under God's umbrella. But if God sees you're determined to go your own way, at some point He'll let you." Tears filled my eyes as I looked into his. "Mike, I'm afraid you're tearing down your protection."

Mike looked down and took a deep breath. "I know, Mom," he said quietly.

"Honey, will you promise me you'll think about this? I believe you're in danger, but it's not too late. You can make different choices starting today if you want to."

He smiled weakly at me and uttered his standard response: "Hmmm." Neither yes or no, just, "I heard you."

I gave him a hug. He bent down and held me tight. There was a tender moment of connection then he walked away.

Homesick

It had been a difficult evening. I paced the floor of my bedroom trying to calm down, but I was so angry my ears were ringing. Mike's door slammed. A moment later, Joe came into the bedroom.

"I can't get through to him," he said. He sat on the bed, shoulders slumped, and wiped his eyes. Seeing my tall, strong husband reduced to tears broke me, and I sat beside him, crying too.

"Karen, would you lock the door?" he asked.

I knew what he wanted: a few moments peace before calling it a night. A few moments without confrontation. Without hostility. Without being slapped in the face by the reality that your kids are in trouble.

Fifteen minutes earlier, Mike had come home from work completely inebriated. Cited with a DUI in May, he'd worked off hundreds of dollars in fines and hours of community service. We'd allowed him to drive our car to work and back only after his solemn promise there would be no more drinking and driving. So much for promises.

I was beginning to regret what I'd asked: that God would reveal the truth about what was going on with our boys. When Mike was arrested for the DUI, he'd spent the night in jail. It shook him up. We hoped the experience would be his wake-up call, but it obviously hadn't been much of a deterrent.

It upset David enough that he admitted his own share of pot smoking and drinking. It wasn't good news, but at least we knew what we were dealing with. The boys still claimed I was overreacting. "We're just doing what every one else is!" they insisted.

Joe and I agreed on the boundaries for our home, but it all fell apart when it came to handling infractions. Our "good guy/bad guy" routine was hard to leave behind. In the past, I would lower the boom and Joe would offer a way out as a means to get the boys' cooperation. But with counseling, our approach became unified.

We tried everything we could imagine. Restriction. Rewards. More family time. More one-on-one time. But the kids just became more hostile. With sinking hearts, we realized it didn't matter what we did. They weren't responding.

It was ironic. Now that I was in touch with my emotions, the love I felt for my children flowed through me at depths I never dreamed possible. But realizing that now this love wasn't reaching them grieved me to the core. The fact was, our kids were out of control, and we simply didn't know what to do.

One hot night in July, it all came to a head. We told Mike if he continued to flaunt the rules of our house, he would have to leave. He was only seventeen, but his behavior was escalating and David was following his example. That night Michael said, "If you kick me out, I'm taking David with me."

Joe and I were torn between wanting to save both kids and fearing we had already lost Michael. Michael's friends picked him up, and after they left, we realized David had gone, too.

"They've got to come back because they didn't take anything with them. We have to get David out then," Joe insisted. I nodded as he continued. "And you need to call your sister to see if you and David can come for a while."

I didn't think it necessary for me to go once Mike moved out, but Joe disagreed.

"No," he insisted. "You both need to go. There could be an ugly scene when Mike leaves, and it may not be safe for you."

There *was* cause for concern. We'd found a gun under Michael's bed several months before. Though we took it, we had no doubt about Mike's resourcefulness in finding another one. For some time, Joe and I had slept with our bedroom door locked—just in case.

One day we realized we were prisoners in our own home, being held hostage by our own children. It was that revelation that finally gave us the courage to act.

Sharon agreed to take David, but suggested I not come. "Why don't you go to Papa's instead? I think my family will be good for David, but if you're here, all we'll do is battle the dynamic the two of you have going."

Though disappointed I wouldn't have Sharon's daily support, I felt her wisdom was God-sent. Dealing with the boys sapped every ounce of energy I had. There was nothing left to focus toward a long-term plan.

I finalized travel plans that night. The boys returned home shortly before dawn. Several hours later, we woke up David—or tried to. He was foggy and disoriented. Later he told us he was so high on acid he couldn't even hear the words we were speaking. But we roused him, and while Michael slept, Joe, David, and I drove to Atlanta's Hartsfield airport.

With an hour before flight time, we decided to grab lunch before boarding the plane. I sat on one side of a small table. Joe and David on the other. David was scowling, threatening not to get on the plane unless we promised he was coming back. "Yes, David. I promise." Joe said. "You will be coming back home."

"Mom, what about you?" Dave asked. "Do you promise I'm coming back after I go to Aunt Sharon's?"

"David," I said wearily, "At some point you will come home, but I can't tell you exactly when."

I looked at Joe. The "golly Ollie" look on his face seemed out of place. I kept staring at him, trying to figure out what was wrong. Suddenly his mouth twisted and his face crumbled as he lost control. When he cried, we all lost it. I burst into deep, silent sobs. David's sunglasses hid his eyes, but tears rolled down his cheeks.

He hardly spoke except to say that if we kicked Mike out, Mike would kill himself drinking. We had agonized over that same possibility but explained Mike wouldn't allow us to help. "He's in trouble either way," was all we could say.

Somehow, Dave and I got on the plane and ended up in Texas. David caught a commuter flight to Tyler, just outside Lindale. I went on to Wichita Falls. I hadn't told Papa I was coming; he'd have insisted I stay with him, and I just couldn't. Having a general idea of what was going on was a lot different from hearing Joe and me hash out the ugly details. I didn't think it would be fair to him. Also, with my nerves shot, I needed solitude.

I set up camp in the Holiday Inn then hurried over to Midtown to catch Papa before he started supper. Deets and Betty were the only ones in the lobby. Betty looked up from her polishing long enough to nod, then continued to buff her way down the hall. Deets smiled as I walked over.

"Hi there, Deets." I could see he was struggling to place me. "I'm Karen Moderow, Mr. Choate's granddaughter."

He shook my hand. "Well, I thought that was you, but your grampa didn't say nothin' about your coming."

"That's because he doesn't know it yet. I thought I would surprise him," I said, trying to sound cheerful.

"Well, that'll sure be a fine surprise. He's right down the hall." Deets nodded toward the rec room. "Just saw him and the others a few minutes ago playin' pool."

Papa did a double take as I walked into the room. He ran as best he could to embrace me. "Hon, what are you doin' here?" he asked, steering me away from the boys.

"We've got some problems with Mike and Dave, and I came here to figure out what to do."

Papa's eyes were alert and piercing. "Let me put up my stick and we'll go upstairs," he said.

"No. I'd rather you finish your game. I'd like to get a cup of coffee, sit down, and watch you play some. Then I'll tell you about everything else later, if that's okay."

"Sure. That'd be fine," he said, putting his arm around me. He pulled around one of the big soft chairs for me to sit in. "We'll just tell the boys you came to visit for a spell," he whispered in my ear. "They don't need to know nothin' more than that."

I smiled thinking of Papa looking out for my reputation. If only he knew. I was past caring what anybody thought about my family or me. My only concern was getting my kids back on track.

Time Out

Papa was disappointed I wasn't staying with him, but he didn't pressure me. I called him around noon the next day.

"Hey, Papa, did you win this morning?" I asked. Papa's hearing aid screeched into the phone. He fumbled around a bit then answered, "I'm sorry, hon, I didn't hear you."

I repeated the question.

"I didn't play this morning," he finally responded.

"No? Why not?"

"Well, I didn't sleep too well last night, so I just wasn't up to goin' down."

Probably worrying about me. Or else he wanted to be sure he didn't miss my phone call. Just in case, I decided just to meet him downstairs from then on. Then he could keep to his routine and save us both the ordeal of a phone call.

"Do you feel okay to go to lunch?" I asked.

"Yeah. Sure. I'm always up for good food. How about Pat's? We could go there."

"Pat's? I thought they closed down."

"They did but they opened back up again. They're just a few blocks down from where they used to be."

"Well, that's good news. Let's do it then!"

"Okay!" Papa's voice carried excitement. "Won't take me but a minute to get downstairs," he assured me. True to his word, he was waiting at the back door as I drove up.

Papa looked small and frail as he pushed on the heavy door. Tears sprang to my eyes just seeing him. I hadn't realized until now how hard being in a hostile environment had been on me. Papa's touch. His kind words. The acceptance I saw in his eyes. They were balm to my spirit. His eyes lit up when he saw me, and I jumped out of the car to hug him.

"I see you got a bigger car this time," he noted, giving my full-size Buick the once-over. I had gotten grief last time for driving a compact. "Those things ain't nothin' but a tin can on wheels," he said. Economy cars were a tough sell to someone who'd driven a Chevy truck all his life.

We buckled up and pulled out onto Burnett Street. "Look over there!" he said gesturing with the back of his hand to the property across from Midtown Manor.

The bulldozers and construction crews were busy building the new convention center. The old tenements were gone. I'd been so distracted the previous day I hadn't even noticed. What a difference it made. You could tell the center was going to be spacious. Big. Texas style.

"They're really cleanin' things up around here," Papa said. "Guess they figured nobody was gonna come if it wasn't safe. They've got more patrol cars around. Luby's even hired their own security man. For a while they was robbin' all the old people there, so it got to where none of us wanted to go. But it's okay now."

And Pat's new place, now located on Scott and Fourth, was better than ever. They fussed over Papa while cleaning off his table.

"Mr. Choate, what are you doin' here on a Thursday?" Christie asked.

"Got my own transportation today!" Papa said proudly.

Since Pat's was too far to walk, Midtown Manor bussed residents over for lunch once a week. It wasn't often enough to suit Papa but it was better than nothing. He was still a regular.

"Let me take your granddaughter's order, Mr. Choate," Christie said pulling out her pad. "Your burger's already on the grill." Papa shook his head in approval like some mafia don sure of his domain. He was one happy guy.

I smiled at Papa, amazed at how just being someplace you are welcomed could lift your spirits.

Before I knew it, two weeks had flown by. When I first got to Texas, all I wanted to do was sleep. Part of it was just catching up on my rest, but depression was also knocking at the door.

From experience I knew it signaled the need for me to connect with my emotions. For months I'd not allowed myself to feel anything but anger. Now I needed time to grieve.

In my hotel room, I came to God pouring out everything I felt without censure. Fears. Questions. Fury. Heartache. It jumbled out in torrents. I prayed for solutions but was drawn to Psalms 131, which seemed to have nothing to do with anything.

Surely I have calmed and quieted my soul,
Like a weaned child with his mother;
Like a weaned child is my soul within me.
…hope in the LORD From this time forth and forever.

What kind of an answer is that? I wondered. I was desperate for concrete direction, and instead God was saying, "Shhh. Settle down. Don't worry. I'm here."

While I understood the importance of expressing my emotions, the possibility that I didn't have to live in that despair encouraged me. I found it interesting that the verse didn't say God would calm and quiet my spirit. It was something I was to do. "Surely I have calmed and quieted my soul," it read. Based on my choice to hope in God, peace was available.

I took this passage to heart then went about doing what needed to be done. Without the cloud of panic, I was able to think more clearly. Early mornings I set aside for time with God. Mid-mornings found me on the phone, researching schools and facilities for David and talking to anyone I felt could give us information or perspective. To relieve some of the tension, I added a swim or a workout in the hotel gym to my daily routine, usually in the evenings. The afternoons belonged to Papa.

After a game with the boys, Papa and I always ate supper together. The discipline helped keep me together. Also, Papa gave me something outside of myself on which to focus. He was the perfect companion. He was present. Willing to listen. Willing to let me engage or not as I needed.

"Did ya get your phone calls made this mornin'?" Papa asked when I picked him up one afternoon.

"Some. The good private schools don't want David if he's in trouble, and I'm not too impressed with what's left. We want him with us, but so far he's saying he's not willing to go to a different school or make different friends. Unless that changes, we're looking at sending him away to a therapeutic high school."

My voice sounded detached. Distant. I was in my "business" mode. The persona I used to gather facts. Make decisions. Get things done. I processed the emotions when I was alone.

"Joe got one lead I followed up on last night," I continued.

"In Georgia?"

"No, unfortunately. It's in California." The thought of David being so far away sent a wave of nausea through me, but the program looked solid. Unlike most the places we had researched, Cascade had a strong academic component. Also, it wasn't based on a twelve-step program; it focused on examining core issues that led a child to use drugs and alcohol in the first place. It was peer-based, an approach that, for kids, seemed to make a lot of sense.

I spoke with a man whose daughter had graduated from Cascade. Two years later she was not only drug-free but thriving, excelling in college, and excited about life. That in itself spoke wonders. In talking with other parents, we realized many programs gave kids a fresh start but didn't last long enough to integrate significant change. The majority drifted back into their previous lifestyles within weeks of leaving. This school had a high success rate.

But after the bad experience with Mike's boarding school, I was paranoid about sending David away. Sharon said he was doing well with her. He worked every day with his Uncle Ray and loved it. Detoxed from drugs and alcohol, doing hard physical work, and being in a healthy, structured family environment was doing wonders for him. Maybe we could build on these changes. *God I hope so,* I prayed. I wasn't ready for an empty nest yet. There was so much I longed to give David and Michael if only…if only.

I often felt physically ill as I went through the motions of discerning a "next step." Interspersed were waves of soul-searching and remorse. I was reading through the book of Isaiah and identified with God's people who were reaping the consequences of choices they'd made.

Amazingly, I felt no condemnation from God. Not that I was without sin. But the process God had taken me through the past several years was paying off. As they had been revealed to me, I owned up to my sin and failings as a wife and mother. I had a long way to go, but the changes the Holy Spirit had been working in my life were real. I knew I was forgiven. But that didn't change the reality of consequences. What I needed now was God's mercy in spite of all I'd done wrong.

Joe and I, wanting to put ourselves in a place where God could speak to us, agreed to read the same chapter in Isaiah each day. Isaiah 55:6-9 came alive for both of us.

Seek the Lord while He may be found,
Call upon Him while He is near.
Let the wicked forsake his way,
And the unrighteous man his thoughts;
Let him return to the LORD,
And He will have mercy on him;
And to our God,
For He will abundantly pardon.
"For My thoughts are not your thoughts,
Nor are your ways My ways" says the LORD.
"For as the heavens are higher than the earth,
So are My ways higher than your ways,
And My thoughts than your thoughts."

We accepted that the solution for Michael and David could be hard—and contrary to what we wanted for them—but we determined to follow through on whatever we believed God led us to do. With Joe in Georgia and me in Texas, agreeing on a course of action was difficult. We didn't experience the same things at the same time. We couldn't hold each other. Communication was cumbersome.

Finding peace about our boys required constant vigilance. Our lives were a slap of reality followed by a returning to God's promises over and over again. It was harder for Joe who had little time to process. He was trying to keep it together while working every day. Dazed and broken, he continued to reach out for Mike.

"We had dinner together last night," he told me on the phone.

"How is he?" I asked, my heart in my throat. I was afraid for Mike; he'd already had two close calls with alcohol poisoning. He was a full-blown alcoholic also using a variety of drugs.

When I thought about all the extremes mothers go through to assure healthy children—diet, breastfeeding, homemade baby foods, nutritious meals—it seemed unfair that it could all be undone by a child's free will. What was it all for if, in the end, you couldn't protect a child from himself? My feelings for Michael vacillated between anger and love—a love so desperate I felt it could kill me.

"Did he seem okay?" I asked.

"Sad. Strung out. But trying."

We were grateful Mike was keeping the door open. As Joe predicted, his departure from our home two weeks earlier had been violent. Unaware David and I had flown to Texas that morning, Michael began swearing, yelling obscenities, and throwing things as he packed. But when he learned I wasn't home, he said, "Sorry, Dad. That was for Mom's benefit." After that, he moved out quietly.

I wondered how that little dynamic would fare in family therapy. I cried a long time after hearing it. All I knew was I loved my son. What everything else meant, how it was all playing out, I didn't know.

Joe arranged for Mike to rent a room from a woman we knew. We agreed to pay room and board as long as he stayed in school. Until he was eighteen, we felt obligated to put a roof over his head; other than that, he was on his own.

Once Mike left, we felt a terrible sense of loss and powerlessness. We tried to tell ourselves we weren't giving up. Just letting go. But it ripped us apart. As for David—we'd been waiting, hoping his time with Sharon would pave the way for his coming home. But time was running out.

"Joe, we need to get together—you, David, and I," I finally concluded. "School starts next week, and I don't think we'll be able to make any decisions until we see how David responds to us face to face."

We decided Joe and I would go to Sharon's where we would have a neutral meeting place and good prayer support.

I told Papa at lunch. He struggled to open a little yellow pack of butter then passed it to me. "Hon, could you open that for me?" he asked. "I just about can't open anything with my thumb like it is." His right thumb, frozen with arthritis, was now useless. I pulled the foil lid off the butter and handed it back. He began buttering a crispy piece of cornbread.

I took a deep breath knowing I couldn't put it off any longer. "I talked to Joe this morning, and he's flying in to Tyler this weekend," I began.

A little tremor went through him but he continued buttering his bread.

"Papa, I have to leave for Sharon's tomorrow."

He looked up at me with sad resignation. "I guess I knew you'd have to go sometime."

I reached across the table for his hand and rubbed his swollen knuckles. "These three weeks have been a lifesaver for me, Papa. I'm sorry I've been such a wreck, but if I hadn't had you to come to, I don't know what I would've done."

He sighed and covered my hand with his own. "Sorry there weren't much I could do to change things, but it's sure been good for Papa having you here." We sat there for a long time, saying nothing.

Taking the Bull by the Horns

Papa accidentally killed a buffalo once and learned a valuable lesson. "You neck- rope a buffalo, you'll kill him," he said. "Their wind pipe collapses. You gotta rope 'em by the horns or by the foot. I learned that the hard way."

One day this guy called me and said, "Alva, you wanna buy some buffalo? There's nine of them. Range delivery."

Range delivery meant you buy 'em then you round 'em up yourself. That can be hard work, so I said, "Maybe. What will you give 'em to me for?"

The guy says, "Five hundred for all nine of them."

"Okay." I said. "I'll go get 'em."

But we had a hard time gettin' the buffalo in the truck. I penned all of them but a little bull. It jumped out of the corral, crossed the lake, and went back to the river. He was in the bush where he was hard to get at. When you're on a horse, a buffalo will turn on you. It can kill a horse right quick with those little ol' horns—they're sharp.

There were three of us workin' him, and we finally got him out of the brush and out in the field. One guy neck-roped him, another one roped his horns, and I got his back feet. Then the boy that had the rope on the bull's neck began to drag him and killed him. He didn't know it would kill him. I didn't either, then—I found that out.

This story left me with a graphic picture of our struggle with David. We had to do something to rein him in, but we didn't want to hurt him in the process. Joe and I met with him at Sharon's and explained the options—all of which included a break with current friends and a change of school. His response was, "No way." We realized that unless there was true brokenness and a desire to change on his part, it wouldn't work at home anyway. That left the choice of last resort: the school in California.

When David realized we were serious about sending him away, he was suddenly very flexible. But as we had warned him, it was too late. We didn't trust promises made under the gun.

Cascade—located three hours north of Sacramento at the base of the Sierra Mountains—was a very long way from Lindale, Texas, we discovered. After traveling twelve hours during the night, Joe and I arrived at the school for a 9:00 A.M. meeting, emotionally and physically drained. But we were encouraged by what we saw.

The young men and women looked you straight in the eye. They seemed confident. Happy. More comfortable with themselves than most kids you meet. The setting was isolated but magnificent. We felt tremendous peace about what the school could offer our son.

We enrolled David, and the next day Joe flew to Atlanta. I returned to Tyler, planning to stay a few days with Sharon.

However, there was one more difficult decision to make. In the course of giving the school detailed family history, we were strongly advised to get help for Michael. "He sounds like such a great kid," the counselor said. "You can't just let him go."

"But what can we do?" we asked. "He's going to be eighteen in three weeks."

"That's long enough for a wilderness program—we can recommend a great one in Montana. You never know, it may be enough to take hold."

We knew Mike would never go voluntarily. Doing this meant hiring a professional escort to, in effect, kidnap our own son. We just didn't think we could do it. But as Joe and I talked, we concluded that, for once, we had to stand up and be parents. We didn't want Mike to say to us in five years,

"You cared enough about David to do something drastic. Why didn't you do it for me?"

Because Mike wasn't living at home, things were complicated. It was around 3:30 A.M. on Friday, August 18, 1995. Ollie, a huge former football player, came to our house with two companions, and Joe took the three of them to Mike's apartment. He knocked on the door.

"Who is it?" someone asked.

Joe identified himself praying the young man would let him in. Legally, they couldn't enter otherwise.

"Just a minute," they were told. There was the shuffle of things being moved about, and then the door cracked opened.

"Can I see Mike?" Joe asked. "I need to talk to him."

The door opened wider, and Joe and the escorts rushed into the apartment. Through the haze of pot smoke, Mike and his friends scrambled around trying to grasp what was happening. They weren't in any shape to put up a fight. As instructed, Joe identified Michael.

"We'll take it from here, Mr. Moderow," Ollie said.

Then with the sound of his son crying, "No, no. This can't be happening," Joe walked out the door.

What Joe did was incredibly courageous. For weeks afterward he'd break down and cry thinking about that night, but he was also confident it was the most loving thing he could've done for Michael.

As for David, he was going to be escorted to Cascade by his Uncle Ray. With the hostility between David and me, I didn't think either of us would survive a twelve-hour trip together.

I hoped to stay in Lindale until David left, but because the dynamic between us disrupted the whole household, I decided to return to Atlanta early.

The night before I left, David came to my room. He leaned against the doorframe but didn't enter. "I just want you to know I hate you," he said quietly. "To make me leave without talking to Mike or a single one of my friends is just mean, and I hate you for it."

I looked at my son. Tall. Still blond. So handsome. And thin like his brother. I wanted to hold him and tell him how much I loved him, but I knew he'd turn from me. With the pressure in my chest crushing me, I calmly told him, "I know you don't understand why right now, but this is the way it needs to be."

"Then I hate you," he said again.

"I know you do, Dave," I said and closed the door between us. His words were calculated to make me change my mind, but I had no doubt he expressed exactly what he felt. Short of reversing our decision, there wasn't one thing I could do about it.

We were both in a hard, hurting place, and I cried for both of us.

Everything I'd been through with the boys had been both humbling and humiliating. I felt rejected everywhere I went. The more I tried to do what was right, the worse things seemed to get. But this experience gave me a new appreciation for how God felt when I rejected him.

I thought about the choices I had made against what I knew was right. I made them anyway, all the while accusing God of trying to keep me from a full life. But I'd become aware of another facet of God's character: His mercy. Because of how I felt about my kids, I knew He'd be willing to help our family regardless of whose fault it was.

In spite of their rebellion and their rejection, I loved my children. I wanted to give Michael and David everything I had. My resources. My wisdom. My heart. But I could not. Some things they wouldn't accept and others would only harm them. I saw that the same was true of my relationship with God.

For the first time, I understood that His father-heart was always longing for me. That He was looking for ways to give me what I needed. Most of all, He wasn't asking if I was worthy of His compassion, love, and mercy. They were already mine simply because I belonged to Him.

My gratitude for His generosity stirred within me a love for God I hadn't experienced before. When my own words failed to adequately express my feelings toward Him—or my anguish over my situation—I turned to the Psalms. When I awoke during the night feeling afraid and so sad that I felt I could die, I read them out loud.

I will love You, O Lord, my strength.
The Lord is my rock and my fortress and my deliverer;
My God, my strength, in whom I will trust…
The pangs of death surrounded me,
And the floods of ungodliness made me afraid…
In my distress I called upon the Lord,
And cried out to my God;
He heard my voice from His temple,
and my cry came before Him, even to His ears…
As for God, His way is perfect;
The word of the Lord is proven;
He is a shield to all who trust in Him…
The Lord lives! Blessed be my Rock! Let the God of my salvation be exalted.

excerpts from Psalm 18

The pain didn't go away, but I received strength to endure it for that moment, and it was enough.

Both Michael and David were so angry with Joe and me that communication was out of the question except as monitored by their counselors. Most of what got through wasn't pleasant.

We were brokenhearted but took consolation in knowing that at least for a while, both our boys were safe.

Spring
1996

Pool Room Brawl

Mike began his wilderness experience by leading his team on a sit-down strike that lasted two days. On the third day, he decided to get with the program. By the end of the week, he led his team to their meeting point in record time.

Mike was bonding with the leaders and working on issues at a deep level. With his mind and body cleared of drugs and alcohol, he was rational. He wrote us a letter saying, "I know you had your reasons for what you did."

Joe wrote back, "In the end, it was my choice to send you to this program. I'd almost given up as a father telling myself things like... 'He's almost eighteen...He's living outside the home now.' But then I realized whether you are seventeen, eighteen, or forty, you are my son. I love you and don't want to see you give away your future to alcohol and drugs."

Joe poured out his heart and begged Mike to follow through with the next step: a three-month treatment center in Wyoming. "Use that strong will of yours to choose life," he wrote.

We were told Michael cried when he read the letter. He agreed to try the Wyoming program as long as his new buddy Ollie—the ex-football player who had brought him to the wilderness program—would escort him.

Mike went to the program but, after some confrontations with staff, threatened to leave. We refused to send airfare. "We'll support you in getting help, but we won't enable you to return to the life you had," Joe said.

We discussed several options, none of which Mike wanted. Two days after turning eighteen, Mike ran away.

"I'm not too concerned, Mr. Moderow," the counselor said. "Lots of people leave, but they always return. We call it blacktop therapy. It's fifty miles to the nearest phone here, and there are bears in the woods. He won't want to be out there after dark, believe me," he said with all confidence. "Don't worry, he'll be back."

He was wrong. Mike walked into town and met a girl who let him crash at her place. He then called his friends, who gathered enough money together for bus fare. It took him two weeks, but between hitchhiking and Greyhound, Mike made it from Wyoming to Georgia.

We had no idea where Mike was or what he was doing during this time, but ten days after he left the program, we got a phone call.

"Mrs. Moderow?" I immediately recognized the voice. It was Sean— one of Mike's friends. I was certain Sean was one of the kids bankrolling Mike's return to Atlanta.

"Is this about Mike?" I asked, my heart pounding. I motioned for Joe to get on the line. We wanted to know Mike was okay, but we were also afraid.

Ollie had told us that Mike threatened to kill us when he'd been taken from Atlanta. "I hear that a lot from kids because they're angry," he said, "but I know the people Mike's been hanging out with. For fifty bucks and a night's high, they'll do anything. I don't think Mike would hurt you when he's sober, but if he tells someone else to blow you away when he's high, he might not be able to take it back."

He told us to warn us, but what could we do? Hide in our bedroom forever?

"I don't care any more," I told Joe. "If someone wants to kill us, let them. At least we'll be out of our misery." I guess you could say it was a low for me.

While we'd made progress in reestablishing our relationship with Mike during treatment, we had no idea how he felt now. Two weeks on the road is a lot of time to plot revenge.

I knew Mike was nearby. I felt it even before Sean's call. Like many mothers, I have a sixth sense when it comes to my kids. I can feel when they're in trouble. I can feel when they're in close physical proximity. Another time Mike had run away and was missing for more than fourteen hours. Late that night, while taking a bath to calm myself down, I sensed his presence so strongly that I asked Joe to check the back deck to see if he was there.

"Again?" he asked. "I just looked about a half hour ago."

"I know, but he's here somewhere. I can feel it."

So, Joe looked again and there was Mike, curled up on the chaise lounge trying to get warm. The same feeling enveloped me now. Mike wasn't far from home. For the past two days, I continuously shot glances toward the side door, both hoping and fearing to see Michael's face.

And now the suspense was about to end.

"Mike's alright," Sean said. Both Joe and I sighed with relief. "And he has a message for you."

I stiffened as he continued.

"He doesn't want to live the rest of his life without parents. He wants to know if he can come see you when he gets into Atlanta."

I could hardly believe what I was hearing. Mike was okay and wanted to see us. I wasn't naive enough to think everything was going to be rosy, but maybe there would be some way Mike could still be part of our lives.

Michael came by a couple days later. He called first and sounded respectful though distant. Fall weather had arrived and Mike wore a bulky wool shirt that collapsed into him as he allowed me one stiff hug. He was thin enough that I could have put my arms around him twice. He smiled shyly then asked if he could get some of his things. I said yes, and went upstairs with him. I didn't trust him, and from the way he looked warily over his shoulder, I gathered he didn't trust me either. It was awkward but we got through it.

Mike told me he didn't want to talk about what had happened yet except to say, "It was hell, but I learned a lot."

He came again on the weekend. "I now know that I'm an alcoholic," he admitted, "but I don't need a rehab to beat it. I can do it on my own. You know me, Mom. No one has a will stronger than mine. All I have to say is I'm through, and that's it."

We knew his chances of succeeding without a change of environment were nil, but we affirmed his inclination. Joe impressed on him the importance of choosing friends and situations that would support good choices. All Mike said was, "Hmmm." We left it at that.

The next time we saw him, his demeanor had changed completely. He wouldn't look at us. He was distracted. Unable to sit still. We recognized the signs: he was using again. It made us sick, but we didn't confront him.

All Joe said was, "Mike, we don't think Atlanta is a good place for you to be right now, but we want you to know we love you."

"I know you do," he said.

We let him call us and tried to keep our visits light and positive.

Hugs came a little more often. He'd say, "I love you," on his way out the door. Still there were flares of anger. And some strong-arm tactic phone calls when he wanted something we wouldn't let him have. But on the whole, he walked softly. When he was in bad shape, he'd stay away. When he was okay, he seemed to love being with us.

Mike moved into an apartment with a friend. He got a job. Enrolled himself in an alternative high school and fought the demons by himself. However, the erratic behavior and mood swings increased. We watched helplessly and loved him as much as he would allow us.

"Standing by while someone destroys himself is a hard thing to do," Papa told me on the phone. I had given him the general gist of things, and he understood the dynamic. He'd been watching the yarn unravel for his friend Boone for some time.

"Boone's been drinking again," Papa told me.

"I'm sorry to hear that. I thought he'd been on the wagon for quite a while."

"He had been," Papa said. "Boone never said much about it, but he got real sick a while back. I figure the doctor told him he better cut out the drinking or else. But the scare must've worn off." Papa was silent for a moment then added, "Boone's about to git himself kicked out of Midtown Manor over it."

"Why? What happened?" I asked

Papa said that on one particular Wednesday morning, he and Boone were playing pool when Deets came in and started stacking chairs.

Deet's way of contributing to the community at Midtown *Manor* was to set up and take down the chairs for special events. He did it every Wednesday morning after Tuesday night bingo. It had never bothered Boone before, but Papa could tell the scraping of the chairs against the floor tile was grating on Boone like nails on a chalkboard.

Next thing you know, Boone came up behind Deets and whacked him in the back of the head with the cue stick. Deets whirled around, chair in hand, and Boone hit him again—this time in the nose. Enraged, Deets threw the chair at him with all his might. Boone stumbled back several steps before falling onto the pool table, out cold. It didn't register with Deets that Boone was unconscious—or maybe it did and he just didn't care. Anyway, he ran over to the table and began to pummel Boone's face and body.

Papa tried to pull Deets off of his friend, but since it was a full-time job just to keep himself upright, his efforts were pretty ineffectual. By then, a gaggle of women screamed onto the scene and managed to drag Deets off to the bathroom to attend to his bloody nose.

A steady flow of towels streamed back and forth between nearby apartments and the bathroom as they all waited for the ambulance to come. After a few minutes, Boone came to himself and was helped to a chair, where he sat waiting, head in hands.

The whole place was a three-ring circus. At first, people ran around like lumbering bears in mass pandemonium, but once it was clear that neither Deets nor Boone was seriously hurt, they settled down. Then the humor of the situation began to hit them—two grown men fighting like cowboys at a rodeo. As the story spread throughout the Manor, it was accompanied first with chuckles and finally with uproarious laughter.

Papa could barely contain himself as he related the fiasco. "Boone never did care much for Deets," he said, laughing. Then, a little more somberly, he added, "But he never would've done anything if it hadn't been for the booze. Everybody knew Boone'd been drinkin."

Deets neither apologized nor bragged about the fight, which seemed to suit everyone fine. The accolades were saved for Boone, who—though every one agreed was to blame—came off as both the victim and the hero.

Amazingly, the incident served only to bolster Boone's standing as king of the Manor. Not only did the knock-down-drag-out fight give the residence a diversion for which they were grateful, it reinforced the conviction that "you don't mess with Boone."

When Boone returned from the hospital later that day, the lobby was packed with gawkers wanting to see for themselves the final chapter of this little episode. Finally, Midtown's most notorious resident walked into the lobby, unassisted, with his nose in the air. Both eyes were black and his face was swollen, but his eyes twinkled. Everyone knew better than to gather around him, but they couldn't help asking questions.

"Boone, you okay?"

"Give any of those doctors trouble?"

"Ya get any stitches?"

"Naw, I'm alright," he said, giving them more of an answer than was customary for Boone.

They all watched him walk unsteadily down the hall to his room. The lobby was so quiet they could hear Boone's door close behind him.

It was Papa who broke the silence. "I'd say he was pretty gracious for someone who just got the tar beat out of him."

The altercation kept Midtown Manor buzzing for days. But the new manager was not pleased.

Shopping Spree

Though Papa laughed about the pool room brawl, he was concerned about Boone. This, like many other things, was not going to end the way he would like. Yet Papa handled it with a grace and dignity that I envied. Joe and I found it almost impossible to carry on a normal life when so much was so wrong.

One night, I heard the garage door opening. Joe was home. Though I would be glad to see him, I dreaded seeing his pain. Not having our children at home left us both with gaping wounds. We'd become empty nesters overnight with no opportunity for adjustment or closure, and the slightest reminder of the boys brought tears. Going to the mall and seeing clothes they would enjoy. Driving behind teenagers as they headed home from school. Listening to friends talk about their children who were doing normal things like going to dances, getting a driver's license, or making plans for college.

Sometimes we were too hurt to connect with each other, and I understood why crises are often catalysts for divorce. It's not a lack of caring, but too much pain in one place. When you're in pain, seeing someone you love hurting also is pain times two.

Joe walked through the door, eyes down. He placed his briefcase on the floor and gave me a quick hug. Together we walked to the leather sofa in our family room—the sofa Mike, Dave, and all their friends loved. As we sat down, the soft cushions forced us to sink toward each other. Then we began what had become a nightly ritual.

After reading a psalm, we prayed, pouring out our grief and bitterness with tears. But there were things we couldn't adequately express, and we ran out of words before we were able to get out the turmoil that was inside us. So we began reciting the classic prayers and creeds of the church—the Lord's Prayer, the Apostles' Creed.

Rote prayers, which often felt dead and boring in every day liturgy, came alive. Reaffirming what Christians for centuries had believed helped us not feel alone. Reminding ourselves that God, our heavenly Father, provides, forgives, protects, and ultimately will reign gave us hope.

We even wrote a prayer of intercession that listed our specific requests for the boys.

Eternal Father, we offer you the body and blood, soul and divinity of Your dearly beloved Son, our Lord Jesus Christ, in atonement for our sins and those of the whole world.

For the sake of His sorrowful passion, we pray that Michael and David will soon come to know Christ as Savior and Lord. Amen.

For the sake of His sorrowful passion, we pray that Michael and David will be protected from the evil one in each area of their lives: spiritual, emotional, physical, mental. Amen.

…we pray that the circumstances of Michael and David's lives will cause them to turn to God. Amen.

…we pray that Michael and David will be freed from any and all alcohol, drug, tobacco, or behavioral addictions. Amen.

…we pray that Michael and David will come into contact with people who will point them to Christ. Amen…

The repetition of our requests in simple, sentence prayers grounded us. As we prayed them, we often felt prompted to intercede for other people and different situations. Perhaps because we ourselves had nothing to offer, there was a strong sense of the Holy Spirit praying through us.

We claimed Jeremiah 31:16-17 as the promise for our family.

Thus says the Lord:
Refrain your voice from weeping,
And your eyes from tears;
For your work shall be rewarded, says the Lord,

And they shall come back from the land of the enemy.
There is hope in your future, says the Lord,
That your children shall come back to their own border.

Everything was out of our control now. There was nothing we could do but wait and trust.

Each night we prayed until peace came. By the time we got together the next evening, we were in grave need of peace again, but that time of prayer kept us from imploding. We came away both unified and more independent. Joe and I handled the daily roller coaster of emotions in our own way. We learned that there were still parts of the journey we had to travel alone—questions with which we had to come to terms in our own quiet times with God.

The change in Joe was dramatic. Anything Joe sets his mind to do, he does well; his pursuit of God proved no exception. There was a wisdom, a kindness, a confidence about him that soon became evident to everyone who knew him. His pain was palatable, but so was God's work in his life.

As during his illness, we pulled together. We cut ourselves loose from all but the most necessary commitments so that we could give ourselves the best chance to absorb and deal with what was happening. And because we couldn't help but wear our pain on the outside, we avoided socializing as much as possible. We lacked the energy to maintain even nominal civility.

Still, I longed for meaningful connections. Like a nursing mother whose baby is taken from her, my body ached at having lost my children so suddenly. Every maternal instinct I had was on alert and needed an outlet. By the time I got to Papa's again in the spring of 1996, I was bursting to see him. Sharon picked me up in Dallas and we drove in together.

Not much had changed. Thankfully, Boone was still there. The boys were still playing pool. And Betty was still keeping things clean and polished. But there were some things that needed attention. Since Papa had been in his place almost fourteen years, his apartment needed updating, and I was in the mood to do it. Sharon, always game for a new project, agreed to help.

Papa had the basics. A recliner and large TV had been gifts from my aunt and family. Though every item was purchased over his strenuous objections, if it made it through the door, he seemed to enjoy it.

"There's no point in spending money on me when there's no way of knowin' how long I'm gonna be around here," he insisted when he told him of our plans.

"Papa, you've been saying that for the past ten years and look at you. You're still going strong," I said.

Seeing we were determined, Papa finally conceded with his usual phrase, "You girls go ahead and do whatever you want." We immediately began evaluating what should go or stay. Papa needed a bookshelf to hold all his photo albums. The one he had, a flimsy two-shelfer, was loaded to the gills.

"If I get another one, I want solid wood," he informed us. For someone who not five minutes before thought nothing needed changing, he was suddenly very opinionated. We had to go to the antique shops to find it, but we did land a tall walnut bookcase with carved detailing. Papa was ecstatic. I found a standing lamp with a black shade and long chain pull. He could turn it on and off easily, even though arthritis now crippled both thumbs. A magazine rack held his phone books and numerous copies of the only periodical he cared about: *Western Horseman.* With adequate lighting, he was able to read for short periods of time. A sturdy table in the bathroom gave him a place to leave out his shaving gear, while the shelf below provided a convenient place for guests' toiletries.

Though Papa couldn't pace us as we shopped, he had no intention of missing out on meals. He insisted on eating out in spite of a bitter cold snap. So Sharon and I snuggled Papa into his winter coat, turned up the collar to cover his ears, then, each taking an arm, raised him so his feet barely touched the ground. A gangly trio, we would run into the restaurant as fast as we could.

We added another eatery to our repertoire: the International House of Pancakes. One recently opened nearby, and because Papa liked their chicken fried steak for once he was content to stay close to home. After eating, Papa was ready for a nap. While he slept, Sharon and I shopped as fast and furiously as we could.

We picked up Melmac dishes in a western design we thought Papa would like. "These are light so you can pick them up easily," we told him, "and they won't break." (He didn't say anything, but the next time I visited him I noticed he wasn't using them. When I asked him about it, he simply said, "I don't like eatin' off plastic.")

We tiptoed around the possibility of replacing his worn green and yellow sofa, thinking he'd be reluctant to give away something Mama had loved. But he surprised us. "I just despise that flowered sofa," he informed us. "Mama and I gave a hundred dollars for the chair and sofa twenty years ago, but if I woulda known I was gonna have 'em so long, maybe I'd have chosen a little more carefully."

So much for sentiment. Papa checked out a couple of sofas with us. We found one he really liked, but it was out of our price range. I was beginning to wonder if Papa's highbrow taste reflected his love of quality or if it was a tactical maneuver to keep Sharon and me from buying things. Maybe he figured he couldn't lose either way.

Had Papa been up to shopping with us, he'd have gotten better prices than we did. He still knew families who owned furniture stores, and he still knew how to bargain.

When he was horse-trading, Papa would lay the groundwork for a buy then return home saying, "That horse will be in my barn by nightfall." It usually was.

We suspected that my grandmother picked up a few of his ways over the years, too. Papa always enjoyed buying for her, so whenever he'd make a little money, he'd take her down to her favorite dress shop in Parker Square.

"She'd try on a dress or two then pick one to buy," Papa said. "Mama was so frugal she'd hardly ever buy the best one. But on the way out, I'd tell the clerk, 'Just set that other one aside.' Then I'd go back later, pay for it, and surprise Mama with it in the evenin'."

Mama never said a word about Papa's surprise purchases, but I couldn't help wondering if, as she placed the better dress back on the shop's hanger, she thought—*That dress will be in my closet by nightfall.*

I, however, had no luck getting Papa his sofa. I bargained with the storeowner to no avail. Sharon and I finally gave up and made do with what Papa had.

Papa perked up as we pulled things out we thought he would enjoy having around him. A wooden sculpture of a cowboy. His hat. A bandana. Anything western made his eyes shine.

He noticed his TV stand had a large open shelf on the bottom. "It looks kind of funny underneath with nothin' there," he observed. He studied the space a bit then said, "I wonder how my cowboy boots would look there?…Maybe with my boot jack?"

It was a great idea. We scurried to follow his instructions and soon created a western grouping that pleased him. Papa bent down and picked up one of the boots, running his hands over the fine leather.

"Those are good looking boots," Sharon said.

"Them is Rio boots—made in Sabre, south Texas." He stared off into the distance then continued. "In 1927, you could get a good pair of boots for thirty dollars, but nobody had thirty dollars. Good boot like that with four stitching would cost you five to seven hundred dollars these days."

He set the boot down, turned, and walked slowly back to his chair. He settled heavily into the recliner then drifted off to sleep, no doubt with western skies the backdrop to his dreams.

By the time we left, Papa's little apartment was fresh and functional. Though he was happy, it bothered me that we weren't able to get the sofa for him. Two years later I walked by that store, and it was still there. It was a shame. I couldn't help thinking that if Papa had worked that deal, that sofa would've been sitting in his living room instead.

Hired Hands

P apa isn't doing too well," my aunt called to say. "He's been sick with
stomach aches and diarrhea, then he gets so weak he can't fix his food.
I bring things over for him a couple times a week, but it's not enough. And
he won't let me hire anybody to help him."

Sharon and I agreed to stay a few days with Papa and talk to
him."There's a limit to how much I can push him," she explained. "I'd
appreciate anything you can do."

We were startled by Papa's emaciated condition. And his apartment
was appalling. His stovetop was charred; evidently he'd had a grease fire in
the kitchen. Several burned rags lying nearby suggested it wasn't a one-time
event.

And Papa had roaches. "I've never had roaches in my life!" he declared
with disgust, as one of them skittered across the kitchen floor. "They're
comin' from the guy next door."

He went to the sink and pulled out a box of powdered poison, which
he then liberally sprinkled over the kitchen countertops and the floor.

"Papa, how can you fix food in your kitchen with that poison everywhere?" I asked.

"Oh, I always clean off everything before cooking," he assured us.

Sure enough, before breakfast he was in the kitchen wiping up the poison—but with the same dishtowel we'd been using to dry the dishes. Afterwards he threw the towel in the dirty clothes. He washed all his towels together, including the ones he used to clean up bathroom accidents. No wonder he had diarrhea all the time.

As unobtrusively as possible, Sharon and I began sterilizing the place. We pulled out fresh dishtowels, but they were as heavy with grease as the dirty ones. After two washings we realized they'd never come clean. The only sanitary thing to do was throw them all away. But first we had to get past Papa.

After breakfast, we waited until he went in his room to dress. We didn't have much time because Papa didn't shower every day anymore. As soon as his door shut, Sharon grabbed the towels along with the trash and dumped them all. We thought we had gotten away with it. No such luck.

"What happened to those dishtowels in there?" Papa asked nodding toward the kitchen when Sharon returned. Caught red-handed, Sharon explained they were worn out and that we wanted to buy him new ones. He didn't appreciate the gesture.

"Seems like a lot of things have been disappearing 'round here lately," he noted dryly. He didn't think we were the only intruders either. "There was a big funeral here a week or so ago, and there was all kind of people in here. I think I musta left my door unlocked 'cause after I came back from playin' pool, one of my blue towels was missing."

He said since then he'd made it a point to keep better track of his stuff. That wasn't good news for us. He now eyed every piece of equipment we cleaned, every rag we washed, and every move we made.

It was clear to us that Papa couldn't live alone without assistance. There were other issues besides sanitation. He had trouble dressing and undressing. Papa still wore a western shirt every day and the buttons gave him fits. We asked him about a series of gouges and scratches on his arm.

"I did that trying to unbutton the cuff of my shirt. I finally just picked up the scissors and cut it off!" he said defiantly.

One of his biggest problems was food. Diarrhea prevented him from going out as much and also sapped his strength. By the time he fixed something at home, he was too tired to eat. We thought Midtown Manor might have some resources for meals but didn't ask Papa's permission to inquire. He'd just turn us down.

We decided after the morning round of pool, Sharon would detain Papa for an extra game while I looked up the manager. The boys only played once a day now.

"We don't play as regular as we used to," Papa explained. "Seems like one of us is sick most the time, and I'm gettin' to where I shoot so poorly I'm embarrassed to play."

But he still loved the game. A little before 10:00 A.M., Sharon, Papa, and I made our way to the rec room.

Virgil was setting up when we got there. He wasn't glad to see us, but, since it was obvious he came to play, he couldn't very well leave. No one else showed up, so we split into teams—Papa with Sharon, Virgil with me.

When Sharon and I had played a quick game of three-way with Papa the night before, he hadn't missed a shot, but this morning, his luck had run out. He played pitifully. So did Sharon and I.

Virgil played much better than the rest of us, but we lost the game when he scratched the eight ball early on.

"I don't know how that coulda happened," Virgil complained, "but we'll get you this time. You wait and see. We're gonna get ya for sure!" It sounded more like a threat than friendly banter.

Sharon racked the balls under Virgil's critical eye. He made us all nervous.

"You go first," I said to him showing deference.

He took me up on the offer. He knocked in a stripe then strutted around like a little banty rooster sinking one ball after another. I was hoping he'd run the whole table so I wouldn't have to shoot, but he didn't. We had two balls left. Sharon shot and missed, so it was my turn. Virgil, who had been telling me how to play all morning, was quick to put in his two cents worth.

"Go for that twelve ball," he ordered. "Whatcha gotta do is hit that ball real thin on the left. Real thin. It's a clear shot. All you gotta do is hit it thin."

I took a deep breath, lined up my shot, and hit it softly. The cue ball wobbled toward the twelve and just missed the target spot. The twelve rolled to the side—where no one short of a pro could dig it out in one shot.

Virgil stared coldly at the ball and shook his head. "You couldn't hit it thin if your life depended on it," he said with disgust.

I might have gotten my feelings hurt, but I looked at Sharon and her surprised expression gave me the giggles. I tried not to laugh, knowing Virgil would think I wasn't taking the game seriously. But Sharon saw my mouth twitching and coughed to hide her own laughter. That did it. We both struggled to keep our composure for the rest of the game.

Needless to say, Virgil didn't stick around for another. I used the opportunity to excuse myself to let Sharon and Papa play as we had planned.

"I'll meet you upstairs later," I said as I took off.

"Don't ya need a key?" Papa called after me.

Of course I would, if I were going straight back to the apartment, which I wasn't. But I went back for the key, hoping he didn't put two and two together. I then made a beeline for the front desk to catch the manager before lunch.

Papa wasn't too keen on the changes that had taken place at Midtown Manor since Mr. King left. "The new manager's a nice woman, and she's tryin' to do a good job, I reckon," he said, "but it's not the same. First thing they did was let go all the old security guards, and they got these fellers in there that don't do nothin'."

He was particularly incensed with the new night watchman. Several times we'd come in after dark and he hadn't been at the front desk.

"That's what he's supposed to be gettin' paid for, but he don't care about nothin'," Papa said. "He's so uncurious he wouldn't pay a nickel to watch a rat eat a bale of hay."

I didn't know if a security guard or office staff person was supposed to be manning the front desk now, but I waited ten or fifteen minutes before someone came. Finally a middle-aged woman greeted me with a smile. Her name was Martha. She wasn't the manager, but yes, she could give me some references of people and agencies that helped other residents in Midtown Manor.

As she searched through her files, a gentleman came by with two Styrofoam containers of food.

"Can I leave these here, Martha?" the man asked. "Two of the folks didn't answer their doors today."

"Sure. No problem. I imagine they'll be down for them directly," she said.

"If they're not here soon, you go ahead and enjoy them. No point in their going to waste."

After he left she said, "He's with Meals on Wheels, and, come to think of it, that might be something your granddaddy would be interested in."

Just then, who should walk in but Papa? He'd decided he wasn't up to playing another game. He preferred to track me down instead, and, of course, he spotted me at the front desk right away.

"What's this?" he asked pointing toward the container.

"Food, Mr. Choate, from Meals on Wheels," Martha said. "Would you like to try one? I was just telling your granddaughter that this might be a good thing for you."

Papa lifted the lid and sniffed at the hamburger patty, corn, hash browns, and a dinner roll. It looked delicious to me, but Papa turned up his nose.

"No thanks. I don't want any food that's been sittin' around who knows how long."

"But Papa, this food could be better than no food…" I began.

"I don't want nothin' from Meals on Wheels," he said. "Now, let's go get some real dinner."

So we went to Piccadilly. After the three of us were seated, Papa said, "I didn't mean to hurt anybody's feelings over Meals on Wheels, but that food just isn't very appetizing to me."

"It couldn't have been too bad. Look at your plate, Papa," I said. "You ordered the exact meal they were serving."

He looked down at the hamburger patty, corn, potatoes, and dinner roll on his own plate and began to laugh. He didn't change his mind though.

It's a good thing we didn't push the issue because the next morning we encountered a problem that had to be taken care of whether or not Papa wanted to cooperate. And he didn't.

Papa was in his recliner, putting on his socks and shoes. Sharon was sitting on the sofa across from him. As he lifted his foot toward the sock, she saw that his toenails, thick and yellow, had grown over the end of his toe and curled underneath.

Alarmed, she asked, "Papa, how long has it been since you had your toenails cut?"

He turned red. "I don't bother with 'em 'cause I can't see to cut 'em," he said.

"Have you told Aunt Marie? She'd be glad to cut them for you."

"No, I haven't told Marie. She does enough already."

Sharon knelt beside him to look more closely. His toenails were cutting into his skin. "Well, Papa, I think a doctor's going to have to take care of this now."

When Papa heard the word "doctor," he lost it.

"I ain't goin' to no doctor. There's no need for it," he insisted with anger in his voice. He got up and went into his room to finish dressing.

I called my aunt.

"He's been complaining about his feet," she confirmed. "He said he had trouble walking, but I thought it was arthritis." Papa always had shoes and socks on when she saw him, and she hadn't thought to check his feet.

"Sharon called the doctor, and his nurse said it might require surgery," I told her. "There's no way to know for sure until they see him."

"What did Papa say?" she asked.

"He's saying he won't go."

"Well…" I heard my aunt take a deep breath and knew she'd been this route before. "I guess we're going to have to take him anyway."

"Do you want Sharon and me to do it?" I asked.

"If you wouldn't mind. He's going to be upset with whomever takes him, and it would be nice to have it not be me for once."

We assured her we would take care of it, but we underestimated Papa. When I told him he had an appointment to see the doctor that afternoon, he sat up ramrod straight in his chair and seethed. Literally. Sharon came beside him and rubbed his back as we talked. The hostility in his tear-filled eyes pierced me like a poisoned dart. It was the first time Papa's anger had been directed at me, and it wasn't a good feeling.

"Papa, you have to get this done sometime," Sharon said. "It's better to do it while we're here in case you need us."

He refused to speak to us. We tried cajoling him. We tried ignoring him. But he would have none of it. He was angry enough to spit. And the humiliation in his eyes broke our hearts.

But when it was time to go, Papa put on his jacket and shuffled out the door like a chastened child. Once in the doctor's office, we held our breath, dreading the moment of truth. The doctor examined Papa's foot silently then issued the verdict. "I think we can handle this here," he said.

He went to work, and within twenty minutes it was over. No pain. No discomfort. No surgery.

"Sometimes all that digging around is painful," the doctor said, "but your grandfather's circulation is so bad he doesn't feel much."

Poor circulation was the last thing for which we would have expected to be grateful, but we were. Papa was a new person.

"I can walk now!" he exclaimed. He said he'd suspected his toenails were to blame and deliberately didn't tell my aunt because he feared surgery. I guess he was just going to let them grow into his foot and out the other side.

"Hon, I'm sorry I gave you such a hard time throwin' a fit like I did this mornin'," he said to me. "I didn't mean to get so angry at you."

"That's okay, Papa," I said, giving him a hug, but he continued to apologize.

After we got Papa home and settled in his recliner, Sharon asked him if he'd thought about what the next step might be for him. Since he felt so bad about the grief he'd given us, we thought he might engage in a discussion about his future.

"I want to stay here as long as I can," he said.

"Papa, if you had help, your chances for staying here would be a lot better. Do you realize that?" Sharon asked.

His mouth hardened. "I can't afford help and neither can Marie. My rent and medicines cost as much as my social security check. I only got 'bout twenty dollars a month left for groceries and everything. Marie's already pickin' up the slack on a lot of it."

I said, "I know that Papa, but we can help out. Just let Aunt Marie find someone to come in several days a week, and we'll see what it costs. You may be eligible for some government assistance—Aunt Marie will check on that. Between us, we can work something out. What do you say?"

He stared at the carpet, hands folded in front him as if in prayer, and sighed deeply. "I guess so," he said quietly.

Tears welled up in his eyes. "I don't know why you kids are so good to Papa, especially after the way I treated y'all this mornin.'"

I patted his hand as he talked.

"I know all this stuff you're wantin' to do is for my own good, and I sure appreciate it."

I was glad to be back on good terms with him and even happier that he'd recognized his fit had been necessary.

I couldn't help drawing a parallel between the struggle with Papa and my standoffs with Michael and David. Would they ever say, "I realize now all you did was for my own good"? Better not hold my breath on that one. Still, I felt an obligation to do what was best for them, even if they fought me all the way.

It seemed I was continuously making people I loved go somewhere they didn't want to go or do something they didn't want to do. It wasn't a fun role. The only thing that kept me going was knowing I couldn't live with myself if I took the easy way out.

With the boys, nothing was easy, and the results were mixed. Our conversations with David were alternately intimate and hostile. He came clean about the things in which he'd been involved, and we were shocked. What we'd seen had been just the tip of the iceberg. In the past two years, taking LSD, Ecstacy, and a variety of other drugs had been as much a part of David's daily routine as brushing his teeth. But he was responding to the nurturing and accountability of the peer-based counseling at Cascade. He still begged to come home, but Joe and I held firm. By now we realized that we were unable to give David the structure he needed to choose a new lifestyle. We saw that as a failure on our part, but it was the truth.

As for Michael, he graduated from high school by a hair's breadth. He'd been accepted by a college in South Carolina and was excited about a new start.

"I know I can't drink, and do drugs and make it through college," he said. "I promise I'm quitting cold turkey when I get there."

But having witnessed the cycle so many times, we had little confidence in his well-intentioned vows. Again we suggested treatment, but he refused. "I don't need help," he insisted. "All I have to do is make up my mind, and it's over."

We prayed he was right.

"Unclouded Day"

Sharon and I didn't expect to be leading any more sing-alongs with Mr. King gone, but a groundswell movement from the residents brought an invitation from the new management. We asked Papa if he'd rather we decline. Getting out in the evenings was a chore for him now, but he insisted we do it.

"I want to get there early, so I can get one of those big chairs," he said. So we arrived twenty minutes ahead. Deets was busy setting up chairs and putting out hymnals. I pulled a comfy chair into the front row, but Papa's frown told me something wasn't to his liking.

"Is this where you want it?" I asked.

"No, put it up there, by the piano."

Since there was no PA system, Deets had moved the piano from against the wall to the center of the room—so Sharon and I could be heard. Papa wanted to be up front with us, where the preacher would be. So that's where we put him.

The rec hall filled quickly. As Patsy rolled by, she teased Deets about having to bring her own chair. Ida, her wig slightly askew, sat quietly at a table up front. Her husband had died recently. Maybe the night would do her good. Frank and Muriel came in together right at start time and took seats along the side. Shirley and her cronies all sat at the same table, books open, ready to sing. She pointed to her watch letting us know it was time to get the show on the road.

Sharon opened in prayer then asked for song requests. They came in one after the other. "Mansion Over the Hilltop." "Stand Up for Jesus." "In the Garden." "In My Heart There Rings a Melody." Several lesser-known songs were requested by the Methodist contingent and sung with a glaring lack of enthusiasm. Another unfamiliar song was called out and someone said, "We don't know that one!" That angered the lady who had requested it, and from then on it was downhill.

Sharon suggested "The Old Rugged Cross" since everyone knew it. After that, Ida asked for "In the Garden" again.

"We already sang that," Shirley informed her.

"No, we didn't," someone else piped in. Things quickly degenerated into a shouting match between those who thought we had sung it and those who insisted we hadn't. We sang it again to be sure. After that Sharon chose the songs herself. After we'd sung the old standards, Sharon said, "Karen and I have been leading these sing-alongs for several years now and we all know each other pretty well. So, if it's okay with you, there's something I'd like to talk to you about."

There was a murmur of assent as Patsy called out, "Sure, honey, you go right ahead."

Sharon smiled and continued. "You already know that the longer we live, the more things happen to us beyond our control. Someone we love gets sick or dies. Our bodies fall apart. Our minds don't work as well as they used to. We look down the road and don't like what we see."

Heads nodded in agreement.

"Do you ever look back at what you used to do when you were healthier and stronger? Maybe you were good at cooking, or taking care of a family, or a business. Maybe you worked hard on a ranch or farm like my grandfather. Some of you may compare that time to today and think, *I used to really be somebody then.*

"Sometimes we think that if everyone has to give to us and we can't give back then we're nothing. We might even feel embarrassed or angry about it. But do you realize that the times we find ourselves totally dependent on God and others are very precious moments in God's eyes?"

The room suddenly became very still.

"Do any of you have great-grandchildren that are infants?" she asked. Many hands went up.

"And how do you feel about them?"

Just thinking about their babies brought smiles to many faces.

"Do you despise them because they can't feed themselves? Do you punish them because they can't dress themselves? Or get angry with them because they can't talk? No. You love them even more because they're totally dependent on you. And how do you feel if that baby falls asleep in your arms? You know it means that baby trusts you. She feels safe. And doesn't that make you happy?

"That's how God feels when we trust Him. His heart bursts with love and joy. He doesn't abandon us or despise us because we are helpless, He just snuggles us in closer. In fact, the less we are able to do for ourselves, the more of an opportunity we have to rest in God's arms.

"Being dependent is often the only way we come to understand that, in God's eyes, we are always 'someone.'"

"Think about it!" Papa shouted, as he dabbed his eyes with his handkerchief.

"The next time you feel hurt or humiliated by what you've lost," Sharon concluded, "picture yourself as a newborn baby, being held in God's arms."

A spirit of reverence rested on the place as Sharon prayed a short prayer. Then we concluded by singing an old favorite, "Unclouded Day." I sang with the others longing for that day every bit as much as they.

O they tell me that He smiles on His children there,
And His smile drives sorrows all away;
And they tell me that no heartaches shall ever come,
O that lovely land of unclouded day.

A Dying Breed

The next morning, no one showed up for pool. A tray of stale glazed donuts sat alone on a table near the kitchen.

"Where is everybody?" Sharon asked.

"I doubt Virgil will come; he feels so poorly all the time he can't muster up the energy. But Boone will be here directly," Papa said. "Most days it's just him and me anyway. Just as well, I reckon, since I can hardly see to play anymore—but I kinda miss having nobody to pick on."

"What about Walter?" I asked. "Where's he been? I haven't seen him since we got here."

"Oh, he's gettin' over surgery."

"Really? On his neck?" Walter had been complaining about bone spurs that bothered him when he played.

"No. Hemorrhoids."

"Well, I'm glad you told me, I could have brought it up and embarrassed us both."

"I wouldn't worry about that," Papa laughed. "I'm sure he'd be happy to give you all the details."

"How long since his surgery?" I asked.

"Oh, 'bout three months, I expect."

"And he still can't play pool?"

"Guess he doesn't want to rush things," Papa said.

Just then Boone came in, all smiles with hugs to go around. He was overly friendly, but I couldn't tell if he'd been drinking or not. It was awfully early in the day if he was.

Sharon racked the balls, and we were set to start when Virgil breezed into the rec room to snatch a donut from the pastry tray.

"Nothing slows him down when there's food around," Boone said under his breath. Then he called, "Hey, Virgil, got time for a game?"

Virgil looked at his watch.

"Gotta make sure he's got time before his next meal," Papa noted. More likely he was buying time to figure out if Sharon and I were playing. I decided to put his mind at ease. "I'm sitting this one out, Virgil," I said. "Go ahead. You play."

"Why don't you and Alva take on me and Sharon?" Boone suggested.

Under those terms, Virgil finally consented.

Boone shot first and had a run of four balls before missing.

"Now ain't that a shame," Virgil taunted.

"You were so upset I had to do somethin'," Boone retorted. "Don't want you to go home muttering, tears fallin' all the way up the stairs."

It was Papa's turn, but he made no move to play.

"Papa, it's your turn," Sharon prompted.

Papa looked around. "Is it your shot, Sharon?"

"No, Papa, it's yours. Boone just shot, so it's your turn."

Papa seemed confused and stood there trying to figure out what was going on.

"Alva," Boone said authoritatively, "it's your shot."

Papa reluctantly picked up his stick. He shook his head as if to clear the cobwebs and shot. He missed the cue ball all together.

"Go again," Boone said.

So Papa lined up the shot again and missed. Sharon was next. She didn't pocket a ball, but the cue ball tucked in behind the eight, leaving no shot for Virgil.

"Good lead," Boone said with a wry grin.

"That's not fair, that's just not fair."

I noticed Virgil had a habit of repeating himself. It was as though he felt compelled to keep talking but didn't have the creativity to come up with something new. He blustered as he walked around the table looking at the situation from one angle then another.

"That's just terrible," he said. "Look what you done. That's dirty pool alright. Dirty pool."

Boone winked at Sharon, "She learnt that from you."

There was nothing Virgil could do. He scratched and also had to put up a ball.

The game stayed close all the way, but Papa had the first chance to shoot for the win. He aimed then shot. The eight ball fell into the pocket as easy as you please, giving Papa and Virgil the game.

You'd have thought Virgil had just won the lottery. Papa said little, but his eyes twinkled with their old shine. Virgil didn't stay for a second game. Guess he wanted to savor the victory. The rest of us played a while longer—Boone and Papa against Sharon and me. We girls lost but didn't mind.

We went to Piccadilly for lunch, happy to celebrate Papa's good day.

"Papa, did you say Virgil hasn't been playing much?" I asked.

"Yep. Outside of playin' with us yesterday and today, it's probably been three or four weeks."

"You're kidding. He made some pretty incredible shots today."

"That's just Virgil," Papa said. "He's streaky. When he gets goin' he can play almost as good as a pro, but it stops just as quick as it starts. It makes him so mad he can't see straight, but it's sure funny to watch."

We took our usual nap after lunch and spent the afternoon hanging out in Papa's apartment. Papa seemed relaxed and energetic.

"How long before we go for supper?" he asked.

"However long you want it to be," Sharon said. "Why?"

"You girls up to catching a quick game of pool before we go?"

Within minutes we were on our way.

We exited the elevator and were surprised to see Frank in the lobby by himself. He was seldom without Muriel. "I'm waiting for my son," he explained. "He's taking me out this evening."

A good ten years younger than the average resident here, Frank had become one of Midtown's more involved citizens. He drove the bus to Pat's every week, as well as to any other planned outings. He also took people to the doctor when they needed a ride. Papa had said he was a good man, and Frank was living up to his reputation. In spite of Papa's disapproval of Muriel, she must have been good for Frank; he looked just as vital as the day we met him.

Papa seemed wistful as the four of us reminisced about Frank and his wife's friendship with Mama and Papa. It occurred to me that maybe the reason Papa didn't like to be around Frank and Muriel wasn't so much a dislike for Muriel as his own discomfort. Maybe being with another couple was just too painful.

"Where you headed now?" Frank asked us.

"To play some pool," Sharon said.

A worried look crossed Frank's face. His eyes darted toward the direction of the rec room, but he said nothing.

"I've been on a roll," Papa teased, "so I thought I'd see if I could win one more game before the sun sets."

The three of us meandered down the hall when we heard the familiar noise of billiard balls being soundly scattered. *That's odd. Who plays pool besides the boys?* I wondered. Then we entered the room and saw Boone, Virgil, and Walter engaged in a game of three-way side ball.

Bewilderment, anger, then shame flashed across Papa's face as reality hit him: the boys had been playing in the afternoons, but without him.

Struggling to gain his composure, Papa started toward them but stumbled sideways. Fortunately, Sharon and I, standing on either side of him, stabilized him without obvious effort.

The boys looked like they'd been caught with their hands in the cookie jar. Sharon and I tried to cover it by making a big fuss over greeting Walter, and he made a big fuss over us.

"Ya'll come play with us!" he insisted.

"No," Papa said "We'll be just as happy to watch you all play for a spell."

And that's what we did.

There wasn't the usual banter, though Walter and Boone made an effort to be friendly. Papa sat in his chair, his Indian face as unrevealing as stone.

"Papa, I think we'd better get us some dinner," Sharon finally said after a decent time had passed. "I'm getting hungry."

Papa sighed and with our help began the slow work of getting himself out of the chair. He smiled kindly at us and said, "Okay. I'm ready whenever you girls are."

We walked out to the parking lot, got in the car, and drove to Pat's without a word. When we arrived, I opened the heavy door for Papa. The entry had an incline that gave him trouble, so Sharon stood behind him in case he toppled backwards. It was early in the evening, and there was only one other customer in the place. We saw a waitress, a young dark-haired girl, cleaning a station. She didn't look up. Papa stood waiting for his usual greeting, but there was none.

"Go ahead and sit wherever you like," the girl finally said.

We squeezed into Papa's booth and waited. Eventually the waitress came over to take our order.

"Ya'll ready?" she asked looking at Papa.

Papa looked toward the kitchen.

"Is Pat here?" he asked.

"No. She had to run an errand."

"What about her daughter?" I asked.

"Christie? It's her day off."

The news flustered Papa. It had probably been a decade since he'd had to give his order. He tried, but he had trouble remembering all the particulars. A cheeseburger—bun warmed but not toasted. French fries, soft. A half order.

"No onions," we said trying to help. "Medium Dr. Pepper." The waitress seemed annoyed. It took a little while but we got Papa's dinner ordered. Ours, too. The girl quickly tore the sheet out of her pad and turned on her heel to prevent the addition of any other directives.

"She's new," Papa said, as if that explained it all.

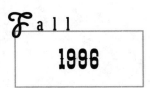

Fall
1996

Catastrophe

My internal "mother's radar" had been active all night. Thinking about Mike and unable to sleep, I read my Bible and prayed until peace came. I had just turned off the light and closed my eyes when the phone rang. It was 2:30 A.M., Wednesday, July 17, 1996.

"Mrs. Moderow?" a woman's voice said.

"Yes."

"I'm a nurse from Georgia's Athens Regional Medical Center. Are you the mother of Michael Moderow?"

My heart stopped. "Yes."

"You need to get here right away," she said. "Your son's been injured in a car accident, and his condition is critical."

The first thing I was aware of was God's quiet voice. *This is My mercy,* He seemed to say. At that moment I had assurance of two things: that Mike would not die and that God intended to use this to give something good to Michael and to us.

"Who is it? What's happened?" Joe asked.

"It's Mike," I mouthed while trying to hear what the nurse was saying. I asked questions, but she kept saying, "Just get here as soon as you can." After giving me directions, she hung up. I relayed all I knew to Joe as we quickly dressed, then I began packing a suitcase.

"Karen, what are you doing?" Joe asked. "We need to go. Now. We don't know how much time we have."

But I was so surrounded by peace that I felt no fear. I wanted to get to Mike as soon as possible, but it was as if someone else had taken over and was giving me instructions to follow.

Clothes.

"We'll need clothes for a few days at least," I said to Joe, voicing the specifics.

Medical and family numbers.

"I'll bring doctor and insurance information." I was still listening as I threw clothes, toiletries, and our personal phone directory in my bag.

Prayer support.

Yes, of course. I added my Bible and notebook, then I called my sister. There was no time for consolation. I asked Sharon to alert our family and friends and ask them to pray. Within fifteen minutes we were ready to go.

As we pulled out of the garage, a car screeched into the driveway behind us. It was a neighbor, the father of one of Mike's friends.

"There's been an accident," he cried. "Did you get a call?"

He told us it had been a one-car accident. Five kids from Atlanta were in the vehicle. "They're all injured. Only one is hurt critically, but they wouldn't tell me who it was."

We told him it was Mike. He left saying he'd contact the other parents to let them know. Then Joe and I took off on the longest two-hour trip of our lives.

In the emergency room, we were taken to the curtained cubicle where our son lay on a hospital gurney. I ran to him. Afraid to move anything, I bent down and kissed Mike's arm. Joe kissed his forehead. We both began sobbing, telling him we loved him.

Michael's head was tilted back, and there were tubes in every orifice. Gastro nasal tube. Catheter. IVs. He was on a ventilator. Still, he looked handsome. There wasn't a mark on him. The real injury, we'd been told, was to his head. He had suffered a TBI, a traumatic brain injury.

Though Mike was in a coma, the moment we walked into the room, he responded with classic "posturing." Mike stiffened, and his shoulders, arms, and hands rolled inward. We later learned that posturing is a primal response to stimuli, usually pain. When the body is crashing and has no other way to communicate, posturing is a red-alert signal—a way of saying, "Stress…stress…help. I'm not handling this."

Because Mike's condition was unstable, we were asked to wait outside the emergency room until the doctor came.

After some general information about Mike's injuries, the doctor confirmed drugs and alcohol had been involved. I had seen a note beside Mike's bed noting alcohol, marijuana, and possibly cocaine in his system. But when it came to explaining what could happen next, the doctor was very vague.

"Your son is going to be in a coma for quite a while."

"How long are we talking about?" I asked.

"With brain injury, there is no way of predicting."

"I'm not asking for a date, just a general time frame," I said, annoyed by his hedging.

He was still hesitant. I wondered if he was weighing the benefit of the truth against our ability to absorb shock.

"We understand Mike's very seriously injured," Joe said, "but we do better dealing with reality. Please, be honest with us about the prognosis."

The doctor looked into Joe's eyes, then mine. "It could be days or weeks, but most likely it'll be two or three months—maybe more—before he wakes up."

I took in a sharp breath then forced myself to ask, "Is there any way of knowing if there's paralysis or mental impairment?"

The doctor shook his head no. "There is going to be significant damage, but he'll have to emerge before we know what he's got left."

"'What he's got left'? What does that mean exactly?"

"Speech. Movement. Intelligence. Processing. All could be affected. There's no way to know."

And there would be no answers. Not for a very long time.

Joe and I held each other and cried.

Throughout the day there were many practical things to handle: medical consultations, insurance certifications, canceling of scheduled activities, family updates. We vacillated between clinical detachment and emotional brokenness. We prayed often, though we weren't able to concentrate enough to offer extended prayers. They were more like pleas shot into the heavens like arrows.

Father, You are in control. Help us. Help Mike.

God, why wouldn't he listen?

Lord, we gave Michael to You before he was born, and we trust You to do what is best for him and for us. Whatever that is.

Holy Spirit, somehow let Mike feel our love. We've never been able to reach him. Hold him for us now.

Father, Michael is Your son, too. Does this break Your heart like it's breaking ours?

We knew God didn't do this to Michael. Mike had been hell-bent on destroying himself, yet for some reason God had spared him.

The more details we discovered, the more we realized his survival was a miracle. The car didn't crash, so there was no loud noise to awaken the few residents of the rural area. When the driver lost control on a curve, the car sheared a couple trees then flipped. In flight it passed over a creek then between two massive trees, rolling two or three times before landing right side up in a grassy field. Somewhere along the way, the manifold slammed into the front passenger side where Michael had been sitting. If any number of things had happened differently, we would have been in a morgue instead of a hospital. Had the car not cleared the trees. Had Mike not been thrown from the vehicle. Had the car not been big and heavy—an old Cadillac classic. Had there not been a house on the rural property. If the woman living there had not been up to hear their cries and call 911. If competent medical help hadn't arrived quickly. If…if…if. There were too many "ifs" to be coincidental.

Thankfully, the other four passengers didn't have life-threatening injuries. The two girls were home by the weekend. The two young men, though in serious condition, were released within a couple weeks. But for Mike, it was touch and go.

We wanted to move him to Atlanta, but the doctors preferred he not be transferred until he could breathe on his own. Then he developed an infection.

"If we're going to transport him, we'd better do it now," the doctor said. "If this gets worse, we won't be able to."

Three days after his accident, Mike was transferred to St. Joseph's in Atlanta.

That same day, David came home.

He was torn in a million pieces—devastated at what had happened to his brother but happy to be home. It certainly wasn't the homecoming we had envisioned.

We'd been to California on monitored visits, but David hadn't been in Atlanta for almost a year. He was thriving at school; he couldn't help but show his enthusiasm for Cascade's nurturing environment and challenging academic program. In between there'd been a lot of honest communication. A lot of restructuring of not only our family system but of David's personal life. We had the beginnings of trust. Now we had to take a chance. We knew Dave needed to be with Mike and with us.

Joe picked him up late Friday night and brought him to St. Joseph's hospital where I was waiting. David had grown a half a foot since I'd last seen him. He was no longer a boy. Over 6'1", he towered over me. He hugged me, placing his chin on top of my head. "Love you, Ma…" he said simply.

With our arms around each other, the three of us walked toward the intensive care unit—to the same room Joe had been in two years earlier.

It had been a rough day for Mike. He hadn't stabilized since the transfer that morning. He had a high temperature and an elevated heartbeat and pulse rate. The infection, which they believed to be in the lungs, wasn't responding to antibiotics. Mike's right lung had partially collapsed. We were warned he could be going into respiratory failure. There was a lot of posturing. Tremors in the arms and legs. Violent hand movements. Possible mini-seizures. These weren't good signs.

We learned that comas don't have on/off switches where one moment you're in and the next moment you're out. Unlike what you see on TV, people seldom emerge without aftereffects. If the body goes into a coma, the underlying cause is usually traumatic enough to cause residual damage.

People who've emerged from comas describe them like being under water: The closer you rise to the surface, the more clear things become. But a person's struggle to get there is a process. On the way up, varying things emerge, and there's no way of knowing what, when, or to what degree.

The Rancho Scale, used by doctors to measure the depth of coma, has ten levels with Level One being "No Response" and Level Ten being "Purposeful and Appropriate Response." Mike was not quite at Level Two. If he were in a ten-foot pool of water, he'd have been almost on the bottom.

Though Mike was capable of only one general response—posturing—we thought it significant that he postured when people entered the room. The staff said it was unlikely that it indicated awareness; still, we were asked to leave the room if Mike couldn't settle down.

"Posturing is not a good thing," the doctors warned us. "It's not a response we want grooved into the brain's circuits."

We were convinced that Mike, at some level, was aware when we were with him. When we talked lovingly to him, he usually calmed down. I felt that, even if he couldn't understand the words, he was picking up the vibes—the way a newborn does when he senses his mother is near.

We didn't know if Michael would respond to David, but Dave could hardly wait to see him. We tried to prepare him for Mike's condition, but there was no way to soften the blow. David took one look at Mike and threw himself across his brother in a giant hug, sobbing quietly. Mike began posturing, then tears poured from the corners of his closed eyes down onto his cheeks. I don't know what Mike knew, but he knew something.

The room was so filled with grief that words were impossible. But sorrow could not choke out the good that was also present. Love. Resolve. Commitment. All the things Joe and I had pledged to each other on the day we married had been held in trust for our family. All we'd been through to this point had strengthened us, and now our mettle would be tested.

Joe and I took each other's hand. And, as David held Michael, I realized that for the first time in a very long time our family was together.

Between a Rock and a Hard Place

In the waiting room, Dave leaned forward in a chair, his head in his hands. "I should've saved him," he cried. "I'm the only one who could have."

I placed my hand on his shoulder. "Honey, nobody could have saved Michael," I said. "You just would have gone down with him." Dave found that hard to accept.

We were all struggling with ambivalent feelings about Mike. Joe and I asked ourselves a million times, *Could we have prevented this had we done things differently?* But a reality check confirmed that other parents had made more devastating mistakes than ours without such tragic consequences. I didn't feel guilt. Remorse and sorrow, yes. But not guilt. As dark as this was, there was some sense of light. This didn't feel like punishment or condemnation. It felt like mercy.

We believed it was the only way Mike could have been stopped. Yet the reality of how this would affect our lives was a somber one.

I was angry—very angry—with Michael.

I kept replaying a conversation we'd had in which I had begged him to consider the consequences of living on the edge.

"It's my life," he said. "If I end up hurting myself I'm the one who'll pay the price."

"No, Mike, we all pay the price," I responded. "What happens if you have an accident and can't take care of yourself? Or what if you hurt someone else? What then?"

He hadn't answered. And now we were facing the very nightmare we had feared.

We did see God's hand in bringing people and resources to help us. At school, David's friends and counselors helped him deal with his guilt and process his emotions on a day-to-day basis—and much more effectively than we could have.

My brother and sister and their families were all able to be with us the first couple weeks—a great gift. Mike's accident occurred two days before the 1996 Olympic Games were to begin in Atlanta. The family already planned to be in town. After the accident, they called to ask if they should cancel, but we wanted them to come. Aunts, uncles, and cousins arrived in force, offering support and practical help in ways we never would've anticipated.

As we cleaned out Mike's apartment, they helped us wade through the ugly reality of what Mike's life had become. Drugs. Weapons. Arrests. Immorality. Evidence of cocaine and heroin use was in plain sight. There was nothing with which he hadn't been involved. The truth was, had there not been an accident, Mike would have likely gone to jail.

The frustration and pain of untangling Mike's legal and personal matters added to the emotional burden I was already carrying. In my quiet time one morning, a verse in Psalm 37 stood out for me. "Cease from anger, and forsake wrath," it commanded. "Do not fret—it only causes harm."

I was at a crossroads. I knew acknowledging my anger was necessary, but then what? Ahead was a significant amount of work for me, not only in whatever lay ahead for Mike's recovery but also in settling his affairs. Was it possible for me to do what needed to be done without tearing myself apart over and over again? Not if I continued to feed the anger. The person who would be hurt most if I gave over to bitterness would be me. *Is this how you want to live through the next few months?* I asked myself.

I went to the hospital later that day and pondered my choice as I stood beside Michael's bed. As always, love surged through me when I looked at him. It was when we were apart that resentment knocked. *Was I willing to nail shut the door to bitterness?* That was the question. It would never be easier than now, when every mothering instinct I had drew me to him.

So, I made my decision. Bending over Mike and kissing his forehead I whispered, "No matter what you've done, you're my son and I love you."

It was a small gesture, but it freed me. And that release of negative energy made a big difference in my outlook. It didn't change the facts. Joe and I were facing a tragedy that would affect our future in devastating ways. That was a given. The only variable was how we would handle it.

A first step was expressing gratitude for the good things coming our way—and there were many. Encouraging phone calls. Visits from family and friends. The generous and continuous support of our church and social community. The cooperation of our insurance company.

But every day brought new challenges. We were devastated when Saint Joseph's told us they couldn't do anything more for Michael. "He needs to be somewhere equipped to handle brain injury," the patient coordinator told us. She walked to Michael's bed and pointed out what we had also noticed: his feet were turning in. Muscles were beginning to atrophy.

"Our nurses come in once a day and place splints on his legs," she said, "but Mike needs therapy three or four times a day. He probably needs it on his arms and torso, too, but we just don't have the staff or training to do it."

Through her referral, we reluctantly visited the Shepherd Center. Immediately we recognized it to be one of the ways God intended to provide for us.

The Shepherd Center, one of a few model hospitals in the nation specializing in spinal cord and brain injuries, was located just forty minutes from our door. There, Michael was treated by a medical team whose competence was only surpassed by their compassion and creativity in treatment. Unlike most facilities, which often discount what cannot be scientifically proven, the staff at Shepherd recognized there was no way to measure what part intangibles play in recovery.

At 6'3" and 125 pounds, Mike was a skeleton the day he arrived. His white cell count was high. He wasn't breathing on his own, and he had a bedsore—a common and potentially serious complication for people who are immobile. But within four days of being at Shepherd, Mike was weaned off the vent. The infection in his lungs subsided, though he was still receiving oxygen through his tracheotomy. A feeding tube replaced the IV allowing him to receive better nutrition. After three weeks of aggressive treatment, the bedsore healed and he began to gain weight. Soon the trach was removed so that, except for a feeding tube and condom cath, Mike was "tube free." He opened his eyes at times now but remained catatonic.

Sunshine greeted me one morning as I came into his room. Michael stirred in the bed. His eyes, half-opened, remained murky and unfocused. He no longer postured, but his mouth made a grimace—a look we called his "lion" face.

"Hi, sweetheart," I said, running my fingers through his beautiful long hair. "Looks like you've already had your bath. Would you like some lotion?"

More shifting. Mike pulled up his shoulders but couldn't lift his head. I dug the bottle out of my bag, squeezed lotion into my hand, then passed it under his nose.

"I brought a new kind. Do you like it?"

I continued talking to Mike as I rubbed the lotion on his arms, his hands, and then his chest. He lay quietly. As I took in the masculine scent of the cream, I felt certain Mike also enjoyed it.

We worked hard to find things that Mike would like. He couldn't have anything by mouth; we didn't know yet if he would have a gag reflex to prevent choking. But the therapists said that anything that stimulated the other senses—sight, hearing, smell, or touch—increased the possibility of response. So we tried to incorporate this strategy in every contact we had with him.

Friends and family signed up in three-hour shifts, seven days a week, to visit Mike and interact with him in various ways. Reading books. Playing music. Tuning in a TV show. Showing him pictures of people he knew. Keeping him up-to-date on current events. A favorite task was massaging his tight, spastic limbs. We went through creams and lotions by the gallon.

Our instinct told us Mike needed people around him. He'd always been very social, and he seemed less agitated when someone was near. Though he couldn't speak, several of us were able to tell if Mike was unhappy or uncomfortable the moment we walked in the room. A quick check would reveal a problem. His cath had pulled loose and he was wet. Sometimes he was cold. Or his sheets were bunched up under him. We learned to communicate without words, a skill that, to my surprise, wasn't as hard as one would think.

My love for Michael flowed into him as if by a direct line. I sensed him receiving it and felt his love returning to me. Because of what we shared, I didn't dread going to see him. It hurt me to see him suffer; it took two therapists to straighten out his contracted limbs morning and night. But pain wasn't the core of our relationship. Being together and communicating what was in our hearts was what mattered.

I closed the bottle of lotion, returned it to the shelf, and picked up the notebook at the end of Mike's bed. We'd asked visitors to sign in and to note any response or changes in Mike's condition they had observed. There was nothing new. Then George, Mike's nurse, and Eddie, an aid, came in.

They nodded at me but spoke to Michael.

"Hey, Mike. How ya doin' this morning?" George asked. "We're here to get you out of bed for a while. What do you think about that?"

Mike stared ahead. Eddie grabbed a clean shirt from the locker and put it on him. We'd been told that getting Mike dressed and up as soon as possible would help him establish a day/night pattern, as well as jumpstart a routine of daily living. This was the first time Mike was well enough to do it.

Eddie left and returned with a large piece of equipment. I moved my chair against the wall to get out of his way.

"This is a Hoyer lift," he explained. "We'll be using this to move Mike."

George and Eddie tucked a mesh cloth under Michael by rolling him on one side and then the other until Mike lay evenly on top of it. This netting attached to hooks on the Hoyer and formed a bundle, which could then easily be swung in an arc from the bed to a chair.

George turned the Hoyer handle, and the net holding Michael began to rise. Eddie held Mike's head while George cranked higher and higher. As I watched, I was suddenly overwhelmed by the reality that my son, who weeks ago was strong and able-bodied, was now being loaded into a wheelchair like a sack of potatoes.

The fact that one so precious to me had been forever altered seemed more than I could bear. I caught myself gasping for air and realized I'd been holding my breath—an instinctive attempt to not "take in" what I was seeing, I suppose.

Michael looked like a bag of vegetables. Lumps in odd places. Inert except for the occasional tumble of gravity. But I rebelled against the image. *No! This is my son!* I screamed inside. I didn't even try to hold back the tears. I cried for Michael. For us. For the sad fact that unless someone were around to challenge their view, most people would look at my son and not see "some*one*," but "some*thing*."

In that moment, with all the rage of a mother's heart beating inside me, I realized I could not let that happen. I could make a difference in Mike's world by being his advocate. I wasn't naive. Such a role would take a big chunk of my life for a time. Maybe forever. Yet how could I not take it?

In whispering, *This is My mercy*, to me the night of Mike's accident, God had given me faith to believe that through this tragedy, He intended to bring good to each person who was impacted by it. The first blessing was given to me that day in Mike's hospital room. It was the answer to a question I had put before God many times in my life: *Who am I in Your eyes?* I hated so many things about me that I had a hard time believing God could love someone so flawed.

But now I had the sense I'd been created the way I was for a purpose. That God not only loved me, He loved how He had made me. I was "beloved" to Him, weaknesses and all. For the first time, I saw that the parts of my personality that gave me trouble would now work to my advantage. The very qualities that made it difficult for me to "go with the flow" had a flip side.

My stubbornness gave me tenacity. My unwillingness to take no for an answer made me resourceful. The indignation that caused me to act rashly at the sight of the weak being preyed upon by the strong now motivated me to fight for Michael in whatever way was needed.

For years I had felt that as Mike's mother I'd been a failure. We seemed painfully mismatched. Now I wondered if perhaps God put us together knowing that one day Mike would need a mother like me. Perhaps I was where I was because God trusted me. It was a humbling thought.

If so, He must've been counting on me to pick up the cross that came as part of the deal. I thought of Jesus in the garden, waiting for what He knew would be an agonizing death. There was no spiritualizing or idealizing what lay ahead. Just a gut-wrenching plea for strength and a submission to God's will based on the conviction that the cross was not the end of the story.

In Matthew 16:24, Jesus says to His disciples, "If anyone desires to come after Me, let him deny himself, and take up his cross, and follow Me." But I'd only recently realized that this instruction prededes another well-known verse: "For whoever desires to save his life will lose it, but whoever loses his life for My sake will find it." Taken together, the implication is that the path to finding one's life can only be found by taking up the cross. One follows the other.

Something inside me said, *Yes! I'm beginning to understand.* As broken and helpless as I'd been the past two years, being with God at a deep, real level had brought peace and strength to my spirit. I was learning that the way to know God was to trust Him. And now I was being called to trust Him with the pain of this moment and the uncertainty of the future. Not just for Michael, but myself. I was called to believe that God had and would equip me in temperament, spirit, and faith to meet whatever challenges lay ahead.

I watched my son slumped in his wheelchair, straining against the headband holding his head in place. I felt sad. Incredibly sad. But I also felt more loved and secure than I'd ever felt in my life.

Prayer Warriors

Dr. Leslie, the physician in charge of Michael's case, stopped me in the hospital lobby. "Karen, how are you and Joe holding up?" he asked. We'd been asked to consider a long-term facility for Mike, and he knew we were upset about it.

"We're having a hard time with this because we see progress," I said. "The other day when Mike heard my voice, his eyes popped wide open. That's a direct response, isn't it?" My voice sounded desperate. "This doesn't seem like the time to give up."

Dr. Leslie patted my arm gently and explained, "Here's the problem. Because Mike is physically stable, your insurance won't allow him to stay here unless he can participate in therapy. That means he must be able to move in response to a command or answer 'yes' and 'no' appropriately. He can't do that yet."

It had been three months since Mike's accident, and we were being told Mike might not emerge from the coma. It was time to consider a nursing home.

This flew in the face of everything we felt God had impressed on us about Mike's situation. Joe asked, "Why would He spare Mike just to have his life be a series of tube feedings and bed turnings? I've sensed God calling us to a place of light. Why would He change everything now?"

I felt the same way. We had received many confirmations Mike was going to be okay. To me that meant Mike would have some sense of who he was and would be physically functioning. I hadn't asked God for these confirmations. They weren't our expectations. As we prayed for God's best for Michael and us, His promises to us about our son had been freely given. Now we wondered if we had misread what seemed to be God's assurances.

The next day was Saturday. As usual, Joe spent the morning with Michael. A nurse said later that she was with Dr. Leslie on rounds when they entered Mike's room. To their surprise, Joe was snuggled in bed beside Michael.

We often cradled Mike because, like a baby, he seemed more contented when held. Joe was talking softly to him, pulling his shoulder-length hair back away from his face. Dr. Leslie took one look at them and had to leave the room.

The nurse told me, "With tears in his eyes, Dr. Leslie said, 'I have never seen such a tender and committed dad.'"

During the months of Michael's hospitalization, Joe made every family meeting, consultation, and conference relating to Mike's recovery, in addition to being with him hours each week.

We met other families of patients with traumatic brain injury while we were at Shepherd. For most fathers, the fact that they'd not been able to protect their son or daughter—and that long-term care needs were beyond their emotional and financial resources—weighed heavily. Some tried but were overwhelmed. Some dealt with the pain by detaching emotionally. Others left. There were few fathers who were willing to engage with their child (and the other parent) in a meaningful way.

Dr. Leslie said, "The moms tend to hang in there, but it's unusual to see a man with the level of emotional, day-to-day involvement Joe has."

I was now seeing Joe for the remarkable person he was. His loyalty, dependability, and commitment literally made the difference in our survival. He shared every responsibility of Mike's care—from laundry to dressing to hygiene—as well as any mother could.

Under the harsh light of a terrible reality, my husband shone like pure gold.

Joe returned home from the hospital one Saturday and caught up with me in the kitchen. He was upbeat. "I feel certain Mike is going to be okay—that there's a purpose for all this," he said.

I told him I sensed this, too. After he left, I was in the kitchen alone. Suddenly the Holy Spirit spoke to me very clearly. It wasn't audible. But neither was it a still, small voice. It was strong and emphatic. He said, "You will have your son back."

Again, there were no specifics about what that might mean, but I took the message at face value.

On Sunday, a friend handed me a note at church. Though unaware of the prognosis we'd received, she'd written out Romans 4:17. It speaks of Abraham's faith that God would give him a son—even though he and his wife were beyond the age of bearing children. Abraham trusted "God, who gives life to the dead and calls those things which do not exist as though they did." The Scripture says that Abraham, "contrary to hope, in hope believed."

I went to bed that night mulling over the implication of the news we'd received: that Michael wasn't expected to emerge from the coma. The thought kept coming to me, *Will I believe God or man?* A phrase from Psalm 20:7 stated the same message in another way:

> *Some trust in chariots, and some in horses;*
> *But we will remember the name of the LORD our God.*

As I slept, I dreamed that Michael was trying to walk. As long as I could hold him up, he could walk, but I didn't have the strength to keep him going. I woke up aware that no matter how much any of us had to give to Michael, it wouldn't be enough. Any trust I placed in what I or someone else could do would come up short.

Joe and I concluded that we should explore every resource. Be willing to mobilize whatever natural and spiritual tools were available to encourage Michael's body, soul, and spirit. Pursue the best medical care possible. But the bottom line was this: There wasn't anyone or anything that could make Mike whole apart from the power of God. Our trust had to be in Him.

From the beginning, I'd kept in touch with a group of faithful supporters via e-mail. Now I shared our conviction that God was still at work. He would have the final say. The faith to believe for Michael's healing—in spite of the discouraging news—grew steadily.

Michael celebrated his nineteenth birthday in the hospital on September 6, 1996. Shepherd worked out an arrangement with the insurance company to delay transferring him to a nursing facility. Michael was given four more weeks to emerge enough to participate in therapy.

Dr. Leslie then suggested I take some time off. At first I felt uneasy about it. Mike knew when I came. His eyes, wide open and the deepest blue, would drink in my face like he couldn't get enough.

"You need a break," Dr. Leslie insisted. "While Mike's in the hospital, you know he's well cared for. Once he's discharged, time away is going to be a lot harder to come by."

I hadn't thought about that. He was right. We trusted Shepherd with Mike's care, and we had a good friend who would attend to Mike's spirit. Judy was the mother of one of Mike's best friends. She loved Mike like he was one of her own children, and she shouldered a lot of Mike's care with me.

I asked Joe about going with me.

"I just can't," he said. He had taken a month off already and didn't want to impose on his company's generosity. "Besides, I can't stand the thought of a trip. I'd rather stay here."

Sharon and her family were returning to the mission field, so he encouraged me to visit her family while I had the chance. I decided to spend several days in Lindale then drive with Sharon to Papa's.

It was fun to participate in normal life again. I watched my nephew and nieces play tennis and basketball. I enjoyed having a meal around a table with a large family. On the weekend, the Lindale community hosted an event to raise mission support for my sister's family. People came from as far as California. My father, who had remarried, flew in with his wife. It nourished my spirit to spend time with them, as well as other family and friends.

I kept thinking about an elderly couple, peers of my grandfather in both age and faith, who lived nearby.

Jewell and Tom Cunningham had been icons in the Assembly of God denomination. As a girl, Jewell and her family traveled that Oklahoma-Texas-Arkansas route preaching the gospel in the early days of Pentecost. Jewell soon established a preaching ministry of her own. When she married Tom Cunningham, they continued their work as they raised three children. Their son, Loren, would become the founder of the largest missions organizations in the world, Youth With A Mission. One of their daughters, Jannie, married a family friend of ours and lived in Lindale.

Tom and Jewell were renowned prayer warriors. Now ninety years old, they were no longer in active ministry, but I felt I should ask them to pray for Michael. At my request, Sharon arranged for me to see them.

Several friends and family members came with me. Jewell, who'd had a stroke, was sitting in a chair. Tom greeted us with his booming voice and was thrilled to reminisce about old times and people we'd all known.

Then I asked if we could pray for Michael. Jewell and Tom's eyes lit up. They loved to pray. As we stood to form a circle, I walked over to the Cunninghams.

"I'd like to stand between you," I said. "You're giants of the faith to me, and I would feel privileged if both of you would lift up my son." I moved between them and took their hands, closing the circle.

Tom said, "Thank you for saying that. I needed the encouragement."

His words surprised and humbled me. I'd come asking something of them, never thinking I had anything to offer them. But I was learning that was how God often did things. Those who give, receive—while those who receive somehow give.

I strongly felt the Holy Spirit's presence as we bowed our heads, then Tom's voice exploded with authority. As others joined him, I startled. I was used to praying quietly. Politely. In my church, we took turns praying one person at a time. I'd forgotten that the old Pentecostals pray out loud, all together at once. I'm not sure how many were praying in that manner, but they sounded like an army. They shouted. They cried. And as they gained power and momentum, I felt the strength of their prayers flying upward. *This is what Papa means when he talks about bombarding heaven,* I realized. Though I had heard him use that expression many times, I didn't understand what he meant until this moment.

Suddenly, I felt a tingling sensation moving up and down my body that lasted several seconds. It washed over and over me like a mild electrical shock. I didn't know what it was, but I was certain it was of God. As we drove home I told Sharon, "I feel like something happened to Michael as the Cunninghams prayed. There's been some kind of release."

The next day was Tuesday, October 22. Sharon and I drove to Wichita Falls and arrived at Papa's just in time for dinner. When we got back from Picadilly, the phone was ringing. It was Joe.

"It's Mike," he said crying. "He can talk!"

I felt joy. Disbelief. Relief. So many emotions ran through me that I couldn't think.

"Mike's talking!" I told Sharon and Papa. Papa sat down on the sofa and began to sob, "Thank you, Jesus. Thank you, Jesus."

Joe said that Cheryl, one of Mike's therapists, had come in late that afternoon. When Mike saw her, he began making the same sound over and over. She came close to him and realized he was saying, "Mom...Mom."

"Do you want your Mom?" Cheryl asked.

Mike nodded yes.

Stunned, Cheryl realized this was a huge breakthrough. She explained that I had gone out of town for a few days but would be back soon. Then she asked Mike a battery of questions to ascertain what kind of information he could access. Mike counted from one to ten. Recited the alphabet up to "G." Told Cheryl her top was red, her jeans blue. Cheryl picked up the photo album we'd compiled and pointed to family members and friends. He named them all. Michael's speech was garbled, but Cheryl, a trained listener, was able to understand him.

After Joe related all he knew, I told him what had happened in the prayer meeting the day before. We cried together—this time with joy.

I then phoned the hospital, hoping someone would be there. Judy answered, and I could tell from the noise that the room was full of people.

"Mike's exhausted now," she warned me, "but he wants to talk to you."

I was shaking so hard I could hardly hold the phone as I listened for my son's voice. His words, though unclear, were the most beautiful I had ever heard.

"Mom..." he said struggling to get them out. "I love you."

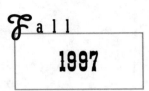

Fall
1997

Homecoming

David, Michael, and I stood outside the Dallas airport and watched the third bus to the rental car lot pull away. Over a year had passed since Mike's accident. David was doing well as a senior in a private high school in Atlanta, and Mike was living with us in a basement apartment we had modified for him. Visiting Papa was our first adventure away from home as a threesome.

We had waited almost an hour for the handicap accessible bus. The airport rental agent assured us it was on its way, but it never came. Finally, I left the boys, got the car myself, and, after winding around in the unfamiliar airport, connected with them again. Such frustrations were a daily part of our lives.

I jumped out of the car to help Michael, but David said, "I've got him, Mom." David countered Mike's weight with his own as he transferred Mike from the wheelchair to the car seat. I collapsed the wheelchair and maneuvered it into the car trunk. David loaded the suitcases. Without his help, this trip wouldn't have been possible.

I was exhausted even before we began, and it was dark by the time we started the three-hour drive to Wichita Falls. I would've preferred taking the commuter plane, but it wasn't an option. Mike was in daily therapy at the Shepherd Center hoping to regain enough balance to walk, but right now, if he toppled he'd be 170 pounds of dead weight. Walking Mike up the long flight of stairs to board the airplane was too dangerous.

Though Mike worked hard to improve, he refused all assistive devises and was always trying things beyond his capability. True to his personality, stubbornness often won out over wisdom. Mike couldn't be trusted to be prudent about what he could and could not do. But we had prayed Michael would still be Michael, and our prayers had been answered. I couldn't very well complain.

On the up side, Michael's determination pushed him to do things he was told he'd never do. He was able to eat and drink. To feed himself. He was continent. Every one of those things made a huge difference in his life and ours. But he still required full-time care.

Mike had processing problems that limited his ability to work with information that had to be learned, remembered, and applied. But mentally, he was as quick as ever. He was funny. Witty. No nuance of a joke or situation escaped him. He would brag that one advantage of hanging around with him was that you never had to worry about getting a good parking place.

Michael was fun to be around, making him a favorite with caregivers and a delight for us. The hard shell—the rage and defensiveness that defined him before the accident—had completely dropped off. What remained was a sweet, vulnerable, and loving young man who seemed to be growing up again in an accelerated fashion.

As Mike began to emerge from the coma, he sensed he had blown it with us and was petrified he would never come home again. Whatever insecurity fueled him to reject all home represented before his accident also created a deep longing for it. I recalled that, even when the final showdown came and Mike moved out, he'd left dragging his heels all the way.

Perhaps the desire to return home is coded into our genes the same way it is for salmon that fight to spawn in the place of their birth. To hear my grandmother tell the stories of people from the state mental hospital who wandered onto their property at the barn, one could certainly make a case for it.

"You could always tell where they were from by how they were dressed," she said. The ladies wore bobby socks with dress shoes and carried funny little purses. Jackets and sweaters on both men and women tended to be several sizes too small or too big. They'd be walking as fast as they could, their eyes fixed on some imaginary place.

When Mama or Papa intercepted them, they willingly offered an explanation for their hurried state. Usually it had to do with getting home. "My mother's fixin' supper and I'm late." Or, "My daddy was supposed to pick me up hours ago but I can't find him," they'd say with panic in their voices. "Do you know where he is?"

Most of those who got out of the state hospital had what we now know to be Alzheimer's. They were harmless but in danger themselves of being hurt or taken advantage of. So, Mama and Papa would try to find out where they were headed then call the hospital to pick them up. Those folks didn't always remember where they'd come from, but they knew they weren't where they belonged. And home was where they wanted to be.

That was the sense we had about Michael. The accident had erased most of his memory of the previous two years—along with much of his anger. Four months post-accident, you could spend the morning with him, walk out of the room, and when you returned, be greeted with a surprised smile that told you he'd forgotten you'd been there before. But his long-term memory and that innate longing for love and home seemed more deeply engrained than ever. We couldn't help but respond.

For months we had bathed Mike in love (and lotion!) and he had responded with childlike delight, giving hugs as tightly as his awkward and often-casted arms would allow. We were as foolish about Michael as a parent would be about a newborn because that's how he seemed to us—like a child for whom everything is fresh and wonderful. He learned new things every day: how to brush his teeth, comb his hair, and use a specially designed controller for the TV. We greeted every step toward independence with praise and joy. And Mike drank it in.

One of our most poignant moments with him was when he learned he was coming home. It was just before Thanksgiving. Joe and I were in Mike's room together.

"Michael, do you know where you're going when you leave Shepherd?" I asked.

From his wheelchair, he looked up at me with the innocence of a doe. His eyes locked on mine as he shook his head no.

"You're coming home," I said. Emotion flooded his face, but I couldn't read it. "Mike, what do you think about that?"

"Happy," he said then pointed for his spell board, a laminated sheet of paper that had all the letters of the alphabet on it. Because his speech was difficult to understand, Mike spelled out words by pointing to each letter.

He asked a lot of questions, carefully tapping out each word to make sure he got it right. *I am coming home? With you and Dad?* he spelled. *At your house?*

"Yes, that's right, Michael."

His eyes sparkled. He wanted to know if he could come home now. "You can come home," Joe said, "but not now." Mike shrugged as if to say, *You can't blame me for trying.*

He began working furiously again. *I love you,* he spelled, then looked up at me with eyes smiling. I gave him a hug. He laughed and hugged me back.

"Did you know that soon after you come home, David will be coming home, too?"

Then you and Dad will have two boys.

Joe looked at me. It was a day we looked forward to as well, though with more than a little fear and trepidation. We were almost afraid to hope it would work out. But the desire to have our family together under one roof again was as great in us as it was for the boys.

"Yes, Michael," I replied. "We'll be a family again. Dad and me. You and David."

His eyes, like ours, filled with tears.

Mike spent seven more weeks in Shepherd's Acquired Brain Injury program. On January 14, 1997, Mike came home. The next day he began Shepherd's full-time day program.

In March Mike transferred to a three-month rehab program in Austin, Texas, to learn independent living skills. It nearly killed us to be apart from Michael, but when he returned home, he was able to shower and dress himself. His posture, speech, and balance had improved significantly. We were still told he'd never walk, but he had made great gains.

In June Michael traveled with us to California for David's graduation from Cascade. The ceremony was outdoors under a canopy. Surrounded by the breathtaking natural beauty of the mountains, graduates began their long procession from the central lodge toward their waiting families. The symbolism of the long personal journeys these kids had traveled was not lost on the mothers and fathers who watched with pride and emotion as their children walked toward them.

David wore the same dark olive suit Mike had worn one year earlier for his high school graduation. Now 6'3", with white blond hair and a winning smile, David looked like he could take on the world. When Michael saw his brother, he wept uncontrollably. He pulled a white handkerchief from his coat pocket and sobbed out loud as David walked down the aisle. Dave had a hard time keeping it together, and so did everyone else.

When the ceremony was over, David flew over to greet us. He had asked for one thing for graduation: that his brother would stand up by himself and give him a hug. Michael had been working on it for the past few months, and when David came toward him, he unfastened the belt of his wheelchair and was on his feet before we could get in position to guard him.

He and David held each other as though holding onto life itself.

We had no illusions about the path ahead. David would struggle to integrate his new values in a world that was not as safe and intimate as the one he had left. And watching David live his life so fully would make Michael even more aware of his losses. Still, the moment represented the culmination of years of heartache and struggle. We had made it this far. There was hope.

Now, as we took the turnoff from Highway 114 to 287 North toward Wichita Falls, I looked at my two sons in the car beside me, amazed at how far we'd come. I couldn't help but be grateful.

Tuckered Out

Michael, David, and I pulled into Midtown Manor around 10 P.M. I intended to drop the boys off at the Holiday Inn first, but Mike wouldn't hear of it.

"Mike, you're so tired," I said. "Why don't you get a good night's rest and you can see Papa in the morning?"

"I'll sleep better if I see him first," he insisted.

I had called Papa from the road to tell him we'd be late. I didn't want him to wait in the lobby for me as he usually did. But now that we were here, my heart raced at the thought of seeing him again.

I would have laid odds he'd be up waiting for us, but when I knocked on his door, no one answered. After several tries I finally went downstairs into the lobby to find the security guard.

He wasn't the one whom Papa disliked. This man responded quickly.

"I hope your grandpa's okay," he said furrowing his brow. "Are you sure he knows you're coming? I saw him earlier tonight, and he didn't say nothin' about it."

My concern was that Papa might be ill. He'd only been out of the hospital a couple of days—another episode of dehydration and disorientation. He had trouble talking, causing doctors to suspect small strokes again. But, like before, most of his symptoms disappeared with hydration.

Papa's physician, Dr. Pavari, was a kind man who treated Papa with concern and dignity. Papa liked him but had difficulty pronouncing his name because it was foreign. "And wouldn't you know it," my aunt said, "in order to test Papa's awareness, Dr. Pavari asked Papa to tell him his name."

Papa worked his mouth around trying to get it out but couldn't.

"Mr. Choate," Dr. Pavari repeated, "what's my name? Can you tell me?"

Papa looked at him, tried again, then gave up. "What are you asking me that for?" he asked shaking his head. "You know I can't pronounce your name even when I've got good sense!"

They knew then he'd be okay. Aunt Marie laughed and told me later that Papa had been in good form all day. He had been in the hospital a week, and every time a doctor came in, he'd ask Papa what month and year it was. They were checking his orientation to time and space. After the umpteenth time, Papa finally became exasperated.

"What's with these doctors anyway?" he demanded of Aunt Marie. "Don't none of them know what month or year we're in!"

It was an interesting window into medicine from the patient's point of view.

Even though Papa was alert upon returning home, he was physically weak. My aunt had stayed with him until today, so this was the first time he'd been alone for several hours.

The guard and I walked hurriedly to Papa's apartment.

"Howdy," he said nodding to the boys who were waiting in the hall. He knocked firmly several times and put his ear against Papa's door. Nothing. He then pulled a ring of keys off his belt and inspected them carefully in the dim light. Selecting one, he inserted it into the deadbolt and opened the door quietly.

"Wait here," he whispered extending one arm toward me in a "stop" motion. He entered the room as if part of a SWAT team. He checked out the kitchen, the living room, then, from the hallway, peered into the bedroom. His body relaxed, and he motioned for me to follow him.

Papa was in bed, sound asleep. He lay uncovered in his underwear and strap T-shirt, with his hands folded on his chest. His quick, shallow breaths raised and lowered his stomach like billows.

"Papa," I said quietly, as I pulled the sheet over him. He would be mortified if he thought we had seen him like this. He didn't stir.

"Papa," I said a little louder. I touched his arm. It felt like crepe paper, all crinkly and fragile, so I rubbed my hand gently up and down the veins of his hands instead. Suddenly his eyes popped open. Confusion passed over his face as he struggled for orientation, then he looked past me and saw the boys.

His eyes lit up like a Christmas tree. Lying flat on his back, he held out both hands. "Michael! David!" he whispered. I moved out of the way as David wheeled Michael to Papa's side. David came around and hugged his great-grandfather.

"I'm so glad to see you," Papa said patting David's hand over and over. Mike and Papa awkwardly tried to embrace, but between Papa's frailty, the wheelchair, and Mike's frozen right arm, they couldn't quite manage it. Finally they locked arms from a distance and cried.

"I love you, Papa, I love you," Mike kept saying.

I translated it for Papa, but the smile on his face told me it was unnecessary.

Papa wanted to get up, so the boys and I waited in the living room while he dressed. In a moment he came out wearing a pair of stained khakis. As he started toward his chair, he teetered to the right and I ran toward him. The wall caught him first, and he righted himself. I put my arm around him and walked with him to the chair.

"I'm sorry I was asleep when you came," he said. "I thought when you called you said you weren't coming till the mornin'."

"Papa, I'm sorry for the mix-up. I called because we were late, and I was afraid you'd worry. I didn't mean to make things more confusing."

"That's alright, hon. I'm just glad you're here. Did y'all check into the hotel already?"

"No. Mike said he had to see you first."

Papa smiled and shook his head in approval. "Well, that's real good of you Michael, to come see Papa tonight. Especially when you must be tired and all."

The bond between Mike and Papa was powerful and immediate. Though separated by three quarters of a century, they walked in the same shoes. Both knew what it was like to be confronted daily by the limitations of their bodies. And they both knew courage when they saw it.

Ghost Town

I was up before Papa the next morning fixing breakfast for us all. Papa emerged from his room wearing the same khakis he'd worn the night before. As he walked to his chair, the smell of urine and stale body odor wafted behind him.

"Papa, do you want to take your shower before the boys get here?" I asked.

"I can't take a shower every day now," he said. "It dries out my skin, besides it takes all my energy."

My aunt had warned me about that. "Dad says he doesn't feel like doing anything, so he just sits there in his chair all day," she said. "He can't do much for himself. There's a woman who comes in for a few hours Monday through Friday who's supposed to keep things clean, do his laundry, and fix breakfast and lunch for him. It's helped some, but most days he sends her home early."

I could hear the frustration in Aunt Marie's voice. "He doesn't want help, but he needs it. I don't know what we're going to do."

Papa was accepted by an assisted living facility where he'd been wait-listed, but now he needed more care than even they could give. Other family members and Margie were doing their best to fill in the gaps, but it wasn't enough.

"I keep hoping he'll realize he can't go on as he is," Aunt Marie said.

I was glad to help out in the short-term, but the long-term solution was one that none of us wanted to face.

Papa didn't get dressed that day. Even putting on a shirt was a slow, energy-consuming task. Instead he chose to be present with us. He got the boys going with stories about the barn.

Their favorite was Papa's encounter with a man who had escaped from the state mental hospital. Apparently, security there left something to be desired. Though most of the patients were harmless, occasionally someone—almost always male—labeled "criminally insane" would escape.

"I'd see them hiding in the culvert waiting for the opportunity to hitch a ride on the highway," he explained. Papa stopped for a few minutes to quell a coughing jag. He touched his throat as if to soothe the tickle then continued. He wasn't easy to understand, especially with his teeth out, but since I'd heard this story before I could help when needed. Between the two of us, we finally got it out.

"I'd call the state hospital soon as I spotted them, and before you knew it, a sheriff's car would come by to take them back," he said. "But there were a few who'd try to hide out for a few days to wait out the search. Without fail, they'd head for the same place: the bunkhouse. Might as well have put a welcome mat at the door."

Because of their frequent visitors, Mama and Papa remained alert for any sign of an open window or missing jars of canned green beans or peaches. Some escapees were smart enough to hide during the day and come in only at night, but they always did something to tip their hand.

One particular man gave himself away by lighting a fire. Mama saw the smoke from the outside and called Papa. As usual, Papa confronted the situation head on. He walked to the door of the bunkhouse and gently turned the knob. The door, usually locked, swung open easily. Papa walked in calling, "Come on out, I know you're in here."

Suddenly, the door slammed into him, and Papa reeled to the side. He regained his footing just in time to square off with a huge man wielding a baseball bat.

"I was just leaving…" the man explained nervously. "I don't want to hurt you. I was just leaving." He motioned for my grandfather to step away, then he backed out the door and ran toward the culvert.

Once Papa saw the man climb up on the highway, he called the state hospital. "His ride came along before too long, alright," Papa said with a chuckle.

As easily as my grandmother spooked, it was hard to imagine her being comfortable with that kind of activity going on, but she trusted my grandfather to protect her. And he did.

I wondered what she'd think of Papa now. He bore little resemblance to the man who didn't think twice about facing a dangerous man with a weapon. The physical changes I saw in him were startling. His bones were visible through his skin. Though pitifully thin, his stomach was bloated, and Papa held his arm across it sometimes like it was tender.

For the first time I could remember, Papa declined my offer to go to Piccadilly. "Hon, I don't go anywhere's much now," he said. "Most days I'm too tired to go downstairs and get the mail."

"What about pool? Do you still go play with the boys?" I asked.

"Naw. With Boone gone I wasn't much interested anyway."

"Boone's gone?" I asked. That was news to me. "What happened?"

"His son came picked him up one day, and that was that." Papa's mouth turned into a tight line. He looked away, letting me know I could draw my own conclusions.

"How about if the boys and I go get takeout from Pat's?" I asked, changing the subject.

A smile crossed his face. "Yeah. That sounds real good."

"You want a milk shake or Dr. Pepper?" I asked.

"Milk shake. Chocolate."

"You got it!"

Mike kept Papa company while Dave and I made the food run. Christie, who was working the counter, recognized me immediately.

"Aren't you Mr. Choate's granddaughter?" she asked.

"Yes, I am. And this is my son, David. We're here to visit with him for a few days."

"Oh, that's great. Is he still at the senior citizens' apartments? We haven't seen him for a while, so we were all wonderin' if he was doing okay."

The place was beginning to get busy, but Christie was intent on catching up with Papa. "He's a wonderful man, and we've really missed him," she said. Then she called to her mother who was in the back.

Pat brought out our order to us personally. "We sure love your granddaddy," she said as she handed me our bag. "Tell him this order is on us."

Getting a free hamburger from Pat's made Papa's day. David, Michael, and Papa sat around his tiny table while I swiveled Papa's recliner around to face them and held my plate in my lap.

"Mmmmm," Michael said sucking his ice-cold milk shake through a straw. After drinking, he sat the cup down firmly on the table. David and I laughed. Mike always set his glass down with a certain authority and style that seemed uniquely him.

"That is good!" Papa agreed, then, to our astonishment, he set down his glass in the exact same manner as Mike.

The number of facial expressions, mannerisms, and speech patterns shared by Papa and Michael were uncanny. As they talked, both gestured with the back of their hand as though flicking something off a table. They cocked their head to the right as they spoke. Crossed their legs in a particular way as they sat. Both hated plastic plates, cups, or eating utensils. And neither would eat a meal off a cafeteria tray.

One of the weirdest coincidences was that, during the span of one week, each decided to drink a glass of milk, a glass of orange juice, and a glass of iced tea every day. Mike was in Georgia, Papa was in Texas. We never figured out what sparked that phenomenon.

I often came away from a day with Michael feeling I'd visited my grandfather as well. Mike and Papa hadn't spent enough time together over the years to have copied each other's behavior. The only explanation was DNA. The brain injury slowed Michael down to the point where their similarities were obvious because their movements were now at the same speed. Seeing the two of them together, side by side, was unbelievable.

Having spent almost a whole day with Papa, I realized something that pained me to admit. He was incontinent. I explained to David that I'd need to spend most of my time caring for Papa.

"I didn't realize he wouldn't be able to get out when we came," I said. "I know it would be hard for you and Michael to stay here all the time, so what would you think about hanging out at the hotel and meeting up with us for meals?"

David would have done whatever I had asked, but I could tell he was relieved. The hotel had video games, a pool, and a game room. They could stay busy.

"That'll work," he said.

"And are you okay with having Mike by yourself?" I asked. David was familiar with Mike's routine, but Joe and I were careful not to put him in a position of being Mike's built-in caretaker.

David knew that his life, like ours, was forever changed by Mike's accident. In time, he'd likely take over our role as Mike's guardian, but we were trying to teach David to embrace whatever season of life one is in. We expected him to make room in his life for his brother, but we were also committed to seeing that David had a life of his own.

"Be fully present with Michael when you're with him," I encouraged him, "but when you're apart, don't feel guilty."

Perhaps because we had given David the freedom to both love and leave his brother, he was good about helping us out when we were in a tight spot.

"Don't worry, Mom," he told me. "Mike and I will be fine. Just do what you can to help Papa."

Papa was exhausted after our first full day together and went to bed early. I made my bed on the sofa and fell asleep listening to Papa's labored breathing.

The next day, Saturday, Papa slept through the morning. A little before noon, I called my aunt.

"Is this usual for Papa?" I asked. I had never known him to sleep past nine.

"No, it's not like him," she said. "I better come over."

By the time she arrived, Papa was up, but he had trouble eating, drinking, and walking.

"I think he's just really tired," she said after observing him.

I hadn't thought of it until then, but it was the same with Mike. When he became fatigued, nothing worked right.

Aunt Marie helped gather laundry before she left—mostly Papa's clothes, which were soiled from accidents. I did multiple loads throughout the day and tried to keep the bathroom toilet and floor cleaned up. It was a full-time job. Papa had diarrhea which no doubt was why he dehydrated so quickly. If someone weren't with him all the time to monitor it, he'd soon be in the hospital again.

Though Papa's failing senses protected him from the depths of humiliation, his gaze, stoic and keen, told me he was aware of all that was going on around him. The line of his mouth told me he didn't like it, but he didn't complain.

Around him were signs of caring. Margie brought a microwave. Johnny Wayne, Aunt Marie's son, bought him a portable phone. The carved wooden bookshelf he was so proud of showcased a wood horse, a gift from Sharon in Costa Rica. New photos of the great-grandkids told me the family was keeping in touch. But none of it could stop the force of aging.

The things Papa most loved seemed frozen in a time warp. Under the TV, Papa's boots and bootjack sat covered by a thin layer of dust. His hat, stored in the closet, hadn't been worn in years. Mama's purse rested beside his hat as though he were expecting her back any moment. Everything was waiting. Just waiting.

Winter
1998

Dont' Fence Me In

When I called Papa the next week from Atlanta, his speech was slurred and he was almost incoherent.

"Papa, can you hear me?" I asked.

"Yeah, I hear ya fine," he said. But the next sentence came out all jumbled, with bizarre words surfacing like a foreign language. He was back in the hospital by the day's end.

My aunt called as soon as he was stable. "He's dehydrated again and had more of those little strokes," she said. "I can't understand anything he says."

"Is there any paralysis?" I asked.

"No. It's more like he's very weak and just doesn't have enough strength or energy to do anything. They want him to have some therapy."

Therapy had been recommended after the last hospitalization but Papa refused it. He also needed a cane, walker, or wheelchair to get around. He had refused those, too. Now he had no choice.

It took some doing, but Papa finally agreed to several weeks of rehab. He wasn't a very cooperative patient, however.

"I don't have long to live so what's the point?" he asked.

Diagnosed with kidney failure and congestive heart failure, he was biding his time. But as the weeks went by, his body proved to be as stubborn as he was. When Papa finally let me buy him another hearing aid when his old one died, I took that as a sign he hadn't given up.

The last time I was at Midtown Manor, he reminisced about the span of his life. "We've gone from a horse and buggy to the moon in my lifetime," he said proudly, then proceeded to give me the rundown of his last years as a cowboy.

"My last saddle was a handmade saddle with silver mounds. I gave $1500 for it." His eyes narrowed as if to bring the picture of it into view. "When I left the barn, I sold it for $450. It had quarter-inch silver lace on the back, and silver on the horn."

It bothered me that, once Papa decided to leave the barn, he sold everything off so quickly. He was impulsive that way. The more attached he was to something the faster he tried to get rid of it. I think he regretted the rash sales later on, but it was all water under the bridge by then.

"I broke my last young horse at seventy-seven," he continued. "And the last horse I sold, I sold to a German family for $900. Them is the same ones that bought the saddle."

Papa seemed trying to get things in order in his mind and in his home. He had me go through his magazines. Most he wanted to throw out. "I can't read any more," he said, though he did save two favorite copies of *Western Horseman*.

I came across his personal phone book and thumbed through it. There were very few listings. Four or five family members. Aunt Marie's number written in huge letters. Most were doctors' numbers that my aunt or one of us grandkids had penciled in. Written in his hand, however, was the number of the "Wichita Livestock Auction" as well as the "Quarter Horse Registration" in Amarillo.

Papa's address book was evidence in black and white of his shrinking world. Fewer contacts. Fewer people. Fewer ways to communicate.

In a very real sense, his situation was like Michael's. One of the biggest challenges Michael faced was his limited social sphere. We were hopeful surgery might improve his speech, but for now it was unintelligible. He was personable, well liked, but his only outside contacts were medical personnel. There was no natural forum to meet people his own age. Even when he was around them, few were interested in slowing down enough to accommodate him.

The summer after Mike's accident, Joe was given box seats to a Brave's game, a treat for all of us. Not fighting the crowds made getting around much easier. Mike's eyes lit up as his dad wheeled him into the skybox and he saw four or five other young men his age. None of them came over to speak then, but we assumed they were giving us space until we got Michael squared away.

We took turns helping him with snacks and a soda as the game began. As the first inning raced into the third then the fifth, we saw Michael's mind wasn't on baseball. He was watching the kids who bounded easily from their seats to the room for food and drinks.

"Excuse me," they mumbled, passing by close enough to touch him. Mike looked up at them as they neared, but by the seventh inning stretch it was obvious none of them were going to try to connect with him.

In their defense, they were young and unprepared. And we'd observed that because Michael's speech couldn't be understood, people assumed he couldn't communicate. Maybe the boys didn't want to embarrass Mike or themselves by expecting Michael to do something he couldn't. Who knew what they were thinking.

Most likely, they just didn't know what to do. For whatever reason, Mike left the game without one young person offering a word or look in his direction. That hurt. Not because it was a single slight but because it was a microcosm of what lay ahead for him.

One by one most of Mike's friends had dropped off. Some went away to college. Others moved on with their lives. Slowly, as Mike became aware that his disabilities were severe and permanent, he realized loneliness and isolation were slated for his future in a big way.

It was heartbreaking for us, as Mike's parents, to know that, as much as we loved our son, we couldn't be everything for him. As he struggled to come to terms with the reality of his life, there was little we could do other than pray for him.

We'd been told that people with brain injury often had more difficulties with the emotional and social hurdles than their physical challenges. We were beginning to understand why. To help him break through, therapists tried helping Mike recover some personal goals. "What did you do before that you'd love to do again?" they asked.

Often a sport or hobby was the gateway to friendship and some sort of social life. Any passion could infuse the life of a disabled person with purpose. But prior to the accident, Mike's passions were drugs and alcohol. He loved them because they made the emptiness and uncertainty of his life go away for a while, but they robbed him of his dreams. Mike had no hobbies. No interests. No specific goals.

Unable to envision a future for himself, he would often explode in frustration. One day he gestured angrily and spit out words we couldn't understand. In tears, he finally pounded out his rage on his spellboard.

I'm sick of therapy and sick of doing what everybody else wants me to do, he said.

"Then what is it you want to do?" I asked.

Drugs.

My heart sank. "Mike, why would you want to do drugs? That lifestyle got you where you are."

He looked at me defiantly then typed, *At least I was around people then.*

For Michael, getting better meant returning to the life he'd known. Part of him knew it would kill him, but emotionally, that was where he wanted to be. And the more rebuffs he encountered, the more he longed for it.

For Joe and me, this was more devastating than the accident. For Michael to pull out of the coma and be functioning at the level he was seemed nothing short of a miracle. *Would God let us and so many others invest our prayers and energy into Michael only to lose him to the same lifestyle again?* we wondered.

Trust, was the only answer we got. The Scripture that spoke to me was Psalms 147:10-11. "He does not delight in the strength of the horse; He takes no pleasure in the legs of a man. The Lord takes pleasure in those who fear Him, in those who hope in His mercy." Considering the running around I had done with Michael the past year, it didn't take much interpretation to understand that my frantic physical and emotional shoring up was a good translation for "the legs of a man."

God reminded me that Mike wasn't the only one He cared about in this situation. He was concerned that Joe and I were wearing ourselves out. Though we didn't have an answer, I sensed that *trust* didn't necessarily mean do more. It meant, somewhere along the way, we were going to have to let go.

In May, while Mike had been in Austin, I agreed to speak at a women's retreat in California. I thought God had directed me there to help others, but instead I was ministered to in a significant way. As I was leaving, a woman ran after me and handed me a card. "I believe God gave me this for you," she said. I thanked her then tucked the card away in my purse. I didn't find it for several days after returning home. I discovered the card, with words adapted from Hosea 2, at the end of a difficult day.

I will bring her into the wilderness, and I will speak tenderly to her heart. There I will give her vineyards and make the valley of troubling to be for her a door of hope and expectation. And she shall sing there and respond as in the days of her youth.

In the timing and gentleness of the passage, I sensed the encouragement of the Holy Spirit. Again, God affirmed that this wilderness season wasn't just about Michael. My son was not to be saved at my expense. Rather, as I learned to give appropriately—through His power—I would experience the renewal and healing I needed to live out my life in joy. By now, God and I had been through enough together that I could honestly say, "I believe You."

"When the Roll Is Called Up Yonder"

As Sharon and I practiced for what would be our last sing-along at Midtown Manor, Papa asked, "Would you girls sing "When the Roll Is Called Up Yonder"? That's my favorite song." After instructing me to "play it peppy," he sat down and listened to us, keeping time by slapping his hand on his knee.

> When the trumpet of the Lord shall sound and time shall be no more,
> And the morning breaks eternal, bright and fair—
> When the saved of earth shall gather over on the other shore,
> And the roll is called up yonder—I'll be there!

We had a hard time getting through the song knowing that one day, not too far off, we'd be singing it at Papa's funeral.

My grandfather left Midtown Manor for good on March 31, 1998.

Moving into a nursing home had always been one of Papa's greatest fears, but by the time it came about, he was able to accept that it was right for that season of his life.

Still, Papa faces tough times. More loneliness. Dependency. One preacher has said, "The one thing I want to ask God is this: why nursing homes?" But if you believe in God's sovereignty and goodness, you must believe that there is some purpose for each moment a person lives.

I know that Papa still prays for my boys, Joe, and me by name—every day. We need it. And we have no way of knowing what spiritual battles he fights for us. One of his roommates told us that in the night Papa often raises his hands and seems to be worshiping. We may discover one day that such prayers changed the outcome of our lives.

Until then, both Papa and I live with stark reminders that life is difficult.

In the past thirteen years, I have seen my grandfather stripped of everything that once defined him. He's no longer a husband. A provider. A church builder. A deacon. He is simply a child of God.

It's a process my life has paralleled in many ways. Any ideal I had of myself as a wife, mother, career person, or even a Christian has been blown apart by the realities of life.

It took me a long time to figure out that many things which seemed worthy of defining me were not. I was reminded of a horse Papa once bought. He was beautiful. Regal. Papa worked him in the arena, and he found that the horse was gentle and responded well to commands. He seemed trustworthy. So, later on that day, when one of granddaughters asked to ride him he let her.

Tena mounted the horse without trouble then leaned into him signaling for him to move forward. Suddenly the horse reared up into the air and started bucking.

"You'd have thought he was the wildest rodeo bronc on the circuit," Papa said shaking his head. "Tena was lucky. She got thrown but not hurt."

The man he bought the horse from gave Papa his money back. "I got that horse cheap and was wondering why," the man said later. "I sold him again at the auction, and now I still see him at every auction I go to."

Like that horse, some things aren't what they appear to be. I pursued many roles hoping to find myself. And now, the necessity of assuming many other roles could tempt me to define myself in those terms except for one thing: I can't do it all. I cannot be a wife, mother, friend, Mike's caregiver, insurance case manager, medical services coordinator, advocate, and facilitator—let alone give creative expression to the person God made me to be.

If I have to do it all to be a worthwhile person, there is no hope. The sheer overload has forced me to pursue "being" over "doing," and now I embrace that choice gladly. As long as I use the gifts and personality God has given me to love Him and those around me, then miraculously, that which is needful gets accomplished. Yet living in that place requires moment-by-moment choices that don't come naturally to me.

One morning I had a day's worth of work ahead reconciling insurance and medical statements, scheduling appointments, and trying to confirm information for Mike's legal case.

Things weren't going well. Each piece of paper required follow-up. Every phone call involved fifteen or twenty minutes of "hold" time. The people I needed to speak to weren't available. When after two hours I'd accomplished nothing, I felt my blood slowly heating. *Is the rest of my life to be spent in one room, sitting at a desk, surrounded by a mountain of paperwork, holding on an automated phone directory system?* I wondered.

I finally slammed down the phone, pushed back violently from my desk and screamed, "I can't stand this!"

I wanted to get away for a while, but how could I? I already needed more hours in the day than I had. But I sensed the Holy Spirit saying, *Come. Sit with Me for a while, and the work will take care of itself.*

Right! I thought to myself as I envisioned another late night in my office. But having reached the point of diminishing return anyway, I put on a favorite CD and snuggled into the soft cushions of my living room sofa. I closed my eyes and let the music wash over me.

Here I am waiting
Abide in me I pray;
Here I am longing for You
Hide me in Your love
Bring me to my knees
May I know Jesus more and more

Come live in me
All my life take over.
Come breathe in me
I will rise on eagle's wings

Suddenly the words became my own and I found myself weeping tears of weariness and longing. God reminded me that He was big enough to take on the insurance company and any other bureaucracy I might encounter that day. That all His resources—His strength, His knowledge, His wisdom, His patience—were mine. I stayed with Him a long while, breathing deeply, taking in His presence.

Afterward, not yet ready to return to my desk, I walked outside to get the mail. There, between the junk flyers and catalogs, were several benefit statements from the insurance company. I opened one after the other, not believing what I read. Payments had been made on the very claims I'd been tracking that morning.

Before I could file away the paperwork, the phone rang. It was a provider with information I'd requested. Then bankers, doctors, and lawyers that I'd been trying to reach for days began calling. Within an hour, every critical thing on my desk had been taken care of, and I suddenly had the afternoon free!

I was discovering that every time I chose "being" over "doing" God came through for me.

Looking back, understanding the difference between who I am and what I do is a lesson God has been teaching me most my life. It's taken some pretty violent throws for me to catch on.

When what we do flows from who we are, it brings deep satisfaction and a sense of "this is what I was meant to do." There's an effortless feel to the work. But when the deeds must serve our self-image, they lose their light and power. Usually the blend of motives goes along unquestioned until some crisis brings life to a grinding halt. It can be a job loss, a divorce, an illness, a death, or, as in Papa's case, the burden of years. Then we are left to ask, "Who are we when everything by which we've defined ourselves no longer fits?"

That question crystallized for my grandfather shortly before he left Midtown Manor. One Saturday, over dinner at Piccadilly, I inquired about church the next day.

"Papa, would you like to go to Southside this Sunday?" I asked.

It was the Assembly of God church he'd attended when I was a child. I thought he might enjoy going one last time. The way he acted when he turned me down—terse and matter-of-fact—told me there was some hurt about the subject.

"Nope," he said. "No point in it. I don't know anybody there."

"Well, how about Evangel Temple?" It was a large Assembly church that many families had switched to over the years.

"No. Except for two old ladies, I don't know anyone who goes there either."

He paused for a moment and started to speak several times before he actually did. "Most all my friends have died off," he said.

Seeing the tears pool in his eyes I asked, "How does that make you feel, Papa?"

"How does it make me feel?" he repeated. "Bad. It makes me feel kind of bad. Used to be I'd go to church, or Piccadilly, or even walk down the street, and everyone would come up to me and say, 'How ya doin', Cowboy?'

"They knew I could rope the meanest steer in the county and could ride or break any horse they brought me. They knew I'd built a church in Byers. Now nobody knows I ever did anything for the Lord."

He looked at me hard, squinting his steely blue eyes. "They don't even know there's a cowboy inside," he said softly.

Papa got up from the table, leaning heavily on the edge. I crossed my arms and pushed down hard on my side of the table to balance his weight. After he steadied himself, I joined him and offered him my arm. I patted his cold, wrinkled hand and held it for a moment.

"Papa, I know there's a cowboy inside," I said.

He looked off into the distance as if measuring the long shuffle home. Then he smiled his crooked little smile and said, "I know you do, hon. I know you do."

Epilogue

Papa passed away on January 2, 2001, the day after this manuscript was completed. I can't begin to imagine the joys of his new life. We all miss him still.

In 1999, Michael moved near my brother and sister in California to attend a college that includes a quality brain injury program. Mike has benefited from having a broader circle of family support. He now walks and talks. He continues to make significant physical, emotional and cognitive gains. He is making good lifestyle choices. He is strong, healthy and engaging yet still struggles with building a meaningful life. Mike longs for the independence driving and employment would offer him. He wonders if there is a woman out there who will love him. These are the areas for which we trust God now.

David graduated from Westmont College in Santa Barbara in May 2002 and moved in with Mike for the summer. It was a wonderful season for both young men. Dave is now attending the Conservatory for Recording Arts and Sciences in Tempe, Arizona where he is preparing for a career in music production. His dream is to have his own studio one day where he and Mike can work together.

Joe continues to serve as the Vice President of Legal Affairs, Public Relations, and Public Affairs for United Parcel Service in Atlanta. I stay busy with freelance work. In addition to our commitment to our church and family, Joe and I spend a great deal of time advocating for brain injury issues. Together with the Brain Injury Association of Georgia, we are helping build a web based resource center to guide, support and empower those with brain injury and their families through the many phases of recovery.

The Brain Injury Resource Center, due to launch in May 2003 may be found at: www.braininjuryresourcecenter.org.

Papa and Mama, with Kern, Marie, and Atha (1933)

Floyd and Atha, with Sharon, Karen, and Edwin (1955)

The "Three Amigos"

Karen, Sharon, and Edwin (1964)

The barn

Circle R Stables—known later as "the barn" (1998)

Papa, in a photo taken for his eighty-second birthday (1985)

Papa and David at the barn (1988)

Brothers

David, 6, and Michael, 8 (1985)

Riding Paige

Mike rides Paige as Margie walks alongside (1988)

The guys

Michael, Joe, and David (2002)

Back Roads Home

Order from:
ACW Press
85334 Lorane Hwy
Eugene, OR 97405

(800) 931-BOOK

Also available through your online or local bookstore

www.moderow.us